At Work in the Iron Cage

At Work in the Iron Cage

The Prison as Gendered Organization

Dana M. Britton

NEW YORK UNIVERSITY PRESS

New York and London

NEW YORK UNIVERSITY PRESS
New York and London

Library of Congress Cataloging-in-Publication Data
Britton, Dana M.
At work in the iron cage : the prison as gendered organization / Dana M.
Britton.
p.   cm.
Includes bibliographical references and index.
ISBN 0-8147-9883-7 (hc : acid-free) — ISBN 0-8147-9884-5 (pb : acid-free)
1. Correctional personnel—United States. 2. Correctional personnel—
Training of—United States. 3. Prisons—United States. 4. Prisons—United
States—Officials and employees. 5. Criminal justice, Administration of—
United States. 7. Inmate guards—United States.   I. Title.
HV9470.B75 2003
365'.023'73—dc21   2003002710

Contents

Acknowledgments

I am deeply grateful to all of those who contributed to this project. I owe the greatest debt to the women and men I interviewed, who gave generously of their time and insight in helping an outsider to understand their work behind prison bars. I would never have gotten into prison at all without the cooperation of administrators at the institutions and the assistance of staff in the administrative offices of the two systems. Supervisors and administrators at every prison smoothed the way for this research, providing rooms for interviews, taking me on tours of their facilities, and assisting in overcoming hurdles like those I faced at control gates in bringing in my decidedly nonregulation tape recorder. Though guarantees of confidentiality prohibit me from mentioning most of these people by name, I can express my thanks to staff in the Office of Research and Evaluation at the Federal Bureau of Prisons, in particular Bo Saylor, Harriet Lebowitz, and Miles Harer. The views expressed here are of course mine, and do not represent views or policies of the Federal Bureau of Prisons, the U.S. Department of Justice, or the state Department of Corrections.

The original incarnation of this work, which involved officers at two prisons, took the form of my dissertation in at the University of Texas at Austin. That research was directed by Christine Williams and Teresa Sullivan; Mark Warr, Susan Marshall, and Desley Deacon were members of my dissertation committee. I am indebted to all of them for their guidance and, in equal measure, for their tough questions and critique. Financial support was provided at the University of Texas by a University Fellowship, and at Kansas State University by a University Small Research Grant.

Special thanks to Nancy Jurik and Irene Padavic, who read and commented on early drafts of chapters of this manuscript. Kim Morgan, Jessie Daniels, and Christine Williams read, reread, and edited every page and every draft. Though not all of their suggestions and critiques are reflected here, this book has been deeply influenced and enormously improved by their labors. At NYU Press, editor Stephen Magro has been patient and encouraging throughout the preparation of the manuscript; Despina Papazoglou Gimbel expertly shepherded me (and it) through the production process.

Advice, critique, and encouragement have come from a variety of sources. I am grateful to Patricia Yancey Martin, who has been a supporter of my work and of this project from its inception. Her generosity and mentorship have been an invaluable gift. My current and former colleagues and students at Kansas State University provided intellectual and social support, especially Mike Timberlake, Leon Bloomquist, Stacey Nofizger, and Susan Williams. My greatest intellectual debt is to Christine Williams, who has been teacher, mentor, and friend. Her work inspired me to ask the questions that frame this book, and her encouragement and (mostly) gentle prodding kept me going throughout this lengthy process. And for her patience, willingness to listen, and daily support in myriad other ways, I thank Kim Morgan.

I dedicate this book to the memory of my grandparents, Maggie and Kenneth Sullivan.

1

Engendering the Prison

Imagine a prison guard. Whom do you see? If you are like most people, the vision in your mind's eye is probably that of a hulking man in uniform carrying a nightstick or even a gun. Perhaps you imagine him as brutal and sadistic; at the very least, you see someone who would be able to deal easily with unruly inmates, to meet violence with violence, to "bang heads" if necessary. Now imagine the place in which he does his work. Again, if like most of the population you have little experience of prison and prison life, you in all likelihood envision a Hobbesian nightmare of perpetual conflict, a war of all against all in which only the strong survive. If these are the images you saw, then you are not unusual. These notions have considerable currency. They are reflected in both commonsense mythology and popular culture. Films like *Penitentiary* (1938), *Cool Hand Luke* (1967), *Brubaker* (1980), and *ConAir* (1997) have framed prison work and prison life in these terms for generations of moviegoers. As this book demonstrates, however, these images have two things in common: they are largely inaccurate, and they are deeply gendered.

The figures obviously missing from this conceptual landscape are women, yet they are a growing proportion of those working and being held in prisons. As of 1995, 19 percent of all correctional officers (the term now preferred over the more colloquial "prison guard") in federal and state prisons were women: 16 percent of officers in men's prisons and 56 percent of those working in women's facilities.[1] Women account for 6.6 percent of all inmates in state and federal prisons, and their population has recently been increasing much faster than men's. Regardless of the population they hold, most American prisons bear little resemblance to their anarchic fictional representations. Most inmates are nonviolent offenders, and all have at least some stake in the maintenance of prison order, if for no other reason than the preservation of their own lives. It is because of this that mass outbreaks of prison violence are

1

actually relatively rare. And contrary to popular mythology, correctional officers who work in inmate living areas are always unarmed. Given that they are commonly outnumbered by one hundred to one or more, a weapon of any kind is a potential liability.

These images also reflect ideas about gender. In this culture, the use of violence has always been connected with masculinity, whether the violence is illegitimate, as in the case of the "bad guy," who becomes a prisoner, or legitimate, such as the sanctioned use of force by the police or corrections officer. Violence is so closely tied to hegemonic forms of masculinity that to be a "real man" is, by definition, to know how to use violence and to be willing to do so under appropriate circumstances. Given this, it only makes sense that men are the "natural" guardians of other men. The invisibility of women in our images of the prison and prison life also reveals the function of the masculine as an unmarked category. Prisons, in a generic sense, are men's prisons; so, too, are prisoners and prison guards men. Women's violence stands in stark contradiction to prevailing norms around (white) femininity, so much so that nineteenth-century criminologists believed the brains and bodies of women criminals to have been somehow masculinized. The requisites of femininity have the paradoxical effect of making women inmates appear even more aberrant than men, and seemingly disqualify women for the job of controlling prisoners, be they men or women.

While the evidence presented in this book contradicts some of these images, I also explore in more detail how notions like this shape our ideas about prisons and prison life. I propose that the ways that we think about the prison are deeply gendered and reflect an exaggerated version of life in men's institutions, one in which "real men" constantly contend for the prize of masculine physical dominance. Women's institutions are seen, when at all, as exceptions, or anomalies, though our ideas about them are also gendered and sexualized. In addition, in a comparative analysis of work in men's and women's prisons, I examine the ways that the prison, through its structure, practices, and policies, presumes and reproduces gender. Specifically, I show that work in the prison reflects the gendering of the institution at a number of levels, from the preconceptions and experiences that officer recruits bring with them, to training that focuses on violence and men's institutions, to assignments based on ideas about what real officers (and thus real men) are like, to officers' ideas about working with male and female inmates, and their conceptions of themselves as masculine or feminine.

This work draws on an emerging theoretical perspective in the sociology of work and organizations, the "theory of gendered organizations" (Acker 1990, 1992). In simple terms, the theory argues that we should see organizations not as neutral organisms infected by the germs of workers' gender (and sexuality and race and class) identities but as sites in which these attributes are present in preexisting assumptions and constructed through ongoing practice. Thus far, this approach has figured in studies of a number of organizations and occupations, such as law and paralegal work (Pierce 1995), as well as nursing, teaching, librarianship, and social work (Williams 1995). Prisons are, without much question, both atypical organizations and unconventional work environments. In the jargon of the organizational literature, prisons belong to the small class of organizations known as "total institutions" (Goffman 1961), that is, these are settings in which people, at least for a time, live the whole of their lives. Residential schools, nursing homes, and the military are other examples of this type. This fact gives prison work some unique characteristics. Officers deal with a client population that is, by definition, involuntary, and thus understandably hostile and uncooperative at times. At the very minimum, prison inmates have a vested interest in subverting at least some elements of institutional control. Unlike most workers, prison officers are involved with the totality of inmates' lives, supervising and surveilling their meals, showers, communications, and a multitude of normally private aspects of personal and sexual behavior.

Even given this, prisons are in some ways ideal settings for exploring processes of organizational and occupational gendering. Ideas about gender have shaped prisons, literally and figuratively, from their very first appearance as institutions of social control. Nineteenth-century reformers made women's presumed inherent difference from men the primary basis of their case for separate institutions for women, run exclusively by female staff. In a similar way, ideas about masculinity played a role in the architecture and styles of discipline advocated in early men's prisons. In a more general sense, the role of the total institution as a societal microcosm (Goffman 1961), as a small society in itself, means that gendering processes that may be diffuse or hidden in more open organizations may be easier to identify in this closed institutional context (Hearn and Parkin 1987).

Studying work in prisons also presents a virtually unique opportunity to perform a controlled comparison, one that may tell us much about the ways that gender inequality is maintained in more typical occupational settings. There is a considerable body of research on gender and work that relies on the comparative case study method, counterposing, for example, the experiences of fast-food workers and insurance sales agents (Leidner 1991, 1993), nurses and marines (Williams 1989), flight attendants and bill collectors (Hochschild 1983), and lawyers and paralegals (Pierce 1995). In some ways, however, this research is limited by the constraints of the occupational structure itself. The kinds of jobs that men and women do are very different, and it is difficult to directly compare the experiences of men integrating nursing, for example, to those of women lawyers. More light might be shed on the forces that shape workers' experiences in male- and female-dominated occupations if one could compare a parallel case, a pair of institutions, similar in form and function, but in which one is dominated by women and one by men. These cases are rare, and none have yet been examined in a comparative study. The prison presents just such an opportunity. Men's and women's prisons are (at least nominally) parallel institutions, created for the same purposes and oriented toward the same goals. In general, the job of the correctional officer is the same in both settings; officers are responsible for enforcing institutional rules, dealing with inmate problems and complaints, supervising routine daily activities of inmates, and maintaining security. The similarity of the male- and female-dominated forms of the same institution thus allows for a somewhat controlled comparison, one in which, by holding the context constant (or as nearly so as possible), we may be able to identify some of the factors that produce inequalities of results and rewards for male and female workers, regardless of the organizational or occupational setting.

The analysis presented in this book draws on a number of sources. The primary material involves interviews I conducted from 1993 to 1998 with seventy-two corrections officers working in two men's and three women's prisons. Three are located in the South, two in the Midwest. Officers at state and federal facilities each constitute one-half of those in my study. There are twenty-seven women and forty-five men in the sample, and there are fifty-one white officers, fourteen African-Americans, and seven Hispanics. I conducted interviews with each officer that lasted between thirty minutes and three hours, asking them about their paths to the occupation, their training, and a wide variety of questions about work experiences and future plans (see the Methodological Appendix for a complete description of the sample and methodology). These data are supplemented by visits I made to prisons in two additional states. Though I was unable to undertake anything approaching complete ethnographies of these institutions, I was able to do some observation and informal interviewing at each.

The Theory of Gendered Organizations

The approach guiding the work presented here is relatively new, but it grows out of a long-established tradition of scholarship in gender, organizations, and occupations. Almost all this research begins from the same empirical problem: the large and persistent wage gap between men and women workers. Though women now make up 47 percent of those working in the paid labor force, those who work full-time, year-round, make only 73 percent of the salaries of their male peers.[2] Much of this difference is due to occupational segregation, that is, men and women are in different jobs, and the jobs women hold pay less, on average, than those that men occupy. In 2001, about 20 percent of women workers were concentrated in just seven job categories.[3] Male workers are less occupationally concentrated, and the average wages of the job categories in which they are most heavily represented are higher, on average, than those dominated by women.

The overall wage gap has persisted, however, even as women have begun to integrate some formerly male-dominated jobs. The reason for this is that even when men and women are in the same occupation, women still make less. In 2001, for example, women attorneys earned only 69 percent of the salaries of their male counterparts. This difference is largely due to internal stratification; women tend to occupy the lowest rungs of the occupational ladder. Women attorneys are more likely to be found in specialties like family law, public defense, and government law, all of which pay lower wages than those to be had in corporate law, a male-dominated specialty (Pierce 1995). Women correctional officers, on the other hand, make 83 percent of the wages of their male counterparts,[4] and they are more likely to be found in state rather than federal prisons (where salaries are higher).[5] As of 1995, women were 19 percent of officers in state prisons, but only 12 percent of those in federal facilities. Women are also less likely than men to occupy top administrative posts. Fewer than 10 percent of wardens in adult facilities, including women's prisons, are women (Martin and Jurik 1996).

But these well-established findings take us only so far toward solving the puzzle of women's lower wages. Nor do they explain the persistent empirical documentation of women's lower levels of organizational power, status, autonomy, and mobility, a finding that holds regardless of the occupation or organizational setting. Taken as a whole, this research raises at least three further questions. First, why is occupational segregation so persistent, even in the wake of three decades of legal changes that have removed the formal barriers to women's (and men's) entry into occupations formerly dominated by members of the other sex? Second, why is it that the jobs in which women are concentrated pay less? Why are "people" or nurturing skills (disproportionately required by female-dominated jobs) systematically devalued? Finally, what factors keep women at the bottom of the ladder within occupations? Once they make the leap into the pool of lawyers, doctors, construction workers, or correctional officers, why do women sink to the bottom?

Drawing on the theory of gendered organizations (Acker 1990, 1992; Williams 1995), I suggest that the answer to all these questions can be found in the interaction between three factors: the structures of work organizations, the cultural and ideological assumptions upon which they draw and which in turn shape them, and the agency of workers themselves.[6] This approach is grounded in two key assumptions. First, organizations must be viewed from within the context of an unequal society, one in which gender domination exists and is reproduced on an ongoing basis. Gender is not something imported into organizations with workers; it is an inseparable part of organizational structure (Acker 1990, 1992; Williams 1995; see also Smith 1979). Second, in line with the interactionist tradition in the sociology of gender (Kessler and McKenna 1978; West and Zimmerman 1987; West and Fenstermaker 1995), I conceptualize gender as a process, the product of a social construction that can be carried out both at the micro level (by the individual actor) and at the macro level (by social institutions, policies, and practices) (Acker 1990, 1992; Britton 1997a, 2000; Pierce 1995; Williams 1995). From this perspective, gender structures the organization and is reproduced by organizational policies and actors. In a similar way, notions about class, race, and sexuality are also intertwined with the framework of modern organizations. Though my focus will be on gender, this should not be taken to mean that I view gender as somehow more fundamental than these other characteristics. I hope to provide some insight as well into how these other axes of inequality shape organizational life.

Levels of Gendering in Organizations

One can conceptualize the process of gendering at a number of levels. Organizational structures, in the form of policies and practices, assume and build on the gender division of labor and more general notions about men and women. Workers in organizations exercise their own agency by "doing gender," that is, men and women workers reproduce themselves (and others) as organizational actors with "appropriately" gendered characteristics. Culture plays a role as well—as the example of the prison suggests, we think about and represent organizations and occupations in deeply gendered ways. At the outset, however, it is important to note that while these levels will be separated for the purposes of analysis, in reality, they are always connected in dialectical processes of interaction; structure, agency, and culture are all interlinked in ongoing processes of organizational gendering. Gendered policies, for example, may be challenged by organized groups of workers who find themselves disadvantaged as a result. Organizational structures provide the bounded contexts in which workers define and contest occupational masculinities and femininities. Gendered cultural representations and ideologies affect our job choices, employers' preferences for particular kinds of workers, and the practices that take place within organizations themselves. The great power of the gendered organizations approach lies in its potential to help us to understand not only the gendering process at each of these levels but also the interconnections between them.

Gendering through Organizational Structure

Fundamentally, organizations are gendered at the level of structure. In a very basic sense, organizations build on and reproduce a division of labor between the public and private spheres, between production and reproduction (Acker 1992). Most modern work organizations presume that the labor involved in the day-to-day reproduction of their workers may be relegated to the private realm, thus enacting a rigid separation between the work lives of their employees and such activities as childbirth, child care, sexuality, eating, and sleeping (Acker 1992). This division between public and private is on the order of an ideal type, of course. Some employers now provide benefits such as child care and paid maternity leave, though this is a rarity, and those who do so are still widely regarded as having done something extra, beyond the minimum necessary compensation due all workers. Such a division also makes much more sense from the perspective of men, rather than women, workers. Because women are primarily responsible for domestic tasks and child care, they often experience, and deal with the consequences of, the spillover of their duties in the private realm into their working days. Particular employers may be more or less tolerant of this, but again, workers see the former as unusually benevolent exceptions. Male workers typically enjoy much greater freedom from the distractions of the private sphere. Underlying the concept of the "job," then, is the assumption that its holder will be able to honor the separation between public and private presumed by the organization. This means that jobs, the most basic units of organizational structure, are based on notions about gender and sustain its reproduction. As Acker writes: "The closest the disembodied worker doing the abstract job comes to a real worker is the male worker whose life centers on his full-time, life-long job, while his wife or another woman takes care of his personal needs and children" (1990: 149).

The presumptions built into most jobs shape women's paths to sex-segregated occupations. Research fairly consistently shows that, in the abstract, men and women value the same kinds of job characteristics, with salary, autonomy, prestige, and location topping the list (Bose and Rossi 1983; England 1982; Jencks, Perman, and Rainwater 1988; Kaufman and Fetters 1980; O'Farrell and Harlan 1982; Rowe and Snizek 1995; Walker, Tausky, and Oliver 1982). However, women, more than men, are forced to make trade-offs between work and family. This often restricts their options in terms of working hours, schedules, location, transfers, and travel and in practice can make female-dominated jobs appear more attractive. Many of these jobs offer regular hours and at least somewhat flexible schedules, allow for some "crossover," however limited, between home and work life, and impose few penalties for women's movement between locales and in and out of the labor force. Women pay a premium for this flexibility, obviously. The presumption of a rigid separation between public and private domains and its effect on women's (and men's) work affects the division of labor within organizations. This fact alone goes quite a long way toward explaining why women predominate in clerical positions, and men in administrative ones.

But it can also explain stratification within occupations. Workers who are free to put in long hours are generally perceived by employers as more committed and as better candidates for raises and promotions. Data indicate that men work more overtime than women, on average, and men predominate in the kinds of careers that require extraordinary numbers of hours per week. Domestic responsibilities may make women less likely to pursue avenues for upward mobility. This correctional officer, a white woman I interviewed in a men's prison, had repeatedly eschewed promotion for precisely this reason:

> [In my previous job], I went up [for promotion] and then I asked to be put back down. I just didn't want the responsibility. It was just too much all the time. It was like I never had any time for me and my family. I don't want that. *Do you think women are more likely to think that way?* I think so. Because being a mom and . . . a woman is, how do you put it? She's got to be like a Jill of all trades, and that just goes along with being a female. *So maybe it's easier for men to move up the chain for that reason?* I think so. That's the way I see it. It would take a really special person to have the rank and those responsibilities plus a household.

The distinction between public and private spheres is even more strongly reinforced in jobs that require higher levels of responsibility and commitment, such as supervisory positions. In the current context, it does indeed take a "really special" woman to combine this kind of work with primary family responsibilities. The exclusion of the "typical" woman worker reveals the deeply gendered substructure of mobility ladders themselves. Though slots such as "supervisor" or "manager" may be conceived of as gender-neutral, they are built on gendered notions about their incumbents.

In a less abstract sense, organizational structures presume and reproduce gender through policies and practices. These may take the form of explicitly exclusionary rules, such as those that historically barred women from many male-dominated occupations and also excluded men from some female-dominated jobs. Most such formal barriers fell with the passage of Title VII of the Civil Rights Act of 1964 and the Equal Employment Opportunity Act of 1972. Even so, lawsuits were necessary to completely open the doors to some jobs in some fields, corrections among them. Men had always worked as officers in women's prisons, though their assignments were often restricted. Most commonly, men worked perimeter posts, such as gates and guard towers (rather than living areas), and served as the disciplinary threat of last resort for women prisoners. Before the 1970s, however, virtually no women worked in men's prisons. Legislation, by itself, did little to change this. The reason is that administrators were left with a loophole, the bona fide occupational qualification (BFOQ) exemption. Under this rule, an employer who can show that a particular job cannot be performed by a member of one sex may legally discriminate in hiring. Some jobs, such as sperm donor or surrogate mother, obviously fall into this category. Prison administrators initially argued that the occupation of correctional officer (in a men's prison) was another.

This issue reached the Supreme Court in 1977, in *Dothard v. Rawlinson*, 433 U.S. 321 (1977). Diane Rawlinson, a twenty-two-year-old who had recently graduated from college with a degree in correctional psychology, applied for the position of correctional counselor (at the time, a euphemism for prison guard) in Alabama's prison system. Though she exceeded the educational qualifications for the position (which required a high school degree or its equivalent) and otherwise met age and health stipulations, her application was denied because she failed to meet minimum height and weight standards. She filed suit, challenging these requirements as an unconstitutional instance of gender discrimination. While the suit was pending, Alabama adopted a policy barring women from positions involving contact with male inmates in maximum-security institutions. Rawlinson challenged this policy as well. The Supreme Court, with Justice Potter Stewart writing for the majority, upheld her challenge of the height and weight stipulations, noting that they potentially excluded 40 percent of the female population, but only 1 percent of men. Further, the Court held that these requirements were unsupported by any evidence linking them to effective job performance. Though the Court also found that Alabama's "no contact" rule restricted women to only about 25 percent of available correctional counselor positions, the majority held that the rule was justified in the limited case under consideration, as Alabama's men's maximum-security prisons were characterized by a "jungle atmosphere" and were thus "constitutionally intolerable." The paradoxical upshot of this holding was that, while Rawlinson was denied employment, no other states, unless they were prepared to argue that their prisons were also unconstitutionally violent, could rely on this case to deny jobs to women (Collins 1991; Zimmer 1986). The doors were thus opened for women to move into positions as officers in men's prisons.

Though it is possible for organizational policies to be explicitly gendered, legal proscriptions have now made this much less likely. More commonly, gender is invoked by facially gender-neutral policies that nevertheless reinforce inequality, as well as by informal practices that draw on and reinscribe notions about gender. Rawlinson actually presents an example of the former. The height and weight requirements she challenged were generic, explicitly singling out neither men nor women. They were, however, discriminatory in their effect, excluding forty times more women than men from the potential labor pool. This kind of discrimination has been identified in studies of a number of other organizations as well. Di Tomaso (1989) found that new workers in a manufacturing firm she studied were initially required to enter a general labor pool. Only after several years did they enter the lowest rungs of the internal job ladder. Unfortunately, the jobs at the bottom of the ladder were the most physically demanding; once one moved up, jobs got easier and less strenuous. Management saw this sequence as absolutely necessary, but women were not perceived (and to some degree did not perceive themselves) as suitable for the jobs at the lowest rungs on the ladder. The effect was that women remained in the labor pool, only rarely moving into upper management. Still other studies have shown examples of this kind of discrimination in jobs (like those in prisons) that require shift work or nonstandard working hours (Blum and Kahn 1996; Britton 1997a; Skuratowicz 1996), thus making it difficult for women to find reliable child care, and in those that employ seniority rules in determining promotions or assignments (Blum and Kahn 1996; Zimmer 1986).

Joan Acker (1989, 1990) points to a similar problem with formal job evaluation systems, now widely used to set wages by government and private employers. These schemes evaluate jobs, rather than their incumbents, in terms of a variety of characteristics, such as skill, responsibility, complexity, and training. These measurements are then used in determining equitable wages across organizations. Such systems were initially welcomed as a tool for ameliorating the wage gap and are a cornerstone of comparable-worth strategies. By and large, however, they have not lived up to their initial promise (Acker 1989; Steinberg 1990). The primary reason for this is that the ranking process employed by administrators "assumes a congruence between responsibility, job complexity, and hierarchical position" (Acker 1990: 148); jobs at the bottom of the organizational ladder (disproportionately filled by women) are assumed to be the least difficult, least responsible positions. When managers impose this "gender-neutral" standard on actual organizations, the effect is to give scientific sanction to the lower wages and subordinate organizational position of female workers, and to preserve the advantage of male workers and managers. The resulting rankings appear objective, but in reality they reflect managers' presuppositions about the relative worth of male and female workers (Acker 1989, 1990).

Informal practices in organizations may also be gendered. This can happen, for example, through the intentional subversion of formally gender-neutral policies. Reskin and Padavic (1988) studied the assignments of men and women strike workers at a utility plant. They found that though plant superintendents initially made job assignments that were sex-integrated, department supervisors systematically resegregated workers, slotting women into what they saw as more appropriate jobs in kitchen work and cleaning. Even within the same job title, supervisors gave men and women different tasks, with one supervisor justifying this practice by arguing that men are simply "stronger, more stable minded" (Reskin and Padavic 1988: 541). Prison supervisors in both men's and women's prisons sometimes engage in a similar process, subverting a nominally rotational assignment scheme by posting officers in accord with preexisting notions about the gendered characteristics appropriate for particular positions. In one of the men's prisons I studied, for example, women were routinely assigned clerical duties; men were not. When I queried a female officer about the reasons for this, she simply shrugged and concluded, "I guess that's what they think our role is."

Gendering through Culture

Culture is the second level at which organizations and occupations are gendered. The focus here is on the "construction of images, symbols, and ideologies that justify, explain, and give legitimacy" (Acker 1992: 568) to institutions, organizations, and occupations. These images may be found in a multitude of sources, from language, to commonsense notions about men's and women's work, to popular culture. Ideas about gender form an integral part of the ways that we think about particular organizations. The military, for example, has traditionally been viewed as a place where boys are turned into men, and this image has been reinforced ad nauseam in literally hundreds of war movies (Williams

1989; Britton and Williams 1996). So, too, are notions about gender an inseparable part of cultural ideologies surrounding the prison. As I noted at the outset, for most people, the generic prison is a men's institution, a site in which brutal inmates and sadistic guards perpetually battle for dominance. Evidence for this claim can be drawn from any number of sources. One could point to the sheer number of cultural representations of men's prisons versus those of women's prisons. According to the Internet Movie Database (www.imdb.com), by mid-2002, there had been 91 "women's prison" movies (or TV series) released, as compared with 657 "prison" films.[7] Moreover, the content of these fictional representations differs dramatically; men's prisons are depicted as unimaginably violent, while the relatively few representations of women's prisons are awash in sexuality. Even a cursory glance at titles in the "women in prison" genre (e.g., *Chained Heat*, *Reform School Girls*, *She Devils in Chains*) bears this out.

My experiences with students provide but one demonstration of the prevalence and impact of this kind of ideological construction of the prison. I take students in one of my courses on a tour of a local women's prison. I then have them write about this experience, comparing their preconceptions with their observations from the tour. Students consistently attest that the latter contradict the former. For most of them, preexisting notions are based on ideas about men's prisons and are drawn largely from exaggerated media representations. This student writes:

> As I walked up to the [prison gatehouse] my heart was pounding. I was anxious because I had stereotypical views of what prison was like. I have to admit that I had never been inside a prison until this trip. Many of my views came from the movies. I thought the inmates would be behaving like wild animals. I thought they would be screaming at people and that they would be banging on the bars. I also had the impression that prison would be a dangerous place for anybody to enter because all of the prisoners would be armed. I was scared to be near anyone who was convicted of a crime, especially since many inmates on television are portrayed as very violent.

Without exception, students come away from these tours with a perspective that differs dramatically from both representations in popular culture and commonsense notions about prisoners and prison life. The consistency of their initial views, however, reveals much about the persistence and importance of these images in culture as a whole.

Though it is useful to analyze these images simply in terms of their content, these representations have material effects, molding the choices of workers, influencing hiring and promotion practices, and, in the case of the prison, helping to frame views about inmates and shape disciplinary practices. Some occupations were historically constructed in accord with gendered ideals about their intended workers. The requisites of nursing, for example, were held to be concomitant with women's naturally submissive and nurturing personalities and domestic roles; so, too, did these characteristics suit women for jobs as kindergarten and elementary school teachers (Williams 1995). There is little question that these ideas persist to the present, influencing patterns of sex segregation in these occupations and making men in these jobs seem anomalous, or at least requiring them to account for themselves in some way. The same is true for many male-dominated occupations. In talking about the ideal recruit, a male supervisor in a fire department notes: "What we're really looking for is a man with a big 'S' on his chest" (Skuratowicz 1996). Prison supervisors also speak of the necessity of hiring "real men" for the job of supervising male inmates.

Though it is possible, generally, to identify a dominant ideological conception of a particular occupation or organization, this can become contested terrain as formerly excluded groups seek to redefine the hegemonic images of their work. Women police officers, for example, emphasize the benefits of defusing conflict, rather than resorting to physical force (Miller 1999). Similarly, Fletcher (1998) reports that female engineers she studied at a high-tech firm routinely employ relational practices in interactions with coworkers, such as mutual empowerment and team building, which serve to disrupt (at least temporarily) the competitive, hierarchical structure and atmosphere of their work environment. Women correctional officers in men's prisons, through their perceptions and practices, also challenge prevailing stereotypes of the prison as too violent for women.

Gendering through Agency

The final way that organizations are gendered is through the medium of agency. This is the microlevel of gendering in organizations and occupations; it includes all the interactions in which workers are involved that, intentionally or not, invoke gender or reproduce gender inequality, as well as processes of identity construction through which individuals come to see themselves as "appropriately" gendered through their work. Workers bring their own identities, interests, and desires to organizations, and gender shapes all these in powerful ways. Men or women workers may organize to protect gender-based interests. Historically, alliances between male workers have played a particularly important role in perpetuating gender inequality. Heidi Hartmann (1976) details the nineteenth-century efforts of the Cigarmakers International Union to legally bar women from working overtime; during the same period, the International Typographical Union mobilized to deny women apprenticeships and training in typesetting, reserving the use of the newly invented Linotype for its male membership (Hartmann 1976; Roos 1990). Still other unions organized for maximum-hours laws for women (but not men) and equal-pay legislation (Cockburn 1983, 1985). Far from the humanitarian impulses they seem, both of these efforts preserved male hegemony in that employers preferred to hire employees who could work long hours if necessary and, if given the choice between a male and a female worker at the same cost, would invariably choose the former. A similar process was at work in the professions, where race- and class-privileged men organized during the nineteenth and early twentieth centuries to deny training and licensing to women and working-class and minority men (Pierce 1995; Witz 1990).

Other kinds of interactions between workers may also reinforce gender inequality. Sexual harassment, though now at least formally illegal, has this effect. There is some evidence that women in nontraditional jobs experience more sexual harassment than women in traditional ones (O'Farrell and Harlan 1982), and that harassment can serve as an effective disincentive for women to step outside conventional roles. Resistance may take other forms as well. Zimmer (1986, 1987) documents male officers' efforts to deny women on-the-job training as they moved into jobs in men's prisons. Martin (1980, 1995) and Prokos and Padavic (2002) observe similar dynamics in policing. Still another obstacle for women in corrections and policing has been the insistence of their male counterparts that the job is too dangerous for women, and their consequent efforts to protect them (Britton 1997a, 1999; Jurik 1985, 1988; Martin and Jurik 1996; Zimmer 1986, 1987).

Alliances between women could also, theoretically, work to preserve women's dominance in female-dominated organizations or occupations. In truth, however, not only has this kind of resistance failed to materialize, but women have generally welcomed men with open arms. Leaders in fields such as nursing and social work have advocated men's recruitment as a route to increasing the wages and status of these occupations. Similarly, women working as officers and supervisors in women's prisons do not question the presence of their male officers, seeing them as absolutely necessary for tasks such as dealing with violent female inmates. Though women *could* form alliances to resist the integration of men into "their" occupations, this has not been the case. In fact, men are generally welcomed, and their presence quickly comes to seem indispensable.

Gendered agency is also important at the level of individual identity. Men and women "do gender" (West and Zimmerman 1987; West and Fenstermaker 1995) in organizational and occupational contexts by interpreting themselves and others as possessors of appropriate masculinity or femininity (Goffman 1977). Men in male-dominated jobs may derive substantial satisfaction from the confirmation of their masculinity through work. A substantial literature on masculinity and blue-collar occupations suggests that manual labor, in particular, can be a potent vehicle for the expression of masculine prowess, autonomy, and independence from women (Peña 1981; Collinson and Collinson 1989). Men in policing, correctional work, and other kinds of protective service occupations also see the job as a resource for "doing" masculinity. This white man I interviewed in a men's prison gains satisfaction from his work for this reason: "I tell [the inmates], I say, I like my job. They say why? Cause I'm keeping you off the street. Keeping my family safe from people like you. Cause we have a high majority of sexual perverts in here." This man invokes his masculine role as "natural" protector, keeping his family safe from the threat posed by sexual predators. Similarly, men in management jobs benefit from and collude in the reproduction of the stereotype of the successful manager as someone who possesses "a tough-minded approach to problems; analytic abilities to abstract and plan; a capacity to set aside personal, emotional considerations in the interests of task accomplishment; and a cognitive superiority in problem-solving and decision-making" (Kanter 1977: 21). Not coincidentally, all these traits are traditionally associated with masculinity.

As I have suggested throughout, however, agency, structure, and culture are simultaneously implicated in the gendering process. Because most organizational contexts are already masculinized, masculinity tends to be conflated by workers and in policies and practices with the necessary or inherent qualifications of particular jobs or the requisites of organizational success. In this case, structure allows culture and agency to fade into the background. These connections may become visible when women workers contest men's dominance by integrating formerly male-dominated spaces. At such times, men may be prompted to define an oppositional occupational masculinity, framing entire job categories or particular tasks as too dangerous or inappropriate for women and seeking to resegregate the occupation or organization through formal or informal mechanisms. This same process occurs when men find their masculinity challenged by integrating female-dominated occupations. Men in these jobs resolve this conflict through a variety of strategies, such as moving into administrative roles, carving out particular specialties or tasks formerly performed by women as masculine domains, or disconnecting their core sense of self from their work (Pierce 1995; Williams 1995).

Women may also "do" gender through their work, but the consequences of doing femininity differ dramatically from those of doing masculinity. In a cultural and organizational context already stratified by gender, to do masculinity is to affirm dominance. Emphasizing femininity, on the other hand, generally enacts submission and subordination (West and Zimmerman 1987). Evidence of this can be gleaned from women's experiences in both female- and male-dominated occupations. A wealth of literature shows that women (but not men) working in jobs as diverse as secretaries (Pringle 1989, 1993), paralegals (Pierce 1995), nurses (Williams 1989), and flight attendants (Hochschild 1983) are expected to display a host of female-identified traits, such as submission, nurturance, emotional support, tolerance, and patience. Women paralegals, for example, are often required to "mother" attorneys, soothing their egos in the event of a loss in court, smoothing over the interpersonal conflicts they cause, and remaining calm even in the face of spectacularly bad behavior (Pierce 1995). Some women may, in fact, gain satisfaction from doing femininity at work in this way. The problem is that all these gendered abilities are conflated with sex in occupational contexts; they become something that women *are* rather than something they *do*. As such, they are not seen as job skills, nor are they rewarded as part of the package of human capital brought to the job by women workers.

Women in male-dominated jobs also do gender. They can accomplish this by emphasizing the parts or requirements of the job that conform to the requisites of femininity, as when women physicians specialize in pediatric medicine, or when women attorneys practice in the areas of family law or public defense. Perhaps not coincidentally, however, the rewards in these female-dominated specialities are lower than those in male-dominated ones. Women can also do gender by accentuating their difference from male coworkers. Some women carve out what they see as distinctively feminine work styles or emphasize women's unique contributions. Female correctional officers sometimes focus on interpersonal communications skills and their calming effect on male inmates, as does this white woman:

> As far as women with men, I think that, this could be kinda sexist, but I do think that women have a calming effect on men. For the simple reason is that when I work with men, they say about this female, "I don't wanna hurt her, so I'll go ahead and do it for this girl." I've seen a lot of macho head banging going on. You know, who's tougher, the officer or the inmate? See, I can go up, "I'm just a little old girl, come on, don't hit me, I like my face the way it is." And so, it's less of a macho challenging type thing, I've found. It worked for me very well. I worked with super high custody inmates, and real macho men don't have to hit girls. They go after the bigger [targets], so it works for me.

In this case, the officer uses gender to her advantage, defusing conflict and managing male inmates in a way that avoids "macho head banging." This woman does gender by using difference as a resource that helps her to perform her job more effectively.

Culture and organizational structure combine to constrain the boundaries of women's assertion of gendered difference and to limit its rewards, however. Women in male-dominated jobs must contend with preexisting norms and policies based on the biographies and behaviors of their male counterparts. In practice, this often means that women are faced with very few real choices; they must either adopt male-defined requisites for success, and face the peril of being perceived as "unfeminine," or they may reject them, doing so at the cost of success as it has been organizationally defined. Some women, like the correctional officer just quoted, are successful in carving out specifically gendered work styles, emphasizing their difference from men, and using gender as a resource. An already masculinized cultural and organizational context means that the rewards that accrue to difference vary substantially for men and women, however. As Williams notes, regardless of the occupation, "men are rewarded for emphasizing their difference from women; women are typically penalized for any difference they (willingly or not) represent from men" (1993: 3). This observation clearly has resonance in the case of the prison. As I demonstrate, male officers in men's and women's prisons reap considerable benefits from asserting their allegedly distinctive masculine capacity to use physical force. Women's purportedly unique gendered abilities, however, are viewed in a different light. In extreme cases, coworkers and supervisors see these traits as potentially dangerous, as when "too much" communication is held to lead women officers to become overly familiar with inmates. More often, however, organizational policy and practice simply frame women's unique abilities as extraneous, rather than as a part of the essential package of skills possessed by any successful officer.

Overall, the perspective I employ in this book argues that the gendering of organizations and occupations is the outcome of a complex interplay between structure, culture, and agency. Bringing these factors together in a systematic way allows us to provide some answers to the three questions posed at the outset of this discussion. The persistent patterns of occupational segregation we observe in the American labor market are the outcome of the structural expectations built into men's and women's jobs, the cultural ideology that attaches to them and shapes the choices of their potential incumbents and employers, and the historical and ongoing efforts of privileged groups of workers to maintain their dominance. Similarly, organizational structure, through policy and practice, combines with the differential cultural valuing of men's and women's skills to ensure that women workers' assertions of difference do not accrue the same benefits as those of their male counterparts. Finally, cultural ideals about gender-appropriate work, organizational practices that enact these ideas, and the constrained choices of workers all come together to produce a process in which, regardless of the occupation or organization, women generally wind up at the bottom. This book explores the workings of these general processes in shaping our ideas about the prison and the day-to-day practices of the officers within. This analysis demonstrates that gender is as much a part of the edifice of the iron cage that is the prison as its omnipresent walls, bars, and fences.[8]

Chapter Overview

Chapter 2 presents a historical review of the development of men's and women's prisons in America, infused by an analysis of the role of gender in this process. This chapter demonstrates how ideas about masculinity influenced the design and practices of men's prisons from their first appearance in this country. Women's prisons did not appear in America until 1839, and their construction was the outcome of an explicitly gendered struggle in which mostly white, middle-class women prison reformers argued that female offenders would benefit from different, more feminine surroundings and from a maternal mode of care and rehabilitation. The "reformatories" that resulted reflected many of the reformers' ideals in both design and practice.

The next chapter provides a brief social history of the occupation of the correctional officer. The first section draws on historical literature to describe the conditions of work and discipline in both men's and women's prisons. I then move to a discussion of current literature, providing statistics and background about the occupation and the legal struggles over the issue of men's and women's employment in prisons housing inmates of the opposite sex (usually referred to generically as "cross-gender" supervision).

In chapter 4, I trace the paths of the officers in my study to prison work. The sex-segregated labor market fundamentally shapes the routes of men and women to the occupation, with men usually moving from one male-dominated, masculine gender-typed occupation to another. Women come from the opposite side of a segregated market, making their transition to prison work a rockier one. I then move on to focus on the training received by officer recruits and the ways that ideas about violence and masculinity undergird this process.

Chapter 5 explores officers' perceptions of and interactions with inmates in men's and women's prisons. In officers' descriptions of their work, I find little support for the stereotype of the brutal and sadistic guard of media-fed fantasies. The bulk of officers' comments draw on distinctions between women and men inmates, a comparison in which the former are always lacking. I also look at what officers think about managing violence and sexuality in their day-to-day work. The comparison between men's and women's prisons again produces some surprising findings; on both accounts, officers perceive that women are most troublesome.

In chapter 6, I discuss officers' feelings about the work itself, their relationships with coworkers and supervisors, and their hopes for advancement. For most of those in my study, inmates are "the least of [their] problems"; it is these more typical aspects of the work they find most problematic. And as in other male- and female-dominated jobs, the stories of the integration of men and women into prisons housing the opposite sex are characterized by asymmetry. Women face resistance in the form of an ideology that links masculinity and physical strength and practices that translate these into requisites for the ideal officer. Men benefit from accentuating these qualities, even in women's prisons.

I conclude in chapter 7 by bringing together the strands of the analysis to show how the prison, as an institution, is gendered in and through culture, structure, and agency. I then discuss what this analysis implies for the theoretical framework guiding this research and for processes of organizational change.

2

Penology in America

Men's and Women's Prisons as Gendered Projects

Prisons are such a common feature of the American landscape that they have come to seem natural, indeed, inevitable. But prisons did not exist in the United States or in Europe until about two hundred years ago. During the colonial era and the early republic, crime and its consequences were left to the discretion of local communities. The fine and the lash were the most common punishments. The latter was often administered in public in hopes that the offender's shame would be as effective a deterrent to crime as the beating itself (Colvin 1997; Hirsch 1992; Rothman 1990). Punishments were not generally differentiated by sex; women as well as men were subject to the full range of prescribed discipline. Though capital punishment was used rarely in early America, both men and women faced the executioner (Colvin 1997; Lewis 1965; Preyer 1982).

The first American prison opened in Massachusetts in 1785; by the turn of the century, eight of the sixteen states had established their own institutions. Far from self-evident solutions to crime, however, early prisons were embattled from their first appearance. State legislatures were reluctant to provide the funds for prisons' construction and operation, and critics immediately noted their tendency to increase crime through the association of all kinds of offenders (Colvin 1997; Lewis 1965). Our current reliance on incarceration is the outcome of a complex and contested institutional project shaped from the outset by ideas about gender, race, and class.

If one assesses that project in terms of its sheer rate of proliferation, it has been an astounding success. As of the last official prison census, in 1995, there were 1,158 state and federally operated prisons in the United States, an increase of more than 15 percent over just five

TABLE 2.1
Number Incarcerated and Rate of Incarceration by Race/Sex Group, 2000

	Number incarcerated	Incarceration rate (per 100,000 population)
White men	436,500	449
Black men	572,900	3,457
Hispanic men	206,900	1,220
White women	34,500	34
Black women	37,400	205
Hispanic women	10,000	60

SOURCE: Beck and Harrison (2001), tables 14 and 15.

years earlier (Stephan 1997). The total prison population in 2000 was 1,312,354 inmates, a number that gives the United States the dubious distinction of incarcerating more of its citizens than any other country in the world. Throughout the 1990s, the prison population increased at a rate of 6 percent per year (Beck and Harrison 2001).

As has been the case since the first prisons were built, women constitute a minority of America's prison population, currently accounting for 6.6 percent of the total, up from about 4 percent in 1925. Women's rates of incarceration have recently risen at a much faster pace than men's, however, increasing 436 percent from 1980 to 2000, compared with 233 percent for men. The current inmate population is, as it has always been, disproportionately composed of members of minority groups. As table 2.1 indicates, among men, whites account for 35 percent of the total prison population; blacks, 46 percent; and Hispanics, 16 percent. For women, the distribution is similar; whites account for 41 percent of those in prison; blacks, 45 percent; and Hispanics, 12 percent. Incarceration rates present much more dramatic evidence of the racial inequalities at the heart of the American prison system. Black men and women are about seven times more likely to be incarcerated than whites; Hispanics are three times more likely. The poor are also disproportionately represented in prison. In 1997, while 68 percent of male prison inmates and 54 percent of female inmates reported holding a job prior to arrest, their incomes were extremely low. Forty-three percent of men and 54 percent of women reported making less than $12,000 per year.[1]

Speaking of "the prison" in monolithic terms is inaccurate, however. In the course of this research, I interviewed officers at five facilities. Among just these five were both state and federal prisons, men's and women's institutions, prison "camps," prison "farms," a "boot camp," and institutions designed and run utilizing at least some of the elements of the "reformatory" model. This diversity reflects distinct historical legacies. The first prisons were part of what criminal justice historians describe as America's first penal system, that consisting of adult institutions. The second system was the product of the movement to establish juvenile reformatories and marks its beginning in 1825, with the opening of the New York House of Refuge. The third, the adult reformatory movement, is generally held to have been inaugurated with the opening of the Elmira Reformatory in Elmira, New York, in 1876 (Hirsch 1992; Rothman 1990). Though not often recognized as such, the post–Civil War Southern systems of chain gangs, convict leasing, and prison farms can be considered a fourth discrete correctional system. Of these, only institutions holding adults (the first, third, and fourth systems) will be the focus here.[2]

This chapter traces the history of men's and women's prisons in America, demonstrating how gender was implicated in the ideologies of reformers and daily practices in these institutions. Race and class shaped the foundations of American prisons from the outset and interwove in complex patterns with ideas about gender to shape our current prison system. I also describe the institutions that are the settings for this research, placing them in the context of the historical projects from which they developed.

The Birth of the Penitentiary

The adult prison system emerged in a context of dramatic social change. By the middle to late eighteenth century punishments that had been the primary sanctions for criminal behavior began to lose legitimacy in both the United States and Europe. There is disagreement about why, but several factors probably played a role. Industrialization and a rising market economy were engines of change, dramatically increasing the wealth of some groups while worsening the poverty of others. The concentration of wealth in the hands of a new industrial class was a prime contributor to a panic over rising rates of property crime that gripped the American public from 1790 to 1830 (whether crime was actually increasing is a matter of dispute) (Masur 1989). A growing and increasingly mobile population meant that strangers became commonplace in local communities. This had the effect of undermining the deterrent value of public punishments, which depended at least in part on the fear of being shamed before neighbors with whom one had personal relationships (Hirsch 1992). Enlightenment ideas about the rationality of man and an ongoing process of "civilization" (Elias 1978, 1982 [1939]) also led to increasing discomfort around the spectacle of public punishment (Colvin 1997; Garland 1990; Hirsch 1992; Rothman 1990).

By 1820, America had fifteen prisons. These early institutions housed men and women, children, and the insane. From their inception, prisons have disproportionately held inmates of racial and ethnic minority groups and the poor; blacks were one-third of the inmates at Walnut Street Jail in Philadelphia (designated a state prison in 1790) and 24 percent of inmates at Newgate Prison (established in 1796 in New York). Irish immigrants constituted about one-eighth of the population at both facilities (Colvin 1997). The unemployed, uneducated, and lower and working classes made up the majority of the inmate population in every eighteenth-century prison.

Before the 1820s, however, prisons were less part of a systematic strategy for reform and control than a reaction to perceptions of increasing crime rates and accelerating social change. As David Rothman notes:

> A repulsion from the gallows rather than any faith in the penitentiary spurred the late-eighteenth century construction. . . . To reformers, the advantages of the institutions were external, and they hardly imagined that life inside the prison might rehabilitate the criminal. . . . The fact of imprisonment, not its internal routine, was of chief importance. (1990: 62)

Indeed, though many institutions constructed before 1820 were called "penitentiaries," that is, places in which the errant might repent and be transformed, none had in place a rehabilitative program (Rothman 1990).

This changed with the inauguration of the "science" of penology through the introduction of two rival systems of prison discipline. These were the separate (or Pennsylvania) model and the congregate (or Auburn) plan. Both sought to keep inmates from associating with one another, though they did so in different ways. The Pennsylvania model was first implemented at Walnut Street Jail and found its fullest expression at Eastern State Penitentiary in 1829. In Pennsylvania-style prisons, inmates were kept in *complete* solitary confinement. Brought into the prison in hoods, they spent their days engaged in craft labor in their cells and never saw (or were seen by) another inmate. Under the Auburn plan, inaugurated at Auburn State Prison in New York in 1825, inmates labored in congregate workshops during the day and were confined to individual cells at night, all the while observing a rule of absolute silence.

Beyond this key difference, however, the two systems organized penitentiary discipline around the same three central tenets of separation, obedience, and labor (Colvin 1997; Dumm 1987; Rothman 1990). Reformers advocated separation because they believed that prisoners who were allowed to associate with one another confirmed their own bad habits while at the same time acquiring new ones. The doctrine of obedience was rooted in the belief that criminals were the products of disordered lives. A Pennsylvania prison commission in 1835 contended that convicts are "men of idle habits, vicious propensities, and depraved passions" (quoted in Rothman 1990: 102) who had failed to learn respect for limits. The call for hard labor was also rooted in ideas about the etiology of criminal behavior. Criminals, particularly property offenders, were held to be idlers, too lazy to work, who instead stole the property of others. Hard labor would create lasting work habits, removing the motivation for theft. The overall aim of this tripartite system was the reconstitution of the inmate as an atomized, disciplined, hardworking "model" citizen (Colvin 1997).

Yet the citizen imagined was by no means generic. As critics have long noted, the subject at the heart of reformers' discourse occupied a particular class position. Through the mechanism of the penitentiary, middle-class reformers sought to instill their own idealized values around work and respect for property while at the same time producing malleable, individualized members of the proletariat. Thomas Dumm writes:

> The penitentiary was not only a means of keeping track of and controlling the movement of criminals. More important was the way in which it attempted to instill in the propertyless the same interests as informed the behavior of the propertied, without providing them with property. . . . By recreating the tensions that informed the behavior of those of the "great middle class," the penitentiary would become a means of reinforcing the relationships that bound the citizenry and political authority together. (1987: 126)

Reform rhetoric framed crime as a rejection of middle-class values and, ultimately, as a violation of the social contract at the heart of civil society (Hirsch 1992). Then (as now) this had the useful effect of focusing panic over crime and targeting public attention solely on the lower, "dangerous" classes. This was an implicitly (and sometimes explicitly) racialized discourse as well, since blacks, the Irish, and other racialized groups predominated among the ranks of the propertyless.[3]

Penitentiary advocates' identification of criminals as "idle," "vicious," and "depraved" *men* and their formulation of disciplinary techniques to reproduce the model citizen were strategies that also implicated gender. Dominant accounts of the roots of criminality conspicuously excluded middle-class women, as prevailing norms around femininity held that idleness was the natural state of the "refined" woman. To explain the criminality of the working-class and poor women who were housed alongside men in penitentiaries, criminologists offered a different analysis: such women were utter negations of femininity. As Francis Leiber wrote in 1833: "A woman, when she commits a crime, acts more in contradiction to her whole moral organization, i.e., must be more depraved, must have sunk already deeper than a man" (quoted in Rafter 1990: 13). Criminal women, unlike their male counterparts, were beyond redemption, by nature corrupt, and outside the reach of the disciplinary regime of the penitentiary.

Even the rehabilitated subject was implicitly male. The goal of penitentiary discipline was to reconstitute the "ideal" citizen as the atomized individual presumed by the social contractarian ideals at the heart of liberal democracy. Yet women stand in an ambivalent relationship to the social contract and to citizenship itself. Liberal theorists did not view women as free and equal subjects in their own right. Because women were generally denied the right of citizenship, reformers' calls for a program of penitentiary discipline that would "qualify the criminal for the resumption of rights" (quoted in Butler 1997: 135) did not apply equally to women prisoners. As Anne Butler aptly questions, "Since society denied women the processes of full citizenship in general, what rights would women inmates prepare to resume?" (1997: 135). The citizens presumed by liberal democratic ideology are economically productive, rational, male heads of household (Arneil 1999; Held 1993; Pateman 1988). It is this group to whom citizenship was originally granted by the Constitution. It was to their example that penitentiary advocates turned in evoking the model citizen (Butler 1997).

Disciplinary practices in early prisons also illustrate gender differences. Military regimentation permeated all aspects of the system. Prisoners moved to and from cells in the "lockstep" march that was one of the hallmarks of the Auburn regime. While marching, inmates kept their eyes on prison officers; at other times, they were required to stare at the floor or to look only at the work being performed. Eye contact with other prisoners was strictly forbidden. Officers rigorously, and successfully, at least during the early years of these institutions, enforced these rules through the liberal use of the lash. Whereas Pennsylvania-style prisons relied on architecture to avoid contamination of inmates through association, congregate prisons did so through physical brutality (Colvin 1997: 91). Administrators of congregate institutions were ardent defenders of the use of corporal punishment, believing it to be not only a necessary disciplinary mechanism but also an indispensable tool for breaking the spirits of inmates (Colvin 1997).

Women were housed alongside men in institutions of the Auburn type, with the first group of women inmates being sentenced to Auburn Prison in 1825 (Rafter 1990). Neither the physical structures of these institutions nor their disciplinary regimes had been designed with women in mind, however. Administrators treated women either as afterthoughts or as annoyances. Reformers' and legislatures' mandate to separate the sexes in congregate institutions worked to disadvantage women, as wardens placed them in makeshift quarters away from the main (men's) inmate population. At Auburn, for example, women were initially kept in an overcrowded, unventilated, third-floor attic above the institution's kitchen. They were not allowed out for work or exercise. Until 1832, they had no regular supervision and no protection from one another. They were required to labor not at industrial work but at sewing. Although women were "spared" the regime of silence and hard labor, their conditions were nevertheless worse than the men's (Rafter 1990). An Auburn chaplain noted in 1830: "To be a male convict in this prison would be quite tolerable; but to be a *female* convict, for any protracted period, would be worse than death" (quoted in Lewis 1965: 164).

Conditions were not much different for women in any Auburn-style facility of the day. In 1842, women inmates in one Illinois prison were kept "in the cook house in the day time and in a cellar [under the warden's house] at night" (quoted in Dodge 1999: 911). Thirty years later, conditions had hardly improved; between 1870 and 1896, women inmates at another Illinois institution were kept on the fourth floor of an administration building. They were allowed out for a once-yearly stroll and spent their days engaged in knitting and light manufacture, as well as mending and sewing for the male convicts and officers (Dodge 1999). Guarded (when at all) by men, women suffered sexual exploitation and abuse. The case of Rachel Welch, an Auburn inmate who became pregnant in prison and died as a result of a lashing in 1826, was not atypical. State investigatory reports of the period are filled with accounts of pregnancies among long-serving inmates and even some instances of forced brothel servitude by women prisoners for the benefit of male officers and inmates (Freedman 1981; Rafter 1990).

As Rafter (1990) argues, the neglect and abuse of women inmates and their exclusion from penitentiary disciplinary regimes stemmed from a number of factors. First, as noted previously, female criminals were viewed by criminologists and penologists of the day as much worse than male criminals. In 1888, a British penal authority wrote that male prisoners possessed "some reason and forethought," but that a woman inmate behaved "more . . . like a madwoman than a rational, reflecting human being" (quoted in Butler 1997: 27). Minimally, male criminals possessed rationality that could be reawakened by discipline. Women were simply irredeemable. Women were also easy to ignore because of their relatively small numbers. During the late eighteenth and early nineteenth centuries, women typically made up anywhere from 1 to 10 percent of any given prison's population. According to one observer, there were only ninety-seven women in prison in the most populous states during the 1830s (Rafter 1990).

Race and class combined with these factors to ensure the disregard and maltreatment of women inmates. Throughout the nineteenth century, black women were even more disproportionately represented in prison populations than black men. In Ohio in 1840, 49 percent of female inmates, versus 10 percent of males, were black; in Tennessee in 1868, the comparable figures were 100 versus 60 percent (Rafter 1990). Poor women of all races constituted the bulk of the prison inmates in all states. Unlike men, these women suffered under the twin burdens of racist and classist notions about their character, as well as prevailing ideas about their inherent irredeemability. These facts provided ready rationalizations for abuse and made a program of penitentiary discipline irrelevant.

The masculine foundation on which the system of penitentiary discipline was built also contributed to the exclusion of women from its regimes. Among nineteenth-century prison administrators, the sentiment that women prisoners were a "nuisance" was nearly universal, expressed in dozens of institutional reports and communications with state officials (Colvin 1997; Dodge 1999; Rafter 1990). An Illinois prison inspector's report of 1845 is typical: "Past experience, not only in our own State, but in others, [demonstrates that] one female prisoner is of more trouble than twenty males" (quoted in Dodge 1999: 912). Similarly, a male reformer of the period opined that the nine women at the Ohio penitentiary caused more problems than the five hundred male convicts (Rafter 1990). The ubiquity of this view serves as a useful barometer for the extent to which women did not fit within the bounds of the assumptions on which the system of penitentiary discipline was based.

For example, as the Auburn model gained ascendance over the Pennsylvania scheme, so, too, did emphasis on the profit to be made from inmate labor. Maximizing revenue, however, presumed the use of men's rather than women's labor. The "silent and insulated working machines" that Elam Lynds, the first warden of Auburn (quoted in Colvin 1997: 90), saw as the backbone of the congregate system were the bodies of male workers. Women prisoners were disparaged because the products of their labors usually failed to meet the expenses of their upkeep and certainly never generated a profit (Rafter 1990). Of course, women inmates were in a double bind, as they were typically assigned to institutional maintenance tasks, like sewing and mending for male inmates, that were not intended to produce a profit. Even when women were assigned industrial tasks, however, their small numbers meant that it was impossible to produce in mass quantities, and then, as now, their labor was undervalued relative to men's. Nineteenth-century prison wardens, under pressure from the state to maximize revenues, viewed the housing of women as an unprofitable inconvenience.

Women's more thoroughgoing cultural sexualization and embodiment also disrupted prison routines. From the beginnings of the penitentiary project in America, administrators have attempted to suppress inmate sexuality, seeing it first as contrary to institutional order and then as an impediment to the creation of disciplined citizens and workers. For administrators the presence of women in men's prisons had the potential to create unmanageable (hetero)sexual tensions, a particularly dangerous situation given the general immorality of the male inmate population:

> Convicts are a class of men whose principles and tastes have been more
> or less debauched from the course of life they have hitherto led. . . .
> [A]dd to this the presence within the prison walls of a large number
> of depraved females, who, by secret contrivances, are in constant com-
> munication with the male convicts, and you will be at no loss to under-
> stand the temptations to this vice are irresistible to natures already fear-
> fully depraved. (Illinois prison physician, quoted in Dodge 1999: 920)

Women are singled out for disapprobation, as it is apparently they who
encourage male inmates to violate rules by engaging in forbidden communications. This same physician, in line with contemporary medical
wisdom, goes on to condemn women for exacerbating the problem of
"self-abuse" (masturbation) among male inmates, which he believes is
the "direct cause of five-sixths of the disease I have had under treatment" (Dodge 1999: 920). Women were also held responsible for the
scandals that erupted when sexual relationships between male officers
and inmates came to light, or when pregnancies occurred among long-
serving inmates. Pregnancies almost invariably created crises, with wardens often requesting pardons for pregnant women, regardless of their
crimes (Dodge 1999; Rafter 1990). The perceived disruptions created
by women's sexuality and by their bodies more generally are again illus-
trative of the kind of bodies that the system was designed to reform.
The asexual male body was (and remains) the implicit target of penitentiary disciplinary regimes.

Eventually, recurring scandals and protests from prison administrators created sufficient pressure, and states began establishing separate
facilities for women. These prisons were administratively (and sometimes physically) attached to men's facilities, as in the case of the first
such institution, New York's Mount Pleasant Female Prison, built on
the grounds of the Sing Sing Prison for men and opened in 1839. Many
of these institutions were run by women, given the title "matron"
(rather than "warden"), but still under the supervision of male administrators (Rafter 1990). With few exceptions, they borrowed regimes of
labor and discipline from men's prisons. The Mount Pleasant facility
was closed due to overcrowding in 1877, but by then the impetus for
building of single-sex facilities had been established. Most states in the
Northeast and Midwest maintained a separate female department by
the turn of the century. The states of the West lagged behind, though
most eventually did operate such facilities. The South, partly as a result

of the legacy of the Civil War, adopted a somewhat different prison system, to be discussed in more detail later. Even so, women in female departments continued to suffer relative to their male counterparts; women's quarters were the lowest priorities in state correctional budgets, and the facilities were invariably inferior to those provided for men (Rafter 1982, 1990). A Missouri warden described that state's female prison building as "a disgrace to the state . . . ; it is old and dilapidated, very crowded, with no facilities whatever for caring for the sick" (quoted in Rafter 1990: 84).

By all accounts, administrators in early prisons, regardless of the type, were initially successful in implementing their disciplinary regimes (for male prisoners). Separation, discipline, and hard labor were rigorously enforced. However, as time passed and penitentiaries proliferated, the model became diluted. The rule of silence was the first to go, both as a result of the brutality required for its enforcement and because of the difficulties of production among workers who were not allowed to speak to one another. Solitary confinement was next, as overcrowding forced the housing of multiple prisoners in single cells (Colvin 1997). The prison also proved vulnerable to the defects that plague all total institutions (Goffman 1961). Its isolation allowed arbitrary violence to go largely unnoticed. Prison investigations throughout the nineteenth century (in both separate and congregate-style facilities) revealed a thriving contraband trade involving guards and inmates, bribery, and inmate homosexuality. Inmate uprisings further eroded the system of discipline (Colvin 1997; Rothman 1990).

Taken together, all these factors created a crisis of confidence in the new "science" of penology. As disciplinary methods lost their rehabilitative features, prisons became little more than custodial (Colvin 1997; Rothman 1990). Paradoxically enough, however, prisons had by this time become ingrained in American society. As rehabilitative goals were eclipsed, incarceration became the prison's raison d'être, a metamorphosis that was accelerated by the predominance of the poor, "foreigners," and racial minority group members among prison populations. Over time, wardens came to see their primary goal as custody (Rothman 1990). The middle classes, who wanted protection from those below them, were pacified (Hirsch 1992; Rothman 1990). Within the short span of forty years, the disciplinary regimes of the penitentiary had become uncoupled from the rehabilitative ideas that had inspired them and given them meaning, making the prison an end in itself, a literal "iron cage."

The Adult Reformatory Movement

This was the climate from which America's adult reformatory system emerged. The inventors and advocates of the reformatory hoped to rekindle faith in rehabilitation by offering a new version of the science of penology, one targeted specifically at the offenders they believed most capable of reform. Several features distinguished the reformatory from the penitentiary. First, reformatory advocates offered a new account of the etiology of crime, one that Pisciotta (1994) calls "multifactor positivism." Rejecting the prevailing paradigm in which criminals were rational hedonists in need of punishment, they instead viewed criminality as the result of a complex interaction of social, psychological, and (increasingly as the nineteenth century came to a close) biological factors. Each criminal was unique and required an individualized program of "treatment," rather than simply punishment (Pisciotta 1994). Treatment was to take the form of a variety of programs, educational, vocational, religious, recreational, and military. Inmates were encouraged to internalize reform through an incentive scheme that allowed those who behaved well to move into higher "grades" and receive more privileges. Indeterminate sentencing and parole provided additional inducements. Reformatory advocates saw the former as a vital tool, in that their treatment-oriented model dictated that inmates would be released only when they had been "cured." Corporal punishments, which by this time had become virtually the sole reinforcers in penitentiaries, were to be avoided if at all possible (Pisciotta 1994). All these methods were targeted at the least hardened criminals, primarily young first offenders convicted of less serious felony crimes. Serious felons and recidivists were viewed as too incorrigible to benefit from reformatory programs. During the height of the adult reformatory movement, roughly from 1873 to 1935, twenty men's and twenty-one women's reformatories were built (Pisciotta 1994; Rafter 1990). Though these institutions did not necessarily adopt the entire package of reformatory programs, their administrators professed at least an explicit commitment to rehabilitation rather than punishment.

By the 1860s, a crisis of confidence in the rehabilitative capabilities of penitentiaries had prompted a search for new ideas. The reformatory solution sprang from a number of sources. For ideological inspiration, reformers drew on the works of European prison activists, including Elizabeth Fry and Mary Carpenter, and prison administrators, such as Alexander Maconochie and Walter Crofton (Colvin 1997; Freedman 1981; Pisciotta 1994; Rafter 1990). Reformatory practice made its first appearance in America in an adult prison at the Mount Pleasant Female Prison during the tenure of Eliza Farnham, who headed the facility from 1844 to 1848. Inheriting an institution in chaos (inmates had rioted in 1843), Farnham instituted an educational program consisting of lessons in history, astronomy, geography, and physiology. She also introduced a system of prisoner classification based on inmate needs and behavior, and instituted an incentive program designed to reward good conduct. Among the incentives were music, access to a library, and a relaxation of the silent system, still in force for male inmates at the adjacent Sing Sing facility (Colvin 1997; Freedman 1981; Rafter 1990). Conditions improved dramatically during Farnham's time as administrator. Paradoxically, however, she was criticized by the state legislature and ultimately dismissed for inaugurating a disciplinary regime with "nothing *masculine* in its composition" (quoted in Lewis 1965: 248, emphasis in original).[4] Farnham's system was quickly dismantled after her removal; her "feminized" regime had proven incompatible with the masculine penitentiary environment (Colvin 1997; Rafter 1990).

Reformatory methods flourished elsewhere, however. The Isaac Hopper Home, a halfway house for recently released women inmates, was operated by women's prison reformers in New York from 1845 to 1864. It employed many components of the reformatory scheme, including religious and domestic study, and established a program that placed inmates in positions as domestic servants in middle-class homes (Freedman 1981). The Lancaster (Massachusetts) Industrial School for Girls, the first American reform school for girls, opened in 1856. Here the "cottage plan" was introduced. Rather than being housed in tiers of cells in a large cell block, small groups of girls lived in cottages, each supervised by a matron who served as a sort of surrogate mother to her charges. The education program at Lancaster focused on domestic labor, again with the goal of placing the girls as servants (Brenzel 1983; Colvin 1997).[5] The man who is credited as the primary institutional architect of the men's reformatory movement, Zebulon Brockway, visited

Lancaster in 1867. At that time, he was superintendent of the Detroit House of Correction and was inspired by this example to establish a women's House of Shelter adjacent to his facility in 1869. It was run by a matron, Emma Hall, and employed a system of inmate "grading" in which good behavior was rewarded by promotion to higher privilege levels. It also trained women for positions in domestic service. Misdemeanants committed to the House of Shelter were subject to the first adult indeterminate sentencing law. Under this statute, which passed with Brockway's strong support (Brockway initially favored such a law for *both* men and women, but the legislature approved it only for the latter), offenders convicted of the pettiest of crimes could be held up to three years and were released only when administrators were convinced that they had reformed (Colvin 1997; Pisciotta 1994). All the seeds for a systematic program of reformatory practice had been sown by the late 1860s.

In 1869, the legislatures of New York and Indiana both approved the construction of reformatory prisons. The Indiana Reformatory Institution for Women and Girls accepted its first inmates in 1873 and was the first completely separate institution for the housing of women convicts in America.[6] The Elmira Reformatory opened its doors to young male first offenders in 1876. Traditional criminal justice scholarship has focused on Elmira as the first, and archetypal, adult reformatory prison. Pisciotta, in his definitive history, contends: "The Elmira Reformatory led America's search for methods of reform in the late-nineteenth century" (1994: 7). It is true that Elmira captured the attention of American and European penal reformers of the day. This is due in part to the fact that prisons for men have always been the main attraction on the American correctional landscape. Elmira's prominence was also the outcome of concerted self-promotion and institutional promotion efforts of its first warden, Zebulon Brockway, who became "in the eyes of many [of his contemporaries] the arm of the state, the hand of God, and a penological genius" (Pisciotta 1994: 7).

Brockway's regime at Elmira drew on his experiences in Detroit, as well as the ideas put forth in the "Declaration of Principles" passed in 1870 at the first National Congress on Penitentiary and Reformatory Discipline. This document was to become a landmark program for penal reform. As one of its authors, Brockway welcomed the opportunity to put these principles into action at Elmira. The "Elmira system" was composed of several parts. Upon admission, inmates were interviewed by

Brockway, who used information about their lives and crimes to determine the "root cause" of their criminality. He then assigned them an educational class, an industry, and a cell (Elmira housed inmates in cell blocks rather than cottages). Inmates worked during the day (later in the institution's history, when prison labor was banned, mandatory military drills were substituted) and attended classes during the evenings. Elmira offered classes in thirty-six trades by 1896, with options running the gamut from carpentry to fresco painting. Mandatory religious services were held on Sundays. Upon arrival, inmates were placed in the second grade of the institution's classification system; behavior could increase or decrease their rank. After serving a minimum of six months in the first grade, inmates became eligible for supervised parole (Pisciotta 1994).

The Elmira system drew on many of the reformatory ideas first employed in women's institutions, but in a masculinized form. Though making passing mention of the necessity of education and separate facilities for women, the Declaration of Principles focused on the needs of male offenders, urging:

> The prisoner's self-respect should be cultivated to the utmost, and every effort made to give back to him his manhood. There is no greater mistake in the whole compass of penal discipline, than its studied imposition of degradation as a part of punishment. Such imposition destroys every better impulse and aspiration. It crushes the weak, irritates the strong, and indisposes all to submission and reform. It is trampling where we ought to raise, and is therefore as unchristian in principle as well as it is unwise in policy. (Quoted in Pisciotta 1994: 158)

Brockway explicitly claimed that the aim of the Elmira system was to turn inmates into "Christian gentlemen" (quoted in Piscotta 1994: 18). It also sought to transform its charges into breadwinners, offering many male-dominated trades. Military drill and discipline, long employed to turn boys into men, was used at Elmira to habituate "the men to prompt and implicit obedience, deference to their superiors, to the habit of command and to loyalty" (Pisciotta 1994: 23). All in all, inmates "who internalized Brockway's vision of reform accepted full responsibility for their criminal act(s) and attempted to become responsible workers, husbands, fathers and citizens" (Pisciotta 1994: 18). In its ideology and program, the Elmira system clearly aimed at the reproduction of appropriate, "Christian" masculinity.

The reality was much different. As Pisciotta (1994) amply demonstrates, Elmira was really no different than any more traditional prison of the day. It quickly became overcrowded, and investigations throughout its early years revealed widespread staff corruption and brutality. Corporal punishment, often administered by the superintendent himself, was common, as were disciplinary sanctions such as solitary confinement, during which inmates were chained to an iron ring in their cells. Staff misconduct was also routine; sexual abuse of inmates and trade in contraband flourished. Eleven other adult men's reformatories opened by the turn of the century, and conditions in all of them were similar. Despite its rehabilitative rhetoric, the men's reformatory movement essentially created brutal prisons not dissimilar to their predecessors. By 1920, the men's reformatory movement lost momentum, and existing institutions became little more than custodial (Pisciotta 1994).

The reformatory ideal, albeit in a feminized form, enjoyed much greater success in women's institutions. In the tradition of separate spheres that dominated nineteenth-century political activism and reform, men's and women's reformatories developed along separate tracks. The construction of women's reformatories was the product of the organized efforts of groups of middle-class women who saw ameliorating the situation of the woman prisoner as their unique social mission. Spurred to action by revelations of sexual abuse in prisons of the day, women mobilized by the mid–nineteenth century to argue for the establishment of completely separate, reformatory institutions for women. Reformers advocated three key principles: separation of female prisoners in their own institutions; the provision of different, feminine care (as opposed to the regimes of strict discipline, work, and silence imposed on male prisoners); and control over women's prisons by female staff and management (Freedman 1981).

Completely separate institutions were justified, reformers argued, for several reasons. First, sexual exploitation of women could be prevented in sex-segregated institutions, and opportunities for rehabilitation enhanced for both men and women. Second, reformers noted that even in the best integrated prisons and female departments, women were seldom provided training programs or even exercise. Finally, reformers argued that separate institutions for women would allow for more efficient management of female offenders, who if housed in one facility would create an inmate population of sufficient size to allow for classification by type of offender and severity of offense.

The argument for differential treatment was buttressed by the reformers' view of the etiology of female crime. Advocates of women's reformatories turned the dominant discourse, which saw women criminals as worse than men, on its head. In 1875, Susan B. Anthony argued that men turned to crime predominantly out of the "love of vice," while women acted out of "absolute want of the necessaries of life" (quoted in Freedman 1981: 41). Anthony suggested that working women, exploited by low wages in the marketplace, turned to crime as a way of meeting basic needs. Crime was the result of economic marginalization rather than depravity. Still other reformers, whose voices would ultimately be more influential, invoked a moral argument, portraying women as victims of male lust, the double standard, and abuses of patriarchal power in the family. Women criminals were unfortunate casualties of male demands for "fallen women" or were unwittingly led to crime by drunken or violent husbands or fathers (Freedman 1981).

The female offender invoked was never intended to be generic, as Rafter (1983, 1990) points out. Like the architects of the men's reformatory movement, women's prison reformers meant for these institutions to house only those inmates they believed to be most capable of reform. In theory, this meant young first offenders, primarily those convicted of misdemeanor offenses, women who had ventured only a few steps down the "road to ruin." The centrality of sexuality in reformers' arguments about the causes of crime singled out women guilty of minor sexual offenses as particularly appropriate targets for a program of moral and domestic transformation. "Hardened" offenders, that is, women felons and recidivists, were to remain in existing men's prisons and female departments.

For their intended targets, rehabilitation was to be effected through a specifically feminine program of discipline. One reform commission wrote in 1855:

> Women need different management from men; they are more emotional and more susceptible; they are far less likely to be influenced by general appeals or force of discipline, and are more open to personal treatment and the influence of kindness. (Quoted in Freedman 1981: 54)

Early reformers advocated training in cooking, sewing, and religion to foster both piety and domesticity. Unlike the men's prison, however, where the employment of inmates in productive labor was advocated as a crucial element in rehabilitation, the use of women inmates' labor has historically been a more contentious issue. Early reformers argued that women should be employed in domestic pursuits, and training programs at many of the first women's institutions focused almost exclusively on placing women as paid domestic laborers (Freedman 1981). Some wardens rejected this option, however. Katharine Bement Davis, the first superintendent of New York's Bedford Hills women's correctional institution, opined in 1903:

> It is not every woman in our mixed throng who is adapted by nature or taste to domestic service, sewing or laundry work. In the reformatories for men, no one for a moment seriously considers limiting the trades taught to cooking and tailoring, though these occupations are highly respectable, and the remuneration of the chef or custom tailor is excellent. (Quoted in Freedman 1981: 133)

Inmates at Bedford Hills were engaged in gardening, raising livestock, and institutional construction projects. These kinds of practices were not typical, however, and most women's prisons emphasized training programs directed toward traditional roles. Following the models established in New York's Isaac Hopper Home and at Lancaster, most placed inmates as domestic servants in middle-class homes (Rafter 1990).

The reformers' demand for differential treatment was reflected in the design of many of the new reformatories, which was based on the "cottage" or family system, introduced at Lancaster. The surroundings of women's prisons were to be as homelike as possible, with private rooms that could be decorated by inmates. In cottages the family structure reformers argued had been missing for female prisoners could be reconstituted in the institutional setting. The ideal case scenario for reformers is evidenced in an 1888 report on one of the first female reformatories, the Hudson House of Refuge, established by Josephine Shaw Lowell in 1887. According to the report:

> The idea of a family and home life is carried out as far as possible in the cottages. In the evening [the inmates] are gathered together in a circle, of which the supervisor and the assistant form the center. . . . The girls, while knitting or sewing, profit by some appropriate reading or oral instruction. (Quoted in Freedman 1981: 57)

The structure of the family, as well as domestic instruction, was held to be crucial for the rehabilitation of female inmates, rather than the stern discipline to which male prisoners were commonly subject.

The influence of the doctrine of separate spheres was conspicuous in the demand for female staff and administration in the new facilities. This was predicated not only on the history of abuse of female inmates by male keepers but also on the assumption that women could best be rehabilitated by members of their own sex, who would set a proper example and be able to instruct inmates in domestic pursuits. Some state administrators initially resisted this demand, at first denying that women were abused by male staff and then arguing that women officers and administrators would be too weak to control female inmates. State administrators were eventually convinced by the early successes of a number of female-run prisons in Europe, and by the end of the nineteenth century, most of the newly established state women's reformatories were administered by exclusively female staff (Freedman 1981).

In contrast to the almost immediate disintegration of the men's reformatory project, many of the goals of women's reformatory advocates were indeed realized. By the beginning of the twentieth century, Indiana, Massachusetts, and New York had opened separate reformatories for women, and sixteen other states (largely in the Northeast and Midwest) followed suit by 1935 (Freedman 1981). Many of these institutions were designed on the cottage plan; most employed a "feminized" program of reformatory discipline and were run by female staff and officers. Yet as Rafter (1983, 1990) contends, the women's reformatory movement had mixed results for women caught in the system. In their early years, most reformatory institutions housed their intended populations—young first offenders guilty of such misdemeanor morals offenses as promiscuity, "waywardness," "saloon visiting," "idle and disorderly conduct," and vagrancy. However, before the advent of the reformatory, women were not typically incarcerated for such minor offenses; at most, they might serve a short term in jail. Men were never sentenced to prison on these grounds; even men's reformatories housed only young felons. Women misdemeanants were sentenced to reformatories and held there on indeterminate sentences of three years or more. If they became especially intractable, inmates could be (and sometimes were) committed to mental institutions, where they could be held indefinitely. The women's reformatory widened the net of social control over the lives of working-class women and involved the state in a coercive project to enforce chastity and inculcate the values of white middle-class femininity. Throughout the reformatories' early years, inmates were, in fact, overwhelmingly white, native-born, working-class women. Black, Native American, and immigrant women, who made up the bulk of women convicted of felony crimes, remained in men's prisons. The few black women who were admitted to reformatories were generally segregated from whites, as in New Jersey, which opened a "colored cottage" at its Clinton Reformatory in 1915 (Rafter 1990).[7]

As the twentieth century progressed, however, the women's reformatory movement entered a state of decline. Judges, eager to use the new reformatories as tools in the legal control of "wayward" women, soon filled them to capacity, and educational and rehabilitative efforts suffered. Encouraged by what appeared to be early successes, or perhaps frustrated by the dilapidated state of women's quarters in men's prisons, judges began to send more "hardened" cases there as well. Men's prison administrators, who had long viewed women's presence in their institutions as a nuisance, encouraged this trend. By the 1920's the ideals of early reformers began to be replaced by the more custodial orientation demanded by the constraints of state budgets and by the perceived characteristics of the new inmate population. Women released from some of these institutions began to relate stories of cruel and unusual punishments. By 1921, the State of New York had appointed a man as superintendent at Bedford Hills, and many newer state prisons began to utilize male staff in posts that did not involve direct inmate contact. By 1935, the transformation was complete, as most states closed existing female departments in men's prisons and transferred all women inmates to the reformatories, which themselves had now become more like prisons.

Even given its eventual demise, the reformatory ideal approached its most complete realization in institutions for women. Administrators of early institutions eschewed brutal corporal punishments and successfully instituted training and education programs designed to transform their charges in accord with the prescriptions of middle-class femininity. The legacy of the feminine model of care they established has never been completely eclipsed. Even today many women's prisons still emulate the cottage model and bear other marks of their development along a gendered track separate from the equally gendered path that produced men's institutions. Though reformatory ideology never established a firm foothold in American ideas about men prisoners, it continues to occupy an ingrained, if ambivalent, space in our thinking about women prisoners.

Convict Leasing and the Farm System

The final historical antecedent of the contemporary American penal system emerged from the post–Civil War South. During the antebellum period, most southern states established penitentiaries on the Auburn model. Virginia and Kentucky were the first to do so in 1800, but all southern states, with the exception of the Carolinas, had built state prisons by the onset of the Civil War (Colvin 1997). Most housed relatively small populations of white male felons and free blacks. Women were incarcerated with men in these institutions, though their numbers were small; Rafter (1990), for example, counts a total of twenty-one white and three black women in the Tennessee state prison during the years 1831–1859. By law, offenses committed by slaves were subject to the discretion of slave owners. Reluctant to lose valuable labor, slaveholders administered their own punishments, almost always involving the whip (Colvin 1997; Oshinsky 1996).

The end of the Civil War was the point of departure for the development of a unique correctional system. Most Southern penitentiaries had been destroyed by Union troops during the war. The South also faced the problems of the severe labor shortage created by the emancipation of slaves and the responsibility for adjudicating crimes committed by newly freed blacks. Governments turned to incarceration as a solution to both. By all accounts, crime rates rose sharply in the post–Civil War South (Ayers 1992; Colvin 1997), and then (as now) public discourse about its causes was profoundly racialized. White southerners believed that blacks, unable to cope with the responsibilities of freedom and resentful of their former enslavement, were taking out their frustrations through violence and supporting themselves by theft. This sentiment was undergirded by the view that blacks were inherently predisposed to crime. As one planter observed, "All their men are thieves, and all the women are prostitutes. It's their natur' to be that way, and they'll never be no other way" (quoted in Oshinsky 1996: 32). In the terms of this logic, slavery controlled these "natural" tendencies; freedom liberated them. Sensationalist news reporting focused almost exclusively on "atrocities" committed by blacks, with particular outrage reserved for sexual assaults against white women (Ayers 1984, 1992). In response to the white public's hysteria over black crime, southern governments passed "Black Codes" that specifically targeted crimes committed by free blacks.[8] The result was an inmate population that was 90 percent black in most southern states after the Civil War (Colvin 1997; Oshinsky 1996).

Yet lacking prisons (and laborers), the South innovated, establishing a unique, and deeply racialized, correctional system. The first element, the chain gang, appeared in Georgia in 1866. Chain gangs were operated by county sheriffs, who either used inmates transferred from state custody in projects such as road building or field labor or leased them to others. Whites in need of workers could purchase black prisoners, who needed white "sponsors" to avoid chain gang labor. Counties derived handsome profits both from the direct labor of inmates and from their sale and leasing. Most southern states followed Georgia's lead, allowing their own counties to work inmates in chain gangs (Colvin 1997).

At the state level, convict leasing was the most commonly adopted solution to the South's postwar prison crisis. Under this system, which became firmly established at the end of Reconstruction in the 1870s, states granted a contract to a private individual or group that allowed them to lease and subcontract the labor of convicts. Inmates were employed in a wide variety of tasks, from railroad building to mining and, most commonly, on large, plantation-style farms. Leasing quickly proved lucrative for the states and for contractors themselves. In the face of growing demand and rising profits, states were pressed to provide a steadily increasing supply of convicts. They did so through the passage of laws that targeted blacks for the most minor infractions. In 1876, Mississippi passed its infamous "pig law," which redefined grand larceny as the theft of a farm animal or any property worth ten dollars or more and had the immediate effect of quadrupling the state's prison population (Oshinsky 1996). In North Carolina, even the *intent* to steal was made a crime (Colvin 1997), and in Florida, one new convict leasing contract resulted in an increase in arrests for vagrancy of more than 800 percent (Oshinsky 1996). Though the text of these laws was generic, they were enforced almost exclusively against blacks. Black men, women, and children convicted under these statutes were all sent to leasing camps. Penitentiaries, where they still existed, were reserved for serious felons. These housed mostly white men, who tended to be convicted of only the most serious crimes (Oshinsky 1996; Walker 1988). White women rarely saw the inside of southern prisons. Governors who saw them as "too delicate" to endure incarceration typically pardoned them, regardless of their crimes (Oshinsky 1996).

Leased inmates were the sole responsibility of the lessees, who housed them in large camps. Conditions were deplorable. The almost inexhaustible supply and interchangeability of inmate laborers meant that their lives were worth very little. Starvation, overwork, and brutality were commonplace; in Texas, "citizens living near some of the prison work camps stated that 'the groans and entreaties of the convicts *at night* were often so absolutely heart rending as to prevent . . . sleeping'" (quoted in Walker 1988: 38). Mortality rates were staggering. In Mississippi, black convicts died at a rate more than eight times higher than their penitentiary-housed white counterparts, and not a single leased convict lived long enough to serve a sentence of ten years or more (Oshinsky 1996). Women and children suffered under the same conditions as adult men. They were rarely segregated, and in some cases, men and women chained together worked the fields and slept on the same wooden planks in camp shacks (Mancini 1996). Unlike men, however, women suffered the additional burdens of sexual exploitation by both inmates and guards; rape was by all accounts a common occurrence (Ayers 1984; Colvin 1997; Mancini 1996; Oshinsky 1996).

Unlike the penitentiary and reformatory systems of the North and Midwest, no real penological philosophy underlay the lease system (Colvin 1997). It served white southern governments as a solution to the problems of labor shortage and crime, while also offering the additional benefit of reinforcing white supremacy. The lease system was little more than a substitute for slavery, ensuring blacks' return to the positions they had occupied in the antebellum South. Without even the dubious protection conveyed by being held as property, however, the lives of convicts were nearly worthless, and conditions in leasing camps reflected this (Colvin 1997; Mancini 1996; Oshinsky 1996).

In most states, convict leasing was abolished by the early twentieth century. A variety of factors led to its decline, including objections on humanitarian grounds, the decreasing profitability of inmate as compared with free labor, and the enactment of the rigid system of legal segregation embodied in Jim Crow laws (Colvin 1997; Mancini 1996; Oshinky 1996; Walker 1988). This paved the way for the establishment of the final element of the southern prison system, the prison farm. As leasing fell into disrepute and then disuse, states again faced the problem of what to do with a now greatly increased population of black convicts. In his definitive history of Mississippi's Parchman prison farm, which was established in 1904, Oshinsky notes that the ideal solution, according to many white policy makers, was to return blacks to their "natural" environment. In the South, that meant the plantation. As one prominent journalist put it, "To confine the negro [in jail] is to doom him to death. To reform his character is an almost hopeless task. . . . The Negro is a Negro. We must deal with him as he is" (quoted in Oshinsky 1996: 96). The plantation system was thus reborn, as states throughout the South acquired large farms and put inmates to work on them planting cotton, sugarcane, and other cash crops. The state, rather than the planter aristocracy, became the primary beneficiary of the forced labor of blacks.

Prison farms bore little resemblance to penitentiaries. Large plots of land were subdivided into inmate camps. At Parchman, each camp housed more than one hundred inmates and was supervised by a sergeant and two deputies. Inmates, chained together, worked the fields in a "long line," cultivating cotton as it had been done in the South for decades. "Trusty shooters," inmate guards chosen for their ability to intimidate other inmates and their willingness to kill, oversaw the workers and shot those who might attempt to escape. As in northern prisons and reformatories, discipline in the camps inevitably meant the lash, though here its use was justified on racial grounds. It seemed, as Oshinsky notes, "the perfect [disciplinary] instrument in a prison populated by the wayward children of former slaves" (1996: 151). There was no more effective way "of punishing [this] class of criminals," according to Dr. A. M. M'Callum, Parchman's first physician, "and keeping them at the labor required of them" (quoted in Oshinsky 1996: 151). Even given high levels of brutality and overwork, conditions on prison farms were not as appalling as those in the leasing camps. Convicts were generally fed well and housed in permanent structures. They enjoyed other "benefits" as well—Parchman farm was the first prison in America to introduce the privilege of conjugal visits. Initially, these were allowed only for black male inmates, a practice justified on the basis of their supposedly more "highly sexed" nature (Oshinsky 1996).

As with the lease system, there were no rehabilitative principles underlying the disciplinary regime employed at prison farms. Most southern penologists and prison administrators simply did not believe that the black convicts could be reformed. The system was designed, as slavery had been before it, to extract as much profit as possible from a captive labor force. Unlike leasing, the farm system generated little resistance among white southerners and largely functioned as promised, returning profits to the state and appearing to control black crime. In the rare instances that advocates felt compelled to provide an ideological justification for the farms, they did so using a deeply racialized logic. Drawing on arguments that were increasingly bolstered by eugenic rationales as the nineteenth century came to a close, commentators defended forced farm labor as uniquely suited to the menial intelligence and meager skills of blacks, who would surely be idle, and perhaps criminal, outside its system of strict discipline. The prison farm was thus explicitly designed to exploit and control an "alien population, and inferior race" (quoted in Oshinsky 1996: 83).

The thoroughgoing racialization of the system is further underlined by the experiences of the few whites who entered it. In an eerie echo of northeastern and midwestern men's prison administrators' view that women in their institutions were little more than a nuisance, farm officials similarly disdained white inmates, seeing them as infinitely more troublesome than their black counterparts. A Parchman superintendent during the 1930s opined, "One white convict gives me more trouble than three Negroes," and still another official noted that whites "may be a minority here, but they cause ninety percent of the problems" (quoted in Oshinsky 1996: 165). Blacks, whose alleged biological endowment suited them for strict discipline and menial labor, "took to Parchman naturally; the white man never would" (prison physician Dr. A. M. M'Callum, quoted in Oshinsky 1996: 165). Prevailing doctrines of racial superiority ensured that whites would be more resistant to a form of punishment that was designed with blacks in mind. The only recorded "strikes" at Parchman occurred in the 1930s and 1960s when white convicts (who were segregated from blacks) refused to work the line (Oshinsky 1996). As in the case of the prison, the "lack of fit" of one group of inmates serves here as a barometer for assessing the kind of inmate for whom the system was designed. The experiences of white inmates reveal the racist logic underlying the structure and the practices of the farm system.

Women were housed with men on prison farms in some states (as in Mississippi) or on separate farms (as in Texas). Regardless, their assigned work was differentiated by both sex and race. Black women, who in some states made up 95 to 100 percent of the female prison population, did the same kinds of field labor as black men during planting and harvesting seasons. At other times, they did stereotypical "women's work," canning produce, doing laundry, and making clothing and bedding for the farms (Oshinsky 1996). White women, whose numbers were typically minuscule, were segregated and assigned domestic chores. After the 1890s, women were housed in separate camps in all southern states, even on farms that held both men and women inmates. They were guarded by male inmates, sergeants, and deputies, a situation that gave rise, as it did in northern prisons, to abuse. Prison investigations of the period reveal that staff reserved the most inhumane treatment for black inmates. A 1910 inquiry into conditions at a Texas women's camp reported that the few white women there testified that they had never been treated improperly. The seven black women interviewed related a very different story, testifying to brutal whippings, rape, and compulsory prostitution (Walker 1988).

The farm system endures to the present. Though its sheer brutality and blatant racism have abated, largely as a result of inmate-initiated legal reforms, convicts across the South continue to work in large agricultural operations. Camp shacks have been replaced by cell blocks and dormitories, and inmates of all races work and sleep together. But persistent racism in the criminal justice system reproduces old patterns; it is not uncommon, even today, to see long lines of predominantly black inmates working in the fields, guarded by armed, mostly white officers on horseback.

Women are now generally housed in separate prisons, but this occurred much later in the South than elsewhere. A few states established separate quarters for women in their existing men's prisons by the 1890s. Though black women were generally leased along with black men during this period, lessees eventually rejected them as less profitable laborers. States were then forced to house them in prisons and ultimately moved them to prison farms. The women's reformatory movement was somewhat less successful in the South, producing only three institutions (in North Carolina, Virginia, and Arkansas), all of which excluded blacks (Rafter 1990). After the demise of the reformatory movement, southern states were slow to build separate, custodial prisons for women. Mississippi, for example, did not move its women inmates to a separate facility near Jackson until the 1980s (Oshinsky 1996).

The Persistence of the Past in the Present

America's current system of adult incarceration, developed only during the last two hundred years, is the outcome of three distinct historical projects. While each introduced a novel variation on the "science" of penology, all were built on a foundation of ideas about gender, race, and class. From the outset, the practices that constituted their disparate disciplinary regimes were shaped by these notions. Penitentiaries, America's "first" penal system, sought through silence, obedience, and hard labor to reform the rational man and reconstitute the ideal middle-class male citizen. Women in these institutions were treated as annoyances. Ideas about masculinity and femininity shaped the second system, the men's and women's reformatory. Brockway aimed to create "Christian gentlemen" at Elmira but succeeded only in reinventing the prison. The reformatory's initial successes and enduring legacy both stem from the women's institutional branch, though the ideal of reform was viable only for the white, working-class "fallen" woman. Racist logics about black crime and black abilities shaped the prison systems of the South, while racialized notions around gender ensured white women's exclusion from the worst of its brutality.

Remnants of all three systems endure. Prisons, now typically shorn of even the pretense of rehabilitative ideology, are the core of America's current network of carceral institutions. Of the 1,158 state and federal prisons operating in the United States in 1995,[9] 101 (9 percent) house women, 1,046 (90 percent) house men, and 11 are co-correctional institutions.[10] Table 2.2 provides a complete distribution of the 1,147 institutions in the first two categories. Some facilities have more than one function (e.g., they may incarcerate a general population of inmates and also operate a boot camp), so the total number does not sum to 1,147.

In the mold of the penitentiary, the vast majority of institutions for both men and women (87 percent) hold a general adult inmate population. Though military regimentation was part of the penitentiary program (at least for male inmates) from the outset, it had fallen into disuse through most of the twentieth century. In the "get tough on crime" climate of the 1990s, the popularity of military-style discipline surged anew; in 1995 there were 52 boot camps operating in the United States, up from 22 in 1990. The most recent development in this area is the advent of the dubious benefit of sexual equality, as there are now 5 such facilities for women. The remnants of the reformatory movement are in evidence in the category of institutions designated for youthful offenders, as well as in treatment facilities. Though these data do not separate prison farms from other institutions, 349 institutions list "farming" as an inmate work assignment. More than half are in the South,

TABLE 2.2
Distribution of Institutions by Function and Sex of Inmates Housed, 1995

	Men Only	Women Only	Total
General population confinement	910	89	999
% of institutions	87	88	87
Boot Camp	47	5	52
% of institutions	5	5	5
Reception/diagnostic classification	117	34	151
% of institutions	11	34	13
Medical treatment/hospital	152	22	174
% of institutions	15	22	15
Alcohol/drug treatment	159	23	182
% of institutions	15	23	16
Youthful offenders	34	4	38
% of institutions	3	4	3
Work release/prerelease	110	22	132
% of institutions	11	22	12
For persons returned to custody	64	15	79
% of institutions	6	15	7
Other	214	27	241
% of institutions	21	27	21
TOTAL	1,046	101	1,147

SOURCE: Author calculation from U.S. Department of Justice (1998).

with Texas alone accounting for 20 percent of the total (with 70). Men are significantly more likely than women to be housed in these facilities; 32 percent of institutions housing men list farming as a work assignment, as opposed to only 20 percent of those housing women. Some gender-specific programming also remains; in the clearest example available from census data, 81 percent of women's prisons offer parenting classes to their inmates, as compared with only 36 percent of men's institutions.[11]

As I noted at the outset, the five prisons in which I interviewed officers for this book represent a wide range of types.[12] Among the men's prisons, one had been established as a prison farm near the turn of the twentieth century and still runs an extensive agricultural operation. The other is a medium-security, general population confinement facility. Two of the women's prisons also utilize inmates to some degree in agricultural labor. One of these is a prison that holds inmates at all security levels, from minimum to maximum; the other is a low-security prison.

The third is also a low-security prison. One of the women's prisons operates a boot camp as well. That last fact notwithstanding, all the women's institutions I visited bear at least some lingering marks of the women's reformatory movement, whether in their design, in programming (as in the cosmetology class at one or in clerical or sewing work assignments at all three), or in the increasingly contested idea that women offenders require different, "more feminine," treatment and surroundings.

One final note on the prisons that are the focus here bears mentioning. Two are state-run facilities, three federal. The federal system developed along a somewhat different historical track than the systems of the various states. The first federal prison was established in 1928, in Leavenworth, Kansas, to hold military prisoners. As of 1995, the federal government operated 110 prisons (versus the 1,037 state prisons) and housed 78,963 inmates. Strictly speaking, to be sentenced to a federal prison, one must commit a federal crime. Historically, the number of offenses so designated was relatively small, and the size of the inmate population reflected this. However, as Congress widened the net of drug offenses that can be prosecuted as federal crimes, the inmate population exploded, growing 42 percent between 1990 and 1995 alone. There are other differences between the state and the federal systems. Among those particularly relevant to the current study are organizational structure within institutions, recruiting and training requirements for officers, and regulations on inmate and officer behavior; I will note these where relevant in the following chapters. The types of institutions in the federal system, however, do not differ systematically from those that have been described in this chapter.

Notions about gender, race, and class shaped the very foundations of prisons. Practices within them both assumed and reproduced inequalities based on those traits. They continue to do so. As the institutions themselves are gendered, so, too, is work within them. In the next chapter, I describe the historical context of work within prisons, paying particular attention to the evolution of the occupations of "keeper," "guard," "matron," and, now, "correctional officer."

3

From Turnkey to Officer
Prison Work in Historical Perspective

From the earliest beginnings of the prison, the "keeper" has occupied an ambivalent position. Michel Foucault captures the paradox in his account of the late-eighteenth-century French debates over the establishment of the prison. A critic rejects the prison because those who would be keepers are surely "monsters among you . . . and if these odious men [exist], the legislator ought perhaps to treat them as murderers" (1979: 114, quoting Mably). Almost two centuries later, in her best-selling book *Kind and Usual Punishment*, Jessica Mitford asks, "For after all, if we were to ask a small boy, 'What do you want to be when you grow up?' and he were to answer, 'A prison guard,' should we not find that a trifle worrying—cause, perhaps, to take him off to a child guidance clinic for observation and therapy?" (1973, quoted in Kauffman 1988: 171). Given her prescription for little boys, one can only imagine Mitford's treatment for a little girl who expressed the same aspiration.

Depictions of prison officers in mass culture, typically the public's only source of information about life behind the walls, often reflect more about our own cultural anxieties about incarceration than the reality of those who actually do the work. Fictitious though they may be, however, these portrayals have an effect. As Jacobs and Retsky observe:

If, as [Egon] Bittner suggests, "police work is a tainted occupation," then prison guard work is utterly polluted. . . . [C]lose contact with convicted felons seems morally profaning for the guard. Even close friends do not know what to make of the prevailing belief that prison guards are sadistic, stupid, and incompetent. (1975: 10)

This stereotype, combined with often abominable working conditions and low remuneration, means that those who have served as officers in penitentiaries, in reformatories, and on prison farms have often done so as a last resort. It has only been in the last thirty years that judicial, administrative, and worker union pressure have come together in an attempt to elevate the status of the correctional officer. The story of the occupation through most of its history has been one of disorder and brutality.

It has also been shaped by ideas about gender. Just as prison administrators and penologists designed systems of discipline with inmates of specific gender, race, and class identities in mind, so, too, did they imagine the characteristics of the "ideal" officer. Two very different models of this officer accompanied the development of men's and women's institutions of incarceration. As the twentieth century drew to a close, these ideas began to be challenged by forces that reshaped prisons, as well as the roles of those who work within them.

This chapter traces the development of the job of the prison officer. There is scant historical information on correctional officers' experiences in prisons and reformatories and on prison farms. The little we know comes not from the men and women themselves but from institutional reports, committees charged with investigating prison riots, brutality, and scandals, and from biographies and memoirs of prison administrators and inmates. While these capture the excesses and exceptions, none gives us an accurate picture of the day-to-day experiences of the typical officer. However, this record can serve as a rough guide to the outlines of the historical path that the role of the officer has taken into the present. In the final section of the chapter, I provide a review of the current legal context shaping the work of men and women officers.

Men at Work in Prisons, in Reformatories, and on Prison Farms

Officers in the earliest prisons were known as "keepers" and "turnkeys" and were literally responsible only for those duties. While these institutions held both men and small numbers of women, staff were exclusively male. The practice of hiring men undoubtedly derived from the predominance of men in the inmate population, beliefs about men's relatively greater abilities to handle potentially violent inmates, and women's almost complete exclusion from the labor force. From the outset, the job was something of a last resort. Tight state budgets and ambivalence over the project of incarceration were reflected in the conditions and wages of the work (Colvin 1997; Rothman 1990). A former inmate's account of the keepers at New York's Newgate Prison in 1823 noted that, while a few were of good character, many were "small-minded, intoxicated with their power, vulgar, and occasionally cruel." Given that the job involved living inside the prison—with the exception of twice-weekly visits to family—and an annual salary of $500 per year, this observer acknowledged that it was "understandably difficult to expect a capable man to live the life of a turnkey" (Coffey, quoted in Lewis 1965: 38). Low salaries and poor working conditions created similar situations at penitentiaries throughout the early nineteenth century.

Misconduct by both administrators and staff seems to have been the rule rather than the exception in many institutions. Reports of investigating committees in New York, Massachusetts, and Pennsylvania from 1800 to 1825 are filled with accounts of brutality, embezzlement, trade in contraband items such as tobacco and alcohol, sexual activity (both same-sex and opposite-sex) between inmates themselves and between staff and inmates, and condemnations of collusion and fraternization between officers and inmates and a general "laxity of discipline" among the keepers (Colvin 1997: 67; Lewis 1965; Teeters 1955). Escapes, assaults, and riots were commonplace occurrences; Walnut Street Jail, for example, experienced major inmate riots in 1817, 1819, 1820, and 1821. At Auburn during its early years, citizens of the surrounding community organized a military unit that met weekly to train in riot control tactics (Lewis 1965).

The introduction of the Pennsylvania and Auburn systems of prison discipline during the 1820s gave rise to a new way of thinking about the role of the keeper. A paramilitary model gained ascendance, promoted largely through the efforts of warden Elam Lynds and his deputy John Cray at Auburn and later under Lynds at Sing Sing (opened in 1828). Both men had military experience, and the influence of a military model was apparent not only in the regimentation that lay at the heart of the Auburn system but also in the mandate granted officers (Colvin 1997). In Auburn-style prisons:

> Guards wore uniforms, mustered at specific hours, and kept watch like sentries. Regulations ordered them to behave in a "gentlemanly manner," like officers without laughter, ribaldry, or unnecessary conversation while on duty. As Sing-Sing's rules put it, in only a slight overstatement

of a general sentiment: "They were to require from the convicts the greatest deference, and never suffer them to approach but in respectful manner; they are not to allow them the least degree of familiarity, nor exercise any towards them; they should be extremely careful to *command* as well as to compel their respect." (Rothman 1990: 106–107)

The model guard was to be both officer and gentleman; the job is framed in specifically masculine terms. Administrators expected that only such a man could command the respect of those in his charge.

The Auburn system also drew on the association of masculinity with violence. The ideal officer was to be a ruthless enforcer, willing to engage in extreme brutality. Control in institutions modeled on the Auburn system, which required inmates to be silent at all times, was maintained through terror. Elam Lynds believed that physical discipline was necessary to "break the spirits" of his inmates, and he authorized the use of flogging by any officer even for minor infractions. According to Lewis (1965), over eleven months in 1845, there were 173 recorded whippings at Auburn for offenses involving conversation. Dozens of others probably went unrecorded. Keepers were given, and by most accounts freely used, the authority to whip those perceived to be shirking labor in order to force them to work (Lewis 1965). Similar reports of brutality emerged from many Auburn-style prisons of the day. Conditions at Eastern State Penitentiary, the most prominent representative of the "Pennsylvania," or "separate," system, were not much different. One investigating committee in 1834 condemned the use of cruel and unusual punishments; another in 1897 decried officers' commonplace, and administratively sanctioned, use of the cane against inmates (Teeters and Shearer 1957).

Public sentiment against prison brutality rose during the late 1830s and 1840s (Colvin 1997; Lewis 1965). After the 1839 death of an inmate at Sing Sing, a crowd gathered at the prison gate demanding an inquest (Colvin 1997). Similar incidents were publicized and denounced by media and public figures during the mid–nineteenth century (Lewis 1965). Whether the level of violence in prisons actually declined as a result is difficult to assess. What is clearer is that the use of violence became less acceptable as a legitimate part of the overall disciplinary regime. By the 1850s and 1860s, most of the unique features of the Pennsylvania and Auburn systems had disappeared. The costs of maintaining the climate of fear integral to the silent system became unpalatable to legislatures and to the public. Perhaps equally important was the inefficiency in production created by the inability of inmate workers to communicate with one another (Colvin 1997). Regardless, from the 1850s and throughout the next one hundred years, the role of the officer reverted to that of custodian. Prisons became little more than holding pens, and the men who worked within were charged only with maintaining internal security and preventing escapes. Salaries further deteriorated, and working conditions were poor. High turnover among guard forces, a chronic difficulty for prison administrators today, began to occur as early as the 1840s (Colvin 1997).

Conditions were similar in reformatories for men. As in prisons, staff were all male, and their primary role seems to have been that of enforcer. Though in theory reformatory advocates eschewed corporal punishment, it was widely practiced. An investigation in 1893–1894 revealed that superintendent Brockway and his staff at Elmira, the first such institution, routinely administered corporal punishments and beatings as part of reformatory "treatment." Eleven adult reformatories for men were in operation by the turn of the century, and all had problems similar to those at Elmira. An investigating committee's 1893 report on conditions at the Colorado reformatory found that staff, on the authority of the superintendent, punished inmates by suspending them by their handcuffed wrists on a meat hook and engaged in other forms of routine brutality. They wrote: "With one or two exceptions . . . [officers are] not competent and not of the character or education demanded by Reformatory discipline and methods" (quoted in Pisciotta 1994: 96–97). Violence, revolts, escapes, drugs, arson, homosexuality, and suicide were cited as problems at all these institutions. By the early twentieth century, men's reformatories, too, had become little more than custodial, and the duties of the male officers in them differed little from those in prisons.

Little is known about the lives of officers in leasing camps and on early prison farms. Camp sergeants and guards—all of whom were male —were extremely poorly paid and required to live in the camps fulltime. In 1903, Florida guards' wages ranged from eighteen to twenty-five dollars a month plus board and lodging. By 1915, base pay had risen to twenty-five dollars, or thirty-five dollars if the guard provided his own horse (Mancini 1996). Low wages and poor working conditions attracted only the most desperate, as the Mississippi legislature concluded in 1888: "A frequent cause of the maltreatment of convicts is the class of guards employed. They work for twelve dollars and a half a month, and we submit that such a price for such a service can only command a very cheap order of man" (quoted in Mancini 1996: 74). Lessees used the low wages paid by the state to their advantage, bribing sergeants and guards to increase production by driving inmates literally to death. As the leasing system was replaced by prison farms, administrators relied largely on a civilian staff of poor, rural whites to supervise inmates in the field; the sole qualification was the ability "to drive and handle niggers" (McWhorter, quoted in Oshinsky 1996: 139).

In comparison to their prison and reformatory counterparts, the leasing camps and prison farms had even worse conditions. In the absence of even a semblance of penal philosophy, and fed by the knowledge that the supply of black inmates who could be used as slave laborers was essentially inexhaustible, sheer brutality went unchecked. A 1910 investigation in Texas, prompted by accounts of beatings and murders of inmates in leasing camps, concluded:

> The shocking revelations . . . reinforced even further to members of the committee the realization that the authority of guards and sergeants over the inmates was total and absolute. State prisoners existed at the caprice of an arbitrary power that recognized few if any restraints. The nature and degree of punishment was limited only by the imagination of those whose job it was to see that the prisoners received proper care. (Quoted in Walker 1988: 133)

As the leasing system died out at the beginning of the twentieth century, these conditions were transferred to the prison farms that took its place. At Mississippi's Parchman farm, which was divided into agricultural "camps," camp sergeants were empowered to use the strap on inmates as they saw fit (Oshinsky 1996).

There were relatively few civilian staff on prison farms, however. Primary supervision of inmates was provided by "trusty shooters," armed men chosen from among inmate ranks. Their charge was to kill prisoners who attempted to escape; if they discharged this duty, they were usually granted early release (Oshinsky 1996). The practice of using inmates to guard their fellows was not limited to the South, though the practice of arming them was. The use of inmate guards and "building tenders" was commonplace in penitentiaries and reformatories from their earliest appearance through the 1970s. In fact, until this time, the majority of supervision in many men's prisons was provided by inmates themselves. Administrators ultimately discontinued this practice under the pressure of inmate-initiated legal reforms (Martin and Ekland-Olson 1987).

The Call for Matrons—Defining "Women's Work"

Women were initially held along with men in early prisons and on prison farms. Because women inmates were considered even worse than their male counterparts, it was obvious that men were their appropriate guardians (Feinman 1994). The practice of allowing men to supervise incarcerated women was first challenged by reformers in the early nineteenth century. Galvanized by outrages such as the 1826 beating death of Auburn inmate Rachel Welch (who had become pregnant while in prison), reformers called for the hiring of matrons to supervise women in quarters segregated from men. In her 1827 work *Observations in Visiting, Superintendence and Government of Female Prisoners*, English reformer Elizabeth Fry wrote: "May the attention of *women* be more and more directed to these labors of love; and may the time quickly arrive, when there shall not exist, in this realm, a single public institution [where women] . . . shall not enjoy the *efficacious superintendence* of the pious and benevolent of THEIR OWN SEX!" (quoted in Freedman 1981: 23, emphasis in original). Fry's call for the employment of matrons marks the dawn of a very different, and equally gendered, idea of the model officer. Drawing on separate-spheres ideology, which saw (white, middle-class) women as inherently gentler and more virtuous than men, Fry imagines not brute enforcers but mentors and guides, women who could gently set the fallen back on the path of true womanhood.

State legislatures began to hire matrons beginning in the 1820s. Few of them fit Fry's lofty ideal. Rachel Perijo, who was appointed jail matron in Baltimore in 1822, was probably the first woman hired expressly to supervise female inmates. A matron was hired at Auburn in 1832, seven years after separate quarters for women were established (Zupan 1992b). By 1845, when Dorothea Dix toured American jails, she reported the presence of matrons in jails and prisons in Massachusetts, New York, Maryland, and Pennsylvania (Freedman 1981). Matrons in state prisons were paid even less than their male counterparts and were often subject to even worse working conditions. Some were the wives of wardens; others were working-class women, often older and widowed, forced by economic hardship into doing the work. Usually, matrons lived in the institution, often in the women's section itself, and were on duty for twenty-four hours a day, six and one-half days per week (Rafter 1990). Kate Richards O'Hare, a socialist activist who served time as a political prisoner in the women's department of the Jeffersonville, Missouri, prison wrote of the duties of matrons in 1919:

> The matrons were required to live in the prison and were never, except on rare leaves of absence, out of the sights and smells of the prison. They were prisoners almost to the same degree we were, and they all staggered under a load of responsibility far too great for their limited intelligence and untrained powers. They handled human beings at their worst, and under the worst possible conditions, and saw nothing day or night but sordid, ugly things ungilded by the glow of hope or love. (Quoted in Feinman 1994: 167)

These women had neither the authority nor the mandate to reform or rehabilitate those in their charge, and inadequate staff and overcrowding made it impossible to impose the Auburn regime or any other systematic program of prison discipline (Freedman 1981). The matrons' duties were solely custodial (Butler 1997; Freedman 1981; Rafter 1990).

The advent of the women's reformatory movement during the mid-nineteenth century resurrected Fry's ideals, however. American women's reformatory advocates, who were largely white, middle- to upper-middle-class women, drew on the separate-spheres model to argue that women required a different, specifically feminine kind of supervision. This was to be provided by officers who could both guide and discipline the "fallen woman" and serve as examples of virtuous middle-class femininity. Many early women's reformatory administrators did fit this profile. Clara Barton served for a brief time as superintendent of the Massachusetts Reformatory for Women, as did temperance crusader and former teacher Ellen Cheney Johnson and physician Eliza Mosher. Women's reformatory superintendents, unlike their male counterparts, often had advanced degrees and were drawn to prison work through their participation in a wide variety of social reform movements. The disciplinary regimes they imposed relied on ideals of middle-class femininity and sought to inculcate domesticity. Reformers believed that staff should come from the same mold. The ideal reformatory officer is captured here in an 1867 report:

> It is especially important . . . that female officers should be distinguished for modesty of demeanor, and the exercise of domestic virtues, and that they should possess that intimate knowledge of household employment, which will enable them to teach the ignorant and neglected female prisoner how to economise her means, so as to guard her from the temptations caused by waste and extravagance. (Wines and Dwight, quoted in Rafter 1990: 14).

In the cottage-style prisons reformers envisioned, and which were eventually built in a number of states, staff were to serve as "cottage officers," akin to surrogate mothers to their charges. The paramilitary mode of officer organization prevalent in men's institutions was not emphasized in women's reformatories (Zedner 1995).

The salaries offered at women's reformatories—lower than those at men's prisons and reformatories—made it difficult to attract staff, however. Even so, the generally lower wages and meager opportunities available to women in the labor market of the late nineteenth and early twentieth centuries meant that the educational and class backgrounds of staff in women's reformatories were probably higher than those in men's institutions. Katherine Bement Davis, who held a doctorate from the University of Chicago and served as the first superintendent of Bedford Hills, hired a number of college graduates, many from women's colleges, to serve on her staff, as did Miriam van Waters, who also held a doctorate and served as superintendent of the Massachusetts Reformatory for Women from 1932 to 1957 (Freedman 1981, 1996). As late as the 1940s, upwards of 25 percent of women's prison and reformatory officers held college degrees (Feinman 1994). The ideology of moral uplift at the heart of women's social reform movements, combined with a lack of opportunities elsewhere, drew educated, middle-class women to the work. As Georgiana Bruce Kirby, who served as a deputy to Eliza Farnham at Mount Pleasant, wrote:

> It had pleased us to love these low-down children of circumstances less fortunate than our own. We gloried in being able to lift a few of them

out of the slough into which they had fallen, or in which they had been born, and to sustain them while they were trying to take a little step upward in the direction of the light. (Quoted in Feinman 1994: 162)

Even so, there were reports of mistreatment of inmates, some sanctioned by administrators, in women's reformatories. Investigating commissions in New York and Massachusetts from the 1890s through the 1920s reported the use of long term solitary confinement, bread-and-water diets, and some corporal punishments. According to Freedman (1981), however, compared with conditions for women in state prisons, the level of physical discomfort suffered by women in reformatories was relatively mild. The reformatory emphasis on "feminized" rehabilitation and self-control did, for a time, apparently succeed in creating more orderly, humane penal environments.

As the twentieth century progressed and job opportunities for educated women expanded, positions as officers became, like their corollaries in men's institutions, poorly paid working-class jobs. High rates of turnover among staff became a chronic problem. By 1962 to 1963, when Rose Giallombardo studied Alderson, the first federal women's reformatory, the captain of the officer force reported that she was pressed simply to find "warm bod[ies]" (Giallombardo 1966: 29) to fill vacant positions. Twentieth-century women's reformatory administrators were professional women, yet without the extensive backgrounds in social reform possessed by their predecessors (Freedman 1981). They presided over regimes that, while retaining some distinctively "feminized" features, such as training in domestic pursuits, came to resemble those in men's prisons and reformatories. Ideals mandating differential, specifically feminine treatment for women inmates had become embattled by the mid-1930s (Rafter 1990).

Some persistent manifestations of difference remained, however. Throughout the country, women's reformatory officers faced less desirable working conditions and were paid less than their male counterparts. The board of managers of the New Jersey Reformatory for Women decried this inequity in 1940:

Our cottage officers work practically twenty-four hours a day and receive from $50 to $70 a month plus maintenance. Male guards in the reformatories for men work eight hours and receive a minimum of $150 per month. (Quoted in Hawkes 1991: 104)

In New Jersey, as in most state reformatories at this time, cottage offi-cers were hired to work twelve-hour shifts. In reality they were on call at all hours, as, in accordance with the reconstitution of a family ideal, they were required to live and eat in the cottages. These requirements were not relaxed until 1951. Salary inequities persisted, however. By 1955, the salary range for male correctional officers in New Jersey was $3,480 to $4,380, while the range for a female cottage supervisor was $2,520 to $3,120 (Hawkes 1991). It was not until the 1970s that women began to fill posts as "correctional officers" on an equal footing with men. It was also during this period that they came to work as offi-cers in institutions for men, a development that significantly increased the opportunities available to women in correctional work. The effect of increasing opportunities was dramatic; as table 3.1 indicates, the pro-portion of women working in prisons more than doubled between 1970 and 1980.

Race and Prison Staff

Whether institutions housed men, or women, or both, staff at early pris-ons, reformatories, and prison farms were almost exclusively white. As table 3.1 indicates, as late as 1960 about 94 percent of all correctional officers were white. Outright discrimination, fueled by racist ideas about the connections between race and crime, initially barred African-Americans and Hispanics from jobs as guards and officers. Such con-nections were made by prison camp administrators in the South, but they were common in other parts of the country as well. Zebulon Brockway, first superintendent of Elmira, described black inmates in in-stitutional ledgers as of "low type," "ignorant," and "cunning—like ro-dents" (quoted in Pisciotta 1994: 49–50). The attribution of inherent criminality to blacks and other "inferior" races was strengthened even further by the eugenics movement, which gained increasing influence at the dawn of the twentieth century (Gould 1981; Tucker 1994). In the minds of prison administrators, blacks and other "inferior" races were more suited to be the kept than the keepers.

In the rare instances before the 1960s in which black officers were hired to work in prisons, it was to guard black inmates, who were usu-ally segregated and housed in the worst parts of prisons and reformato-ries. In the 1950s at Alderson, for example, black officers supervised

TABLE 3.1

Correctional Workforce by Sex, Race, and Ethnicity, Selected Years, 1870–1999

	Total	% Female	%Black[f]	% Hispanic
1870[a]	13,252	0.1		
1880[a]	38,153	0.2		
1890[a]	78,263	0.4		
1900[a]	103,590	0.8		
1910[b]	78,268	0.1		
1920[b]	115,553	0.3		
1930[b]	159,964	0.6		
1940[b]	219,437	1.1		
1950[b]	237,203	2.2	4.6	
1960[b]	242,229	2.9	5.8	
1970[c]	318,611	5.1	13.5	
1977[d]	490,000	10.2	18.0	
1980[d]	548,000	12.4	16.8	
1983[e]	146,000	17.8	24.0	2.8
1990[e]	184,667	18.9	23.5	6.4
1995[e]	278,000	17.8	28.2	6.4
1999[e]	315,000	23.5	24.9	8.7

SOURCES: 1870–1940, U.S. Bureau of the Census, Sixteenth Census of the United States: 1940, *Comparative Occupation Statistics for the United States, 1870–1940* (Washington, DC: Government Printing Office, 1943); 1950, 1960, 1970, and 1990, U.S. Bureau of the Census, Decennial Censuses; all other years, U.S. Bureau of the Census, *Statistical Abstract of the United States* (Washington, DC: Government Printing Office).

[a] From 1870 to 1900, prison workers were included in the category "guards, watchmen, and doorkeepers, detectives, firemen, policemen, probation and truant officers, marshals and constables."

[b] From 1910 to 1960, the relevant category was "guards, watchmen, and doorkeepers."

[c] In 1970, "Guards and watchmen."

[d] From 1972 to 1982, "guards."

[e] From 1983 to present, data are specific to "correctional institution officers," a category that includes officers in prisons but also those in jails, juvenile facilities, and community-based facilities.

[f] From 1950 to 1980, this category includes black officers, as well as those of all races other than white. From 1983 to 1999, this category includes black officers only.

black inmates in segregated cottages and oversaw their work on the institution's pig farm (Feinman 1994). Blatant discrimination eased beginning in the 1960s; as table 3.1 indicates, between 1960 and 1970, the number of blacks working in prisons almost doubled. These benefits probably accrued largely to black men, who had access to jobs in men's prisons. Opportunities for black women paralleled those for white women, increasing following legal challenges to bars to employment in men's prisons and affirmative action policies implemented during the 1970s (Belknap 2001). Even so, the continuing practice of siting facilities in predominantly white, rural areas has meant that the officer corps in many prisons tends to reflect the demographics of the surrounding population. Racial conflict between staff and inmates is a fixture of daily life in many modern prisons. Inmates, who come largely from urban areas, are disproportionately members of minority groups. Major riots at Attica and other prisons during the 1970s had at their roots long-standing racial tensions between urban minority inmates and rural white guards.

Engendering the Officer

By the mid–twentieth century, two different, and gendered, models of the job we now call "correctional officer" had emerged. Ideologically at least, "ideal" officers working in men's and women's prisons had very different orientations toward their work. In line with prevailing ideas about proper masculinity and femininity, men were to be officers in a paramilitary mold, and to serve primarily as enforcers, ready and able to use violence if necessary. Women, on the other hand, were to be mentors and surrogate mothers, guiding their wayward charges toward rehabilitation. The studies of work in men's and women's prisons that began to appear during this period indicate some of the differences reflected in these gendered ideologies, but some areas of convergence as well. Through the 1960s, men served almost entirely in institutions housing men, with officer corps ranked and governed on a paramilitary model. The first research on officers in men's prisons appeared during the 1950s, 1960s, and 1970s and revealed the existence of a masculine white working-class officer subculture with a distinct set of guiding norms. In line with the attributes of working-class masculinity, men who served as officers accepted violence as part of their work. A prison guard interviewed by Crouch (1980) noted that, prior to the 1970s, if an inmate committed a minor infraction, an officer would just "kick his ass, and that'd be the end of it" (1980: 15). Whether or not individual male officers engaged in these actions (and it is clear that many did not), prevailing norms dictated that if they were to continue to work in the prison, they had to accept them (Kauffman 1988).

This ideology, though consistently demonstrated in studies of male officers during this period (and even now), is paradoxical. As prison administrators, workers, and inmates have long known, no prison can be governed by violence alone. Officers are unarmed and grossly outnumbered. In reality, they maintain order only through a process of negotiation with inmates. As Sykes understood, "Far from being omnipotent rulers who have crushed all signs of rebellion against their regime, the custodians are engaged in a continuous struggle to maintain order—and it is a struggle in which the custodians frequently fail" (1958: 42). Inmates also have an interest in maintaining a secure environment, and many cooperate with officers in the enforcement of rules (Owen 1988). The real basis of the order in any prison is a negotiated one, the result of reciprocal accommodations between inmates themselves and between officers and inmates (Owen 1988). No effective officer does their job completely "by the book." Many prison rules are explicitly contradictory, and many others are unnecessarily petty. Enforcing all such rules uniformly would undoubtedly lead to widespread discontent and perhaps even mass disorder. Administrators understand this and expect officers to maintain order through the exercise of discretion. As Sykes (1958: 56) notes, "To a large extent the guard is dependent on inmates for the satisfactory performance of his duties; and like many individuals in positions of power, the guard is evaluated in terms of the conduct of the men he controls." Given these organizational and structural constraints, no prison could actually be governed by brute enforcers who manage inmates by "kicking ass." The subcultural norm of the authoritarian officer who rules through violence gives way in the light of prison realities to the officer who can do his job only by effectively negotiating order on a day-to-day basis.

Early research also revealed a profound distrust of administrators, whom officers perceived as out of touch with the day-to-day realities of their work with inmates. Suspicion of, and social distance from, inmates was a core value, deriving from officers' views of the etiology of crime:

> In the most general terms, guards perceive inmates as volitional actors who choose crime from among other, presumably equally available, lifestyles. Guards tend to view prisoners as men who, on the streets, were lazy and adverse to work, and who turned to crime as a more expedient lifestyle. (Crouch and Marquart 1980: 79)

Officers maintained a rigid line between themselves and inmates, and any officer perceived to have "crossed the line" by becoming too familiar with inmates risked being rejected by his fellows. Members of officer subculture generally opposed any changes that they saw as an erosion of their authority and were particularly suspicious of programs that increased inmate rights. Loyalty to other officers was also paramount (Duffee 1974; Crouch 1980; Fox 1982; Kauffman 1988).

Racism was normative as the resistance and harassment experienced by black officers who came to work in men's prisons during the 1960s and 1970s clearly illustrate (Owen 1988; Zimmer 1986, 1987). Similarly, the belief that only "real men" could do the work of guarding male inmates meant that the first women to integrate men's prisons during the 1970s faced hostility, exclusion, and harassment (Feinman 1994; Jurik 1985, 1988; Jurik and Halemba 1984; Martin and Jurik 1996; Owen 1988; Zimmer 1986, 1987). Overriding all, however, was a commitment to safety and security, a goal that officers believed they knew best how to achieve. Officers invoked a constant need to be on guard against potential outbreaks of violence. The specter of danger was clearly one of the primary forces that held the officer subculture together. This value also served as a primary source of resistance to the increasing employment of women (Zimmer 1986). Though I studied officers in men's prisons almost four decades after the first of this research appeared, my interviews reveal that many of these values are still alive and well.

There are very few studies of officers at women's prisons (or of women's prisons at all) during the same period, and those that do exist (Giallombardo 1966; Heffernan 1972; Ward and Kassebaum 1965) pay little attention to staff. They indicate, however, that remnants of the ideology that women should be treated differently from men in prison, while embattled, survived, at least among some administrators. Ward and Kassebaum report that the superintendent of the California Institution for Women "said that in her experience women acted differently in prison, had different problems and consequently, they needed different treatment" (1965: vii–viii). Similarly, Giallombardo (1966) found a treatment regimen very much in evidence at Alderson. In both cases, these assumptions by administrators carried corollary expectations for staff, who were expected to participate in inmate rehabilitation. Ward and Kassebaum (1965) reported that women officers, at least in California, were better educated than their male counterparts, being required to have completed at least two years of college before employment.

Little is known about the existence of officer subcultures in women's prisons. Giallombardo (1966) observed that officers at Alderson, like their counterparts in men's prisons, distrusted administrators, whom they saw as out of touch with the day-to-day realities of maintaining routine and security. They also opposed changes that gave inmates more power and autonomy (Giallombardo 1966). Increasingly called on by administrators to perform counseling and treatment, officers expressed insecurity and resistance, pointing to their lack of training in a system that prepared them only to assume custodial functions. Giallombardo (1966) and Heffernan (1972) both report that officers expressed resentment of treatment staff, whose activities they considered disruptive to prison routine and whose allegiance to inmates and their rehabilitation was suspect. There is little evidence in any of these studies of the vision of officer as mentor and teacher that women's prison reformers advocated at the turn of the century. Nor is there any suggestion that officers were systematically prepared for these roles. While these observers report some discontent among white women officers regarding the racial integration of the officer corps, it appears to have been less ingrained and hostile than in men's prisons. There is also little evidence of widespread resistance to the employment of male officers in women's prisons. But perhaps the most striking difference between men's and women's prison staff revealed by these studies is the lack of emphasis on danger and the use of physical force. Then, as now, the work environment in women's prisons was freer the constantly reiterated threat of violence than its male counterpart.

Prison Reform and Professionalization

During the 1960s and 1970s changes began to occur that would fundamentally alter the roles of men and women in corrections. Until the 1960s, with the exception of investigating committee reports and the public scandals and resignations that followed in their wake, courts and legislatures observed a "hands-off" doctrine with regard to the decisions of prison administrators (Crouch 1980). Prison staff, regardless of the institution, were selected using arbitrary criteria, if any at all. They were generally untrained and underpaid, and high turnover was the rule. In 1964, the director of the Federal Bureau of Prisons assessed the situation: "Trained personnel are . . . scarce and except in a handful of prison systems salaries are too low to attract competent people" (Bennett, quoted in Lunden 1965: v). These conditions, combined with the relative insulation of prisons from public scrutiny, meant that misconduct by officers (and administrators) often went unchecked. It was not until the 1930s that full-time, paid training programs for prison guards began to appear, an effort that was pioneered by the Federal Bureau of

Prisons. The expense of such programs meant that many states were slow to adopt them, however. As late as 1967, the President's Crime Commission noted that most officers are "undereducated, untrained, and unversed in the goals of corrections" (quoted in Hawkins 1980: 56). Most states and jurisdictions did eventually introduce formal training programs for officers in the 1970s (Feinman 1994).

This change, as well as a host of others that would transform the conditions of incarceration for American prisoners, came about largely as a result of inmate-initiated legal action during the 1960s and 1970s. Prior to this time, prison inmates had essentially been considered legally dead and had little access to the courts. This changed with the Supreme Court's decision in *Cooper v. Pate* (378 U.S. 546, 1964), a case that had the effect of granting prisoners access to the courts to pursue suits against prison administrators (Martin and Ekland-Olson 1987). A number of high-profile cases followed, all of which exposed abuses and violations of the rights of inmates. Decisions often addressed the lack of adequate, well-trained staff. For instance, in a case originating at Parchman farm, *Gates v. Collier*, 349 F. Supp. 881 (N.D. Miss. 1972), the court required that the State of Mississippi

> exert every effort to obtain competent civilian personnel, making special appeal to the black community for qualified persons. Lack of funds shall not constitute valid grounds for continuing delay . . . the defendants shall submit a statement of compliance with the provisions of this paragraph and also propose a plan for the total and complete elimination of the use of [inmate] trusties for armed guard duty and for other custodial responsibility within six months thereafter, or not later than June 20, 1973. The plan shall include the type and nature of training program recommended for the new civilian guard force and proposals for recruiting personnel upon [a] racially nondiscriminatory basis.

Similar cases across the United States ended with state prison systems under the jurisdiction of judicially supervised consent decrees to improve inmate food, housing, and medical care, to curb brutality by staff, and to recruit more and better trained officers from a diverse pool of applicants. The effect on opportunities for officers of color was dramatic, as table 3.1 indicates. Between 1960 and 1983, the proportion of black officers serving in correctional institutions quadrupled, rising from 6 percent to 25 percent.

It was also during this period that a concerted drive toward professionalization of the occupation began (Jacobs 1977). As Jurik and Musheno (1986) observe, unlike efforts in other fields, which largely derived from campaigns by workers themselves, professionalization in corrections was initially a top-down affair. In response to legislative and judicial pressures, administrators focused on increasing the educational level of staff, as well as implementing lengthier and more systematic training programs. To reflect this new emphasis, job titles in many systems were changed, for example, from "correctional officer" to "correctional counselor" or "correctional service officer." Violence was increasingly decried, and communication emphasized as the primary legitimate tool for inmate management. Unlike other professionals, correctional officers were not given the generally recognized attributes of their titular status, however, such as increased autonomy, authority, and a code of professional ethics. In most cases, the move toward more professionalized staff involved a change in name rather than function. Officers were given no training in counseling, nor was the structure of their job changed to allow them to counsel as well as maintain security. As might be expected under these conditions, this change in emphasis produced resistance from staff, many of whom saw these changes as diminishing their authority (Duffee 1974; Jacobs 1977; Jacobs and Retsky 1975; Martin and Jurik 1996; Jurik and Musheno 1986).

Correctional officers in many states responded by organizing, and their rapidly increasing numbers have often given them considerable political clout. The correctional officers' union in California, for example, is now one of the most powerful such organizations in the state. In a move that contradicts the trend toward the working-class solidarity signified by unionization, however, officers have also embraced the label of professional, attempting to define it in their own terms. An officer in an on-line forum (www.corrections.com/thinktank) defines professionalism in terms of ethical conduct:

> Should there be a universal code of ethics in corrections? The only answer if we EVER hope to be viewed as professional law enforcement officers is YES! Ethics in the profession is crucial to successfully operating in the modern correctional setting and we must constantly maintain and improve our ethical conduct if we hope to gain the respect of the public, fellow staff and yes . . . [e]ven the inmates! The media loves to portray the "Guard gone bad," and if we as correctional professionals want to

bury the "guard" label, we must continually strive to demonstrate that the old days are gone forever and in this new age of corrections the correctional "Officer" conducts his/her daily duties within the highest standard of ethical and professional behaviors. The knuckle-dragging days are dead and gone and a universal code of ethics can only be another sign of that dead attitude and the professional correctional workers' commitment to insure it stays that way!

Officers see adopting the label "professional" as one way to escape the stigma that still accompanies working in prisons. It also carries the promise of positive evolution, a clear signal that the "knuckle-dragging days are dead and gone." However, without substantial alterations in job requirements—still at the level of a high school diploma in most states—and in the structure of the job itself, the adoption of the professional label again promises to be a change more in title than in status. Labor shortages in prisons and the emphasis on custody over rehabilitation mean that the achievement of professional status is unlikely in the foreseeable future.

The Legal Context of Cross-Gender Supervision

Perhaps the most significant development in correctional work in the last three decades has been the increasing prevalence of "cross-gender" supervision, that is, the employment of men and women in prison facilities housing inmates of the opposite sex. As table 3.2 indicates, as of 1995, women were 19 percent of correctional officers and were only slightly underrepresented as officers in men's prisons, at 16 percent.[1] Eighty-four percent of all women who work in prisons, and 97 percent of men, work with male inmates. In turn, women now constitute only the bare majority of officers in women's prisons, representing 56 percent of the total. The current situation, a striking departure from historical trends in the occupation, is the product of a contentious legal history centered around both the hiring and the deployment of cross-gender officers.

The position now known as "correctional officer" has, from the outset, been framed in gendered terms. Men have been seen as the natural protectors of society and thus the appropriate guardians of those who would harm their fellow citizens. In early prisons, this was true even for female inmates, whom society at large viewed as even worse than their

TABLE 3.2
Correctional Workforce by Jurisdiction and Facility Type, 1995

	Men	Women
Total	172,077	39,345
	81%	19%
Men's prisons	166,995	32,908
	84%	16%
Women's prisons	5,082	6,437
	44%	56%
Federal prisons	8,799	1,210
	88%	12%
State prisons	163,278	38,135
	81%	19%
Federal men's prisons	8,515	1,002
	89%	11%
Federal women's prisons	284	208
	58%	42%
State men's prisons	158,480	31,906
	83%	17%
State women's prisons	4,798	6,229
	44%	56%
Working in men's prisons	166,995	32,908
	97%	84%

SOURCE: Author calculation from U.S. Department of Justice (1998).

male counterparts. It was only as a result of the efforts of reformers that a feminized model of the keeper emerged, first in the position of women's prison "matron," and later as reformatory "cottage officer." Against this ideological and cultural backdrop, it seemed almost unthinkable that women would possess the capability to work in men's prisons. It was this ideology that guided the policies of men's prison administrators until the 1970s and serves as a justification for informal practices even today.

Access to Employment

Prior to 1972, only men were hired to work as officers in facilities holding male inmates. Though Title VII of the Civil Rights Act was amended in 1972 to include public-sector employees, early on, administrators apparently hoped that the job of correctional officer in a men's prison would qualify for an exclusion from equal employment requirements on the grounds of a bona fide occupational qualification (BFOQ). Women began to sue in the lower courts for jobs in men's prisons, however, and generally won. The Supreme Court became involved in this issue in *Dothard v. Rawlinson*, 433 U.S. 321 (1977), in which the Court held that at least under some circumstances jobs as correctional officers in men's prisons qualified for a BFOQ exemption from Title VII requirements of equal employment opportunity. However, perhaps because arguing that *Dothard* justifies excluding women from certain types of facilities is virtually the same as admitting that they are unconstitutionally violent (Collins 1991:14), only one other case was decided on this precedent. Most subsequent attempts to restrict women's employment failed. For example, in *Gunther v. Iowa*, 612 F.2d 1079 (8th Cir., 1980), the court held that the BFOQ exemption applied only in the "peculiarly inhospitable" atmosphere of the Alabama maximum-security prison. Similarly, in *Harden v. Dayton Human Rehabilitation Center*, 520 F. Supp. 769 (S.D. Ohio, 1981), the court declared that the state had not supplied the preponderance of evidence necessary to support a BFOQ claim. Collectively, these cases shattered the barriers to women's employment in men's prisons (Collins 1991; Zimmer 1986).

Two other forces combined with legal changes to increase women's access to positions in men's prisons (Martin and Jurik 1996). The first was a severe shortage of male officers. Court decisions in inmates' rights cases in the 1960s and 1970s created the immediate need for large numbers of officers. As the supply of male recruits became exhausted, administrators had little choice but to turn to women. At Louisiana's Angola State Prison, women began to be hired in the wake of just such a staff shortage (Crouch 1980), and the situation was the same in many states during the 1970s. Second, women's presence in men's prisons was seen by advocates as concomitant with the overall drive to professionalize the occupation and "normalize" the prison environment. Drawing on an essentialist paradigm not so different from the separate-spheres model invoked by reformers 150 years earlier, they held that women's presence could "exert a 'softening' influence on inmate behavior and could avert some potential crisis situations before they grow into physical confrontations" (Kissel and Katsampes 1980: 219). Additionally, those who supported the integration of women into officer forces in men's prisons believed that they would have lower tolerance for brutality, or at least less ability to use violence. Women were to gain access to men's prisons, but only through the door of an ideology that reinvoked essentialist ideas about the qualities they would bring to the work environment (Martin and Jurik 1996). As of this writing, all states and the Federal Bureau of Prisons now employ women as officers in these facilities. As table 3.2 indicates, however, in a reflection of the pattern of internal gender stratification in most occupations, women are less likely to be employed at the more lucrative federal level. They constitute only 12 percent of the officer corps in federal men's prisons, versus 19 percent of those in state facilities.

The circumstances surrounding men's work as officers in institutions housing women are strikingly different from those in the opposite case. Perhaps the most notable difference between the two is the lack of a legal struggle around the basic rights of men to work as officers in women's institutions. One reason for this may be that male officers have always been present in institutions of incarceration housing women. Even today, men account for 44 percent of those in women's prisons and are the majority (58 percent) of officers working in women's prisons in the federal system. Opportunity may play a role as well; comparatively speaking, there are relatively few women's prisons, which means that the number of jobs available is much smaller. This makes the issue of cross-gender supervision a much more crucial one for women, who were historically unable to compete for the overwhelming majority of positions as correctional officers. Finally, the lack of a legal struggle around this issue may be due to the relatively lower status of women's institutions. For male officers, women's prisons simply do not serve as the same kind of masculine proving ground as men's institutions.

Issues in Deployment

Though the courts have generally agreed that men and women should be allowed to work in facilities housing members of the opposite sex, the deployment of cross-gendered officers has been much more problematic. The crucial issue has been whether officers of the opposite sex can work in inmate housing units. Such postings are the majority of assignments in most prisons, and being barred from them dramatically decreases job opportunities. The chief difficulty is privacy; officers in housing units routinely observe inmates in various states of undress and are often involved in supervision of showers and toilet facilities. Such posts also usually require the strip- and pat-searching of inmates returning to their cells from visits or work details.

The legal history and current status of men's and women's access to these positions are two very different stories. Initially, women who were hired to work in men's prisons were given positions that did not involve inmate contact, such as administrative office work and the searching of female visitors. Large numbers of women began to move into inmate contact positions during the late 1970s, which gave rise to a series of inmate-initiated lawsuits focusing on the right to privacy. In early cases, courts ruled that male inmates had the right to be free from supervision by officers of the opposite sex. In *Bowling v. Enomoto*, 514 F. Supp. 201 (N.D. Ca., 1981), the court declared:

> prisoners in all-male institutions had limited rights to privacy which included the right to be free from unrestricted observations of their genitals and bodily functions by prison officials of the opposite sex under normal prison conditions. (Quoted in Zimmer 1986: 7)

Similarly, in *Hudson v. Goodlander*, 494 F. Supp. 890 (Md., 1980), the court ruled that an "inmate's privacy rights were violated by the assignment of female officers to posts where they could view him while he was completely naked" (quoted in Zimmer 1986: 7). *Bowling* declared that California officials must strike a balance, protecting inmates' privacy rights while optimizing opportunities for women.

The Supreme Court issued the benchmark ruling on this issue in *Hudson v. Palmer*, 104 U.S. 3194 (1984). Though this case dealt with cell searches rather than cross-gender supervision, it paved the way for the almost unrestricted employment of women in men's facilities. In this case, the Court held that inmates had no reasonable expectation of privacy in their cells and cell contents. This ruling was applied specifically to female officers in *Grummett v. Rushen*, 779 F.2d 491 (9th Cir., 1985), a case that arose from San Quentin in California. At the time, women worked almost everywhere in the facility, including living areas, and also performed routine pat-down searches of male inmates. The court held that where the observation of nude male inmates was "infrequent and casual," no privacy rights of the inmates were violated, nor did pat searches violate inmate privacy, assuming that they were done in a professional manner. In *Timm v. Gunter*, 913 F.2d 1093 (8th Cir., 1990), the Eighth Circuit Court of Appeals held that both pat searches and casual observation of male inmates by female officers did not violate inmates' rights to privacy. The court declared that whatever privacy interests the inmates may have had were overcome by the interests of the institution in maintaining security and in furthering equal employment opportunity (Miller 2000).

The deployment of male officers in prisons for women has been more controversial. In accord with the ideology that has framed the ideal men's prison officer as one willing or at least capable of using violence, men's role in women's prisons has historically been that of enforcer, and their assignments have reflected that emphasis. Even after matrons were hired to supervise women in state prisons, the historical record indicates that they sometimes relied on male officers to control unruly or violent inmates (Lewis 1965). With the hiring of additional female staff, however, men were restricted to assignments outside of the housing and living areas of female inmates, typically staffing gate and perimeter positions in reformatories. Giallombardo (1966) notes that during the time she was at Alderson, 10 of the 102 officers were men. They were assigned to the gate, delivered medical and other items to the cottages, and assisted at patrol duty. It is clear that they served as enforcers, however:

> The male officer symbolizes brute force without benefit of a gun to the inmates. The female officer never exerts any physical force in her dealings with inmates unless she is physically attacked and acts in self-defense. When an inmate "refuses to listen to reason," the officer calls a lieutenant. If the lieutenant fails to secure compliance, two male officers are called and it is they who use physical force if necessary in escorting (in the company of a female lieutenant) a recalcitrant inmate to seclusion. (Giallombardo 1966: 32–33)

Just as women gained access to jobs in prisons housing the opposite sex through gendered routes, so, too, did men. A gendered division of labor has existed since the earliest days of separate incarceration for women. Women matrons, guards, and, now, officers were responsible for day-to-day supervision of inmates, and men for the threat of the use of physical force. As I will show, this is a pattern that persists to the present.

Until very recently, men have not been assigned to positions supervising women inmates in their housing units. As in men's prisons, the rationale for this policy has been inmate privacy. Key recent litigation in this area has focused on the issue of whether male officers should be allowed to pat-search female inmates, and as of this writing, the issue remains unsettled (Miller 2000). The pivotal case thus far is *Jordan v. Gardner*, 986 F.2d 1521 (9th Cir. 1993). The originating suit was filed in 1989 by several inmates at a Washington state prison that had instituted a policy permitting male correctional officers to perform pat searches of female inmates. The policy required officers to conduct random searches of inmates for contraband. In doing so, they were required to run their hands over the inmate's entire body from head to toe, "squeezing and kneading her breasts, probing her crotch by pressing the flat of the hand against the genitals, and squeezing and kneading seams in her crotch area" (Miller 2000: 317 n. 95). The policy had been in effect for less than twenty-four hours when a woman who had previously suffered extensive sexual abuse reacted with severe distress to a pat search by a male officer; her fingers had to be pried loose from cell bars she had grabbed during the search, and she vomited during her return to her cell.[2] Several other women vomited and exhibited signs of shock (Miller 2000). The Ninth Circuit overturned the policy in a decision which held that it violated inmate rights under the Eighth Amendment to the Constitution, prohibiting "the unnecessary and wanton infliction of pain upon prisoners" (*Jordan v. Gardner*, 986 F.2d 1521 [9th Cir. 1993]). Interestingly enough, it was also the Ninth Circuit that had held, in *Grummett v. Rushen*, 779 F.2d 491 (1985), that pat searches of male inmates by female officers did not violate the Eighth Amendment. The court notes this apparent contradiction in its decision in this case, justifying the application of different policies in the case of women's prisons by applying the "reasonable woman" standard it first established in a 1991 sexual harassment case. In that decision, the court had written:

Because women are disproportionately victims of rape and sexual assault, women have a stronger incentive to be concerned with sexual behavior. . . . Men, who are rarely victims of sexual assault, may view sexual conduct in a vacuum without a full appreciation of the social setting or the underlying threat of violence that a woman may perceive. (*Ellison v. Brady*, 924 F.2d 872, 879 [9th Cir. 1991]; footnote omitted)

The justices held that female inmates' greater experience with sexual harassment and abuse should be considered in formulating policies regarding the assignment of male officers in women's facilities.

Though a definitive statement, the Ninth Circuit's decision in this case is binding only within its jurisdiction. The Supreme Court, though it has had multiple opportunities to do so, has never ruled on the issue of cross-gender searches in either men's or women's prisons. In a recent review of case law in this area, Miller observes, "The constitutionality of cross-gender searches is not settled law today and has not been for years" (2000: 326). The upshot of this legal landscape is that a wide variety of deployment practices and search policies now prevail.

Nationally, pressure around this issue continues to mount, particularly around barring male correctional officers from conducting searches of women inmates. On one side are officers and officer unions that favor gender-neutral assignment policies and have initiated legal action and filed grievances against regulations that restrict men's assignments. Such a grievance by female officers was in fact the impetus for the adoption of the policy overturned by the Ninth Circuit in *Jordan.* On the other side, women inmates in a number of states and jurisdictions have lawsuits pending that seek to overturn cross-sex pat search policies, as well as to bar male officers from women's prisons entirely. Recent scandals involving the sexual abuse of female inmates by male officers have fueled this controversy (Amnesty International 1999a, 1999b; Human Rights Watch 1996, 1998).

As the development of institutions of incarceration for men and women proceeded along paths deeply influenced by race, gender, and class, so, too, did prison work. In line with white working-class masculinity, ideal male keepers, turnkeys, and guards were to be officers, gentlemen, and enforcers. Female officers, white and drawn from the educated middle classes, were to serve as teachers, mentors, and examples. Maternal guidance, rather than violence, was to be their primary tool in rehabilitating their working-class sisters. And, though black officers now make up one-quarter of the custody staff in American prisons, African-Americans have been (and still are) seen by many as more suited to be living in prisons than working in them. These prototypical officers are little more than stereotypes, however. It is difficult to know whether actual officers ever lived up to these ideals, of if prisons could have been governed in an orderly fashion if they had. By the mid–twentieth century, legal and structural changes in the occupation blurred the edges of the masculine and feminine styles of correctional work. Male officers are now enjoined to command through communication, while the vestiges of middle-class femininity that once shaped women officers' roles have been eroded by equal employment directives and a growing call for "equal" treatment for male and female offenders (Chesney-Lind 1996).

The day-to-day realities of the lives of officers and the practical complications of doing the work have always belied both the ideals of prison administrators and the stereotypes of the public. It is to those officers that I now turn. Chapter 4 traces the paths to prison work taken by the individuals I studied and examines their preparation for jobs as officers. Though their stories mark the dramatic changes in the occupation during the last thirty years, they also reveal the lasting influence of ideas and social structures built on foundations of race, class, and gender.

4

Paths to Prison

Very few of us work in the occupations to which we aspired
in childhood. As Williams (1995) observes, if we did, there would be
many more cowboys, professional football players, superheroes (whether
of the Xena or Superman variety), nurses, and ballet dancers. As this list
suggests, occupational socialization is a thoroughly gendered process.
Cultural depictions, children's play, and adult role models all shape the
kinds of jobs that children come to see as appropriate for men and
women (Marini and Brinton 1984). This is certainly true for those in my
study. Few people grow up dreaming about future careers as correctional
officers. A 1967 survey found that only 1 percent of youth mentioned
"prison guard" as their preferred occupation. The situation had not
changed much by the time the officers in this study were adolescents. In a
1982 poll, only 0.1 percent of those aged fourteen to twenty-two expressed an aspiration to work as prison guards. While few adolescents
imagine themselves in this occupation, it is an even rarer choice for girls
than boys. Of those who selected prison work, 95 percent were male.[1]

Historically, low remuneration, difficult working conditions, and the
ignominy that comes with doing society's "dirty work" combined to
make jobs in prisons unattractive. The circumstances of prison employment today reflect both continuity and change. Salaries have improved,
though they are still low, with starting pay averaging only $23,000
nationally (Belluck 2001). The drive toward professionalization of the
occupation notwithstanding, most prison systems require only minimal
qualifications of officer recruits: typically, they must be twenty-one years
old, have graduated from high school, and have no felony convictions.
Working conditions have changed for the better during the past thirty
years, but they still vary widely across states and even from institution
to institution within systems. Some prisons are high-tech, climate-con-
trolled facilities utilizing video monitoring of inmates and computerized
access; others are un-air-conditioned in summer, are barely heated in

winter, and rely on steel bars, gates, and razor ribbon wire for security. Most are located in remote, rural areas. Taken together, this package of attributes marks the occupation as a working-class job, albeit one that offers a salary, job security, and all the benefits that accompany government employment.

Demand for correctional officers has been strong and is expected to remain so through 2008 (U.S. Department of Labor 2000). Even given high demand and improving working conditions, the job retains its status as work of last resort, and prison system administrators nationwide find themselves hard-pressed to recruit and retain officers. Prison salaries have not kept pace with the private sector. The median income for a correctional officer in 2000 was $30,524 (U.S. Department of Labor 2001b). In comparison, the median income for full-time, year-round employed male high school graduates in the labor force as a whole was $34,303. High turnover rates have exacerbated staff shortages. As I noted in chapter 3, turnover among prison workers has always been a problem for administrators, but the situation worsened in the wake of strong economic growth during the 1990s. In the United States as a whole, 16 percent of all officers left their jobs in 1999, compared with almost 10 percent in 1991. In some states, the situation is much worse; in Alabama for example, the attrition rate is 42 percent, and administrators estimate that the state is currently short some 412 officers. Nationwide, systems have responded with a variety of strategies. Kansas recently lowered its minimum age for officer recruits from twenty-one to nineteen, and other states plan to follow suit. The building of new prisons has been canceled, states have offered increased pay and benefits and substantial start-up bonuses, and some provide free transportation and room and board to attract workers to remote institutions (Belluck 2001).

Relatively low salaries are undoubtedly accelerating one other change, the shift from a largely white male work-force to one that is now composed of increasing numbers of women and African-American and Hispanic men. According to Reskin and Roos, the composition of a given occupation is the result of a "dual-queuing" process: "labor queues" order groups of workers according to their desirability from the perspective of employers, while "job queues" rank jobs in terms of their attractiveness to potential workers (1990: 29). A mismatch in the ordering of these queues can lead to change in occupational demographics, and this is precisely what is occurring in prison work. In 2000, white male high school graduates who worked full-time and year-round earned a median income of $36,378; for black men this figure was $27,972, and for Hispanic men it was $27,854.[2] For women, the comparable figures are white, $26,007, black, $21,752, and Hispanic, $21,180 (U.S. Department of Commerce 2001, table 8). Though white male workers may still rank at the top of prison employers' labor queue, correctional employment is less lucrative than other opportunities in these workers' job queues, and employers must increasingly look elsewhere. Conversely, race and sex discrimination in the larger labor force mean that prison work is more attractive to women and African-American and Hispanic men. Lower levels of wage differentials by race and sex in the government employment sector have made these jobs even more appealing to workers from formerly excluded groups.

In this chapter, I trace the paths of those in my study to prison work and examine their experiences as they trained for the jobs they were to assume. As the foregoing suggests, those who come to work in prisons rarely do so through very direct routes. I trace the ways that those paths differ by gender and examine the kinds of barriers men and women overcame first to imagine themselves as, and then to become, officers. I then turn to the institution of the prison itself, showing how gendered assumptions about inmates and officers shape training and leave important gaps for officers who do not fit within its assumptions about the generic officer and the typical prison work environment.

Previous Work Experience

Stereotypes abound about how one comes to be a correctional officer. By far the most common is the notion that those who seek out such employment do so because they possess authoritarian personalities and desire to indulge their taste for brutality. In 1922, sociologist Frank Tannenbaum wrote that "the keynote to understanding the psychology of the prison keeper" is "the exercise of authority and the resulting enjoyment of brutality" (quoted in Hawkins 1980: 60). For the officers in my study, both men and women, the reality is very different. Like the adolescents mentioned earlier, few indicate that they are now in the occupation to which they have always aspired. Most report that they "drifted" into the work.[3] None grew up dreaming of working in prisons or even planning to do so. In a reflection of its higher prestige and visibility (or perhaps more favorable fictional portrayals), the three officers who found the closest fit with their childhood dreams imagined careers in policing. One such white man made his way into his current job from a military career:

> From the time I was in grade school, I'd always told my mom I wanted to go into law enforcement. I always have been geared toward that. In high school, I went into Army Reserves then into the Military Police. After a while, I wanted to see the complete law enforcement side that the military had to offer, so I went into corrections in the military. I found out I liked that.

This man, like many others, found out very much by chance that he enjoys correctional work. Though he is unique in that most men did not describe such a direct career path from childhood plans to adult vocation, his combination of a military background and prison work is a fairly common one among them.

Interestingly, the other two officers who saw their work as consistent with their early ambitions were women, both of whom also imagined themselves as police officers. This white woman remembers patrolling her neighborhood from a very early age:

> Like when I was three and four years old, I would ride my tricycle, I mean, I remember a tricycle, not even a bicycle, and I'd act like I was a policeman, I'd go like [makes siren noise]. And I was always fascinated, we had a neighbor who was a state trooper, and I was just fascinated by it. So then I went to college, and I majored in criminal justice. Once I started taking classes, I decided that I liked the corrections end of it more than the actual law enforcement.

This childhood ambition is unusual for girls. Even now (and more so when this officer was a child), policing is one of the most masculine gender-typed and sex-segregated of all occupations. The same 1982 survey cited earlier found that 1 percent of adolescents aspired to work in policing as adults; 78 percent were male. At a cultural level, the ideal police(man) has long been conceived as a tough, aggressive soldier in the war on crime.[4] Cinematic representations like Clint Eastwood's "Dirty Harry" built on and exaggerated this image, and the hypermasculine cop is now a stock character in prime-time television dramas.

This archetype has been joined only recently, and quite begrudgingly, by the equally violent "Dirty Harriet." Even so, images of the "macho" woman officer are still uncommon, and representations of women in policing reflect deep cultural conflict over the relationship between femininities and violence (Rafter 2000). In reality, as recently as 2001, women were only 13 percent of total sworn police officers ("sworn" meaning, among other things, that they are empowered to carry firearms). Since this officer's childhood neighbor was a state trooper, it is worth noting that women are even more of a rarity at this level, constituting only 6 percent of state police (National Center for Women and Policing 2002).

Beyond these rare cases, however, officers in this study, both men and women, overwhelmingly recount a pattern of occupational drift; they find themselves working in prisons more as a result of circumstance than conscious plan. As this white man indicates, very few people ever set out to be correctional officers:

> What appealed to me about this job? Well, I knew very little about it. I mean, I had classes at [the university], criminal justice. That's what I had my degree in, and I had some corrections classes. I wasn't interested in it, I don't think anyone really, ever says, "Oh, I want to be a corrections officer."

Criminal justice and criminology majors are now among the most popular of undergraduate offerings in American universities. Criminology classes at my own institution consistently generate high enrollments, driven by students who increasingly seek courses and majors that they (and their parents) see as having a tangible link to future employment. A number of those I interviewed either had received or were pursuing degrees in this area. This man's account is a fairly typical one among these officers, many of whom start out with interests in other areas of criminal justice, such as policing or work with juvenile offenders, and find that they have an interest in corrections almost by chance.

Table 4.1 depicts officers' accounts of their paths to prison work (because some reported work in more than one category, totals do not sum to the sample size of seventy-two). For most, this is not their first adult employment, and they report experience in a wide variety of fields. Though neither men nor women plan to work in prisons, this table clearly indicates that their routes to the occupation differ. More important, these

TABLE 4.1
Paths to Prison Work

	Men (N = 45)		Women (N = 27)	
Military	20	44%	2	7%
Family in correctional work	5	11%	3	11%
Law enforcement	6	13%	2	7%
Degree/courses in criminology or criminal justice	6	13%	4	15%
Administrative support (clerical)	0	0%	10	37%
Technical, sales, or service	9	20%	10	37%
Other occupation	9	20%	5	19%
Personal recruitment	2	4%	4	15%
Divorce	0	0%	5	19%
Financial support while in school	5	11%	2	7%
No other job or educational experience	1	2%	2	7%

systematically divergent paths reflect the deeply sex-segregated structure of the underlying labor market. In simple terms, men typically come to the occupation from male-dominated, masculine gender–typed jobs; women come from female-dominated, feminized occupations.

For men, the modal category of previous work experience is military service—44 percent had been employed in this category. The same is true of only 7 percent of women.[5] The prevalence of military veterans is only partially accounted for by demand-side factors on the side of prison employers. Both federal and state governments do have explicit hiring policies that give priority to veterans. One might expect that men would be substantially advantaged by this preference, given that they are more likely than women to serve in the armed forces. In this particular context, there is little evidence that this is the case. Growth in the field during the last twenty years means there is little competition for entry-level jobs in corrections. It is thus unlikely that men benefit substantially from these policies, or that the chances of women who seek such jobs are significantly negatively affected.[6] While military experience can be parlayed into advantage in other areas, for example, in assignments or promotions, the experiences of those I interviewed do not demonstrate that it plays a key role in hiring.

On the supply side, men who served in the military generally describe a fairly direct and logically consistent path from the armed forces to work in prisons. The armed forces are still dominated by men, who account for approximately 86 percent of all active-duty soldiers. Military service is also strongly gender-typed as masculine and remains one of the last avenues through which boys are held to be transformed into "real men" (Britton and Williams 1996; Williams 1989). Beyond this, the prison's paramilitary structure mirrors that of the armed forces; the officer corps is supervised by sergeants, lieutenants, and captains. Line officers are generally expected to obey the orders of superiors without question. So, too, are inmates. This is particularly true of men's prisons, which throughout their history have used military regimentation as an explicit disciplinary strategy. The prison work environment is thus highly compatible with prior military experience. This correspondence is the primary reason that this Hispanic man sought out prison work:

> I got out of the military several years ago, and I worked for the city for a while. But I knew as soon as I got out of the military that I was going to be a correctional officer. It was an organization I could get into, something structured like the military. And that appealed to me.

An additional attraction is provided by the fact that many of those with military experience had worked in policing or corrections specialties during their service. The bridge to prison work is obvious, as for this white male officer:

> Well, I joined the army, and I wanted to go in and be an MP [military police officer]. They didn't have any regular MP slots, so they told me at the time that they had a correctional slot. And I got into it, and I liked it. You know, I like working with people, and it's always been something I enjoyed once I got into it. I never really thought about it before I started, though.

In this case, experience in military corrections blends seamlessly with work as a civilian correctional officer. Like so many others (both men and women), however, this man's initial acquaintance with correctional work happened essentially by chance.

Other common categories of previous work experience for men cover a range of occupations. For some, like law enforcement, the connection to prison work is clear. In the "technical, sales, and service" and "other" categories, a few men had also been employed in closely related work, such as private security. Other jobs, such as janitor, miner, welder, and assembly line worker have no obvious connection. With few exceptions, however, these occupations are both male-dominated and masculine gender–typed, traits they share with work in corrections.

For women, the single most common previous employment is clerical work. Thirty-seven percent had worked in clerical jobs of one sort or another; most were secretaries or clerks. As table 4.1 indicates, no man reported this kind of work experience. The size of this difference is large, equaling that between men and women in the "military" category, and reflects the sex segregation of clerical work in the larger labor force. In 2001, women were 77 percent of all administrative support workers and 99 percent of secretaries (U.S. Department of Labor 2002b). Clerical work is also strongly gender-typed as an appropriately feminine occupation, one drawing on women's purportedly greater interpersonal skills, manual dexterity, and tolerance for menial tasks (Davies 1982; Pierce 1995; Pringle 1989). In stark contrast to men's sense of the "fit" between military experience and prison work, the connection to the skills required in clerical jobs is far from obvious. This Hispanic woman was a clerk for a large corporation and had been unexpectedly laid off:

> I was looking for a job. I had worked in bookkeeping for a company for almost ten years, and they called us in one day, and said, "Your department is no longer in existence." So, that's the reason, not that this would've been my first choice as a job, but . . . *Did you have any reservations about doing it?* Sure I did. Lots. Lots. I've never been involved with people of a criminal mind, and that's where you are every day. So, I had that.

Like many women, this officer's previous work had given her little acquaintance with "people of a criminal mind," and she is clear that the job would not have been her first choice. In fact, none of the women in my study perceive that they had made a natural progression from clerical to correctional work.

This is true even for the handful who moved into their positions as officers through a more gradual process, as a result of internal transfers from clerical jobs in prison administration offices to security. In their work as secretaries and clerks, these women had little exposure to inmates, except for the few "trusties" permitted to clean offices and run errands for staff. Their work did give them a window most women lack, however, providing exposure to the institution and to other women working as officers. This African-American woman's story is worth quoting at length because it so beautifully illustrates the process of transformation many of her counterparts experienced in their paths to becoming officers:

> *Why did you decide to get into corrections?* Well, I didn't. I lived five minutes from [a men's] prison. All my life I've been living by it and I didn't even know it was a prison. I thought it was a home for boys. A friend went over there and she called me and told me how good the money was and everything. [At that time] I was a secretary barely making $16,000. So when I found out about the money I said, "Okay, I'll put in as a secretary." I got hired. But it was like walking into a totally different world. A world that I knew nothing about. I was scared to death. The only thing I knew when I went to the prison was how to type. [Then] what happened was that [the prison] locked down all the [inmates].[7] One of the guys that I came in the system with, he said, "In custody they need people to work overtime because they got the [inmates] locked up." I said, "They won't let me work because I'm a secretary." He said, "Yes, they will. Anybody can work." I went up to the lieutenant's office scared to death and said, "I wanna work overtime." They said, "Well, sign your name in the book." I was scared. Then they said, "You're working the cell house." I said, "Okay." I'm not one to back down. If I say I'm gonna do something, I'm gonna try. I went in there in the cell house. I went in and this female, matter of fact, this female who trained me said, "Have you ever worked in here before?" I said, "No." She said, "You do exactly what I tell you and you won't have any problem." I did it for one day, and I said this is not bad. And the money was real good too. So from that point on I would work overtime. They would put me in the cell house because nobody wanted it. So that's how I got interested in working in custody.

This officer now has more than five years' experience and has more than doubled her salary. Her story illustrates many of the themes that run through women's accounts of becoming officers. Like many of them, she was afraid and came to the work by happenstance. In this case, a shortage in the local labor market and the lure of overtime pay pulled her into the job. She ultimately transferred to a full-time custody assignment because of the higher pay and because she found, to her astonishment, that she could do the work.

Beyond clerical employment, the other previous job experiences that women report bear no clear relationship to correctional work either. Women were employed in a variety of female-dominated occupations in the "technical, sales, and service" category, including cook, clothing retail, cashiering, and child care. As a rule, women do not perceive the skills they acquire in such previous employment as directly transferrable to prison work. Most are pulled into the work through circumstances, opportunities, personal contact, or a combination of all of these. As is the case with three other women, this white female officer was personally recruited through a contact in her previous employment:

> *Had you worked in corrections before?* No, this is my first job in corrections. *What did you do before?* Assistant manager of a [retail] store. So, [this is] something completely different. *Why did you decide to do this?* I was looking for a change. Looking for a good opportunity and . . . one of our customers works here and she told me that they were hiring so I did my stuff and got in. She recruited me. *It's quite a change, I imagine.* Very much. Very much. I've enjoyed it.

As this woman's final comment indicates, lack of experience in a related field did not serve as an insurmountable barrier, and she has come to find that she enjoys the work. In her case, as in those of other women I interviewed, a woman acquaintance who already worked at the prison helped her bridge the gap between her previous work in female-dominated occupations and her current job. Such experiences illustrate the well-established importance of "weak ties" in social networks (Granovetter 1995). For most of us, the most useful information comes from those we may know only casually. Such individuals often serve as bridges to other social networks, providing links to opportunities to which we might not otherwise have access (Putnam 2000).

Though most women with experience in female-dominated occupations do not see a clear connection between their prior work experience and their current jobs, there is one intriguing exception to this pattern. This white woman, currently working in a men's prison, had been employed in a day care facility. She now sees little difference between the two: "I was a teacher in a day care center. And it's basically the same except for the kids are a lot bigger." Given most people's preconceptions about men's prisons, this statement seems incredible. It is consistent, however, with many officers' perceptions of themselves as little more than "baby-sitters" for inmates. As Maeve McMahon (1999) argues, while the occupation is strongly masculinized, the actual tasks of the correctional officer are quite similar to those required of a mother (or a surrogate such as a baby-sitter—officers are required to control the behavior of their sometimes uncooperative charges, (often) provide some positive guidance, and do the body work involved in supervising inmates' bathing, dressing, and eating. It is thus not all that surprising that officers, particularly women officers, might see inmates as children, and their job as "baby-sitting." Indeed, this is a sentiment somewhat more common among women than men in my study.

At any rate, the fact that most women do not perceive their previous job experiences as related in any significant way to their current occupations does not mean that there is no connection. The Federal Bureau of Prisons, for example, defines related job experience quite broadly in its requirements for correctional officer candidates. Recruits can apply experience in more than a dozen occupations, including teaching, counseling, welfare or social work, nursing, sales, and, indeed, day care. All these jobs require the management of people, which is the core ability on which correctional officers must draw. Once they enter the work, many women who come from such occupations are surprised to find that they already possess many of the requisite skills for their new jobs. However, because the links between women's experiences in the female-dominated, feminized sector of the labor force are not especially clear, it is undoubtedly true that most women do not consider prison work a logical option.

Motivations

While their paths to the occupation differ dramatically, almost all the men and women in this study cite extrinsic factors such as pay and benefits as the reasons for their attraction to the work. Given the discussion at the outset of this chapter, this may seem curious. Correctional officer salaries must be assessed in light of the qualifications required and local labor market conditions, however. As of 2001, the base starting salary for a federal corrections officer was approximately $27,000. To qualify at this level, recruits must possess a bachelor's degree or at least three years of related experience (broadly defined, as described earlier). In the state system in which I did my interviews, the 2001 salary for a nonprobationary officer (i.e., an officer with more than a year of experience) was approximately $24,000. The position requires only a high school diploma or general equivalency diploma (GED). Though the starting salary, particularly at the state level, seems low, it often compares quite favorably to salaries for other available work. Prisons tend to be located in isolated rural areas in which opportunities for secure, well-paying work are dwindling. Add to the salary the benefits package that comes with government employment, such as health insurance, paid vacations, and retirement, and such jobs can be very attractive indeed. Though I did not specifically ask about the incomes of those in this study (whom I interviewed between 1993 and 1998), they volunteered figures that ranged from the low $20,000 range to more than $40,000 among those with long experience in the federal system.

This combination of salary and benefits is a substantial draw for both men and women. These officers are typical. This white man came to work in the prison from the military:

Why'd you decide to be a CO, to be in security? It was a good-paying job. I had just gotten out of the military. I was in for eight years. Corrections was the best-paying job in this area at the time, and it also offered some of the best benefits.

Similarly, the job compares favorably to other opportunities for this white woman and African-American man:

I went into security because, of course, that's where your money is. You have good retirement, good benefits, good insurance, and it's really the best job around here.

Why corrections? It's just something I stumbled upon. Once I got in, not to say I was trapped, but it ended up being that way 'cause, you know, you spend more than five years and you kinda get used to your pay and salary and everything and it's hard to leave then and find that same pay and salary. Ever since then I've been doing corrections.

None of these officers have formal education beyond high school. For them, and for many like them who found themselves between jobs as a result of planned or unplanned unemployment, prison work was the best available option in the area. As one officer puts it, "This is the best way to make money, at least in this town."

For some women, the lure of the job is made even stronger by financial exigencies produced by divorce. As table 4.1 indicates, five women (19 percent of the sample) came to jobs in corrections after they divorced. All were single mothers at the time I interviewed them. Given the dire economic straits that single mothers face (25 percent of all such households were in poverty in 2000), prison work can be very enticing indeed. This white woman transferred from a clerical position in a men's prison to a custody position after she divorced:

> I'm divorced, and I've got kids to support. *And so, it made sense for you to make this change?* Yeah. *Are there a lot of women here similarly situated?* Well, that's the reason most of them work here as security, is to make money to support their families. *A lot of single moms?* Yeah. *Do you think that has anything to do with the fact that a lot more women are coming into corrections now?* Yeah, probably so. You make a lot more money, and you've got hours to work with your child care needs, the school needs and everything.

This officer's transfer from a clerical to a security position immediately doubled her salary, and the option of working a night shift meant that her extended family could care for her children. Her situation is fairly typical of the women in this study who mentioned divorce as one of the reasons they sought out prison work. Taken together, their stories reveal that the higher pay in corrections becomes even more attractive against the backdrop of the kinds of female-dominated occupations typically available to single mothers, especially those without college degrees. Add to this the benefits that accompany government jobs, and the attraction to work in this male-dominated, masculinized occupation is obvious.

Preconceptions

With the exception of those with family members who are also correctional officers, few women or men enter the job with accurate ideas about what prisons are like. Few have ever even visited a prison. This is as much true for the general public as it is for those who actually become officers. For most of us, television and movie portrayals serve as the background from which we draw our ideas about prison. These two men (one African-American, one white) illustrate the ubiquity of the media as a cultural force in shaping ideas about prisons and prison life:

> Well, I guess like most people I never really thought about it. Prisons were, like, things on television that you see, everybody has a gun, and [there's] fighting every day, and all that good stuff, but it's not. *What's the reality, then, compared to that experience?* Well, it's pretty much like outside really, if you really look at it. It's a lot more organized, I'll tell you, than outside is, also.

> You know, when you come into the prison system, you think, you know you see all these movies and stuff and you think, that's prison life, but it's not. It's not as rough, anyway, at least where I've worked. It's a lot better than what's portrayed on the movies.

Two threads tie these accounts together. First, officers are clear that the underlying theme in media representations is violence. In television prisons, "everybody has a gun, and [there's] fighting every day." The prisons brought to mind for these officers are men's prisons, populated by the media's stock characters—brutal inmates and guards who live and work in a jungle-like environment plagued by assaults, stabbings, rapes, and shootings. The media also paint a gender-stereotyped portrait of women's prisons, though the stock characters—the predatory lesbian and unjustly imprisoned sexual innocent—draw on notions around sexuality more than around violence. Regardless, it is the Hollywood image of the men's prison that occupies center stage in most people's thinking. Such stereotypes can create a formidable barrier for most who consider becoming officers, as one man recalls: "When I started, after seeing prison movies, I was scared shitless" (quoted in Lombardo 1981: 32). Given the deeply gendered associations drawn in such portrayals between masculinity and violence, these depictions undoubtedly have a disproportionate impact on women, for whom stereotypical femininity has never included the ability to "bang heads."

The second theme lies in the comparison of that portrayal to officers' actual experiences. None indicate that actual prisons bear more than a passing resemblance to their fictional counterparts. While violence is an "aspect" of prison life, it is "a lot better than what's portrayed in the movies." No prison could function if the violence in media representations were routine. Many officers perceive this disparity between the cultural construction of the prison and their actual experiences. This should not be taken to mean that COs (correctional officers) do not see their environment as stressful or dangerous, however. In fact, officers' perceptions of the danger of their working environment are the result of a complex interaction between experience, interpretation, and cultural construction. This construction begins during training.

Training

All the officers in my study were required to complete formal training before beginning work in their assigned institutions. In both the federal system and the state system I studied, men and women are trained together, are taught from an identical curriculum, must meet equal requirements, and are expected to pass the same tests. The same applies to officers who will work in men's prisons and those who will work in women's facilities. Training does differ by system, however. Federal officer recruits apply to a specific facility to which they wish to be assigned. They must then complete 200 hours of training within their first year of employment. The first 80 hours consists of "institutional familiarization," a two-week period in which new officers become acquainted with the institution in which they will work. Then, within the first sixty days of appointment, recruits undergo 120 hours of specialized training at the federal law enforcement training center in Glynco, Georgia. The training includes four components: firearms; self-defense; written tests on classroom material covering a variety of topics, such as rules, regulations, and strategies for dealing with inmates; and a basic physical abilities test.[8] Once on the job, all employees must complete annual refresher training and also have the opportunity to take a wide variety of optional courses. During my interviews, I met officers who had taken advantage of opportunities to learn Spanish, receive a commercial driver's license, learn crime scene investigation techniques, and become certified in the use of specialized weaponry.

The state's training, by contrast, is less standardized and offers less diversity. Recruits are required to complete 160 hours of formal instruction. This is given at one of the state's residential training academies or may be completed at any one of several colleges with which the system contracts. The training includes self-defense, firearms, chemical agents, CPR, first aid, physical training, nonviolent crisis intervention, and standards for use of force. Near the end of the training period, recruits are allowed to prioritize the specific facilities in which they would like to work. Officers are then assigned to a unit (which may or may not be among their list of preferences), where they spend two weeks in on-the-job training, working with and observing officers at a variety of posts. State officers are also required to complete annual in-service training. As a rule, they do not have access to the wide variety of voluntary opportunities provided by the federal government. Tight state budgets and officer shortages mean that the state is struggling simply to keep up with demand for officers. This white man, who had worked both in the state system I studied and in the federal system, put it this way:

I believe [federal training] is better because the government puts out more money. They have better training facilities. State is more do it where they can do it. Get them out. They just try to get you in there and get you out.

I interviewed federal officers who had work experience in various states, and their impressions were similar. Most state departments of correction simply lack the financial resources and the luxury of time to offer the kind of training available in the federal system.

Officers' overall perceptions of training vary little by gender. Perhaps the most salient difference in this area is between state and federal officers and lies in the latter group's much higher level of satisfaction. Federal officers are much more likely than their state counterparts to describe training as "outstanding" or "excellent." Both groups do share a sense, however, of the disconnect between the material provided in training and the skills they actually need to do their work. For most, the real learning begins on the job rather than in the classroom. This white woman frames the difference in a particularly gendered way:

What do you think of the training? Do you think it was useful in preparing you for what you do? Not really. This job is on-the-job-training. I mean, you know, they can tell you, it's just like having a baby, somebody can tell you, but until you experience it . . . ! [laughs] Same way with this. So, it's more on-the-job-training.

Similarly, this white man sees the formal training as important, but he believes officers learn what they really need to know while on the job:

> *So, tell me what you think of the training. Do you think it's useful training?* Well, I think I learned quite a bit in [the federal training center]. I learned about the legal aspects of the position. I learned a good foundation. But that year in [on-the-job-training] status is where you actually learn what you need to learn. So, Glynco was good for the book aspect of it, but the hands-on is where I really got my bacon.

This critique is not unique to corrections; employees in many kinds of jobs perceive a lack of fit between formal training and interactions with real clients or customers. In this case, part of the reason is structural; since the largest part of the training takes place in a location separate from the prisons where officers will be working, there is little opportunity to deal with situations involving inmates. Officers' suggestions for improving training invariably focus on the desire to have actual or at least simulated interactions with inmates in a realistic environment.

The upshot of this gap is that if new officers are to be successful, the quality of their on-the-job training becomes very important. Officers receive this kind of occupational socialization through observation, from supervisors, and, probably most important, from more experienced coworkers. Earlier research on the integration of the officer corps revealed considerable resistance among "old guard" officers to the presence of women and minority men. In some cases, white male supervisors and coworkers openly refused to train new officers (Owen 1988; Zimmer 1986). I collected very few stories of this kind about on-the-job training experiences. The few officers who relate such experiences attribute them almost exclusively to white "good old boys" whom they see as a dying breed. This does not mean that exclusionary processes are not still in operation, of course. Many new recruits may leave in the face of hostility. It also suggest, however, that like racism and sexism in culture more generally, the expression of this kind of prejudice may have taken on more subtle, if not less insidious, dimensions. Correctional officers do relate more general accounts of racial and gender tension between officers and between officers and supervisors; these are addressed in more detail in chapter 6.

One final important, though perhaps surprising, source of on-the-job training for new officers comes from inmates themselves. This white man describes his early days on the job in a men's prison:

[The inmates] knew more about it, the fact is there was one out there that trained me. When you go in, you don't know anything. They stuck me out in a dorm the second night there. I'd never even seen the place, I had no idea where nothing was, or anything. So, there was an old [inmate] out there. He knew I didn't know anything, just came on the unit, he eased up there and told me what to do. He went right through the whole procedure. Showed me how to turn the lights off at ten-thirty, when to count, how to count.[9] He did! I had a lot of respect for him. I could go to him and I could find out anything I wanted to know. Really. Of course, I talked to my supervisor too, but really to find out what happens I could just ask him.

This African-American woman's experience, also in a men's prison, is similar:

The inmates are the ones that helped, that taught me how to be an officer. Not the staff. You know, they helped me but the inmates are who teach you. When you're new at this job the inmates are gonna come and tell you, "Ma'am, you left a door open." Or, "Somebody's sick." Because you can't be at two places at the same time. Nine times out of ten it's gonna be the inmates that tells you what's going on.

These accounts may seem incredible, yet they are entirely consistent with the now considerable volume of research that reveals the negotiation process that is at the heart of social order in any prison (Owen 1988; Sykes 1958). Most inmates share officers' interests in maintaining a predictable and stable day-to-day routine, and long-serving inmates know that routine better than most officers. Cooperation is thus sometimes in the interests of both officers and inmates (though this is obviously not always the case). As I demonstrate, this kind of cooperative interaction between inmates and officers is not uncircumscribed and is governed by subcultural norms on both sides mandating a certain social distance between groups. These officers' experiences clearly demonstrate that such moments of convergence of interests exist, however.

While both men and women officers are similar in noting the discrepancy between the material provided in training and their work experiences, gender does play an important role in two other gaps officers perceive between training and their everyday work experiences. The first is a perception that training exaggerates the potential violence of the job and of the work environment. This is a sentiment expressed most vehemently by officers who trained in the state system. In the central training academy, recruits are taught by seasoned male officers, many of whom seem to take particular delight in telling "war stories" about prison violence. In addition, officers are shown several films; the one that seemed most salient had been made during a particularly notorious prison riot in another state. The emphasis on violence leaves many new officers questioning their decision to pursue the occupation, as in the cases of these women, one white and one African-American:

How big was your training class? I'd say it was about seventy-five people, but about five didn't graduate. *And did you lose women or men?* Oh, we lost one woman, she got scared. We saw a film, and they show this inmate cutting another inmate, and basically all of his insides fell out. So, after she saw that film she realized that she wouldn't be able to handle it. *And the men you lost because . . . ?* Some of them, it just wasn't for them. I think basically the same thing happened to them, but they wouldn't admit that. [laughs] After the film, everybody, well, I decided I don't want to do it, it's just not worth it, the money's not good enough. So, I think the film really did it.

Did you lose anybody out of your training class? I think we lost two, that I know of. One was a young guy, and he decided he'd stay working for his dad after he saw a training film. In fact, all of us went, are we sure that this is what we want?

Far from attempting to contradict the violence of popular-culture portrayals of the prison, this kind of training reinforces recruits' fears, painting a gendered visual and rhetorical picture of the prison as a work environment in which male inmates are violent animals and in which officers constantly fear for their lives. Though these officers obviously completed training, many recruits are dissuaded. It is interesting, however, that while these officers suggest that men were affected by the film, not one male CO spoke of it in this way. In fact, very few men-

TABLE 4.2
Numbers and Rates of Fatal and Nonfatal Occupational Injuries,
Selected Occupations, 2000

	Number employed	Fatal injuries	Nonfatal injuries	Rate of fatal injuries	Rate of nonfatal injuries
Correctional institution officers	344,000	8	224	2	65
Firefighting	233,000	41	189	18	81
Farmworkers	768,000	159	14,036	21	1,828
Forestry and logging	109,000	95	1,508	87	1,384
Truck drivers	3,088,000	852	136,072	28	4,407
Cashiers	2,939,000	68	26,921	2	916
Secretaries	2,623,000	12	6,062	0.5	231

SOURCE: U.S. Department of Labor (2001a, 2001c), U.S. Department of Commerce (2002).
Rates are per 100,000 workers employed.

tioned it at all, and one thought that the film was the best aspect of the training process.

This gender difference in perceptions of the film is instructive and points to one of the ways that the training process constructs correctional work as a gendered occupation. It is certainly true that on certain occasions officers must deal with incidents of violence. Mass disturbances or assaults that involve fatalities or serious injuries to staff are relatively rare, however. According to the last prison census, there were 312 riots in American state and federal prisons in 1995. While this number is not trivial, 91 percent of institutions reported no such incidents. During that same year, 76 inmates (of 969,843 incarcerated) died as a result of assaults by other inmates. Ninety-five percent of prisons reported no deaths.[10] According to the U.S. Department of Labor (2001a, 2001c), there were 8 fatal occupational injuries to correctional institution officers during 2000, and 224 job-related injuries and illnesses requiring days away from work. Those numbers translate into an occupational death rate of 2 per 100,000 workers and a nonfatal injury and illness rate of 64 per 100,000. These numbers do not approach the highest among occupations. For the sake of comparison, table 4.2 reports rates for selected occupations.

Among these are male-dominated, masculine gender–typed jobs (farm and timber workers and truck drivers) and some heavily female-dominated occupations (cashiers and secretaries). Even though the latter are not typically considered among the most dangerous of jobs, workers in both have higher rates of occupational injury than correctional officers.

It is not my intention to minimize the threat of violence that officers perceive they face on a daily basis, but it is extremely important to assess the rhetorical picture of the institution created by training (and by culture at large) against the reality of the incidence of that violence.

Officers themselves understand this. Those I interviewed repeatedly emphasize that their job requires more mental than physical toughness on a routine basis. My interviews, as well as other research on the prison, reveal that the core of an officer's job lies in the management of people. The primary role of the officer is custodial and bureaucratic, managing the movement of inmates from place to place and dealing with the countless forms and regulations that structure life in any total institution. The actual experiences of officers consistently belie the violent messages of training, leaving some, like this white woman who worked in a men's prison, feeling like the gullible recipients of trainers' tall tales:

> Okay, to me, they hyped it up to be, I mean this is not a good place to work, but they hyped it up to where, maybe some units were like what they were talking about, but this unit was nothing like it. *Some units were like . . . what were they talking about?* Well, the violence . . . a lot of things they said as far as . . . I'm not sure how to put it. They were full of a lot of these, you know, the fishin' tales, [where the fish] keeps getting bigger and bigger? *Fish stories?* Yea, that's pretty much the way that was. You know, they'd tell about their days, you know, give us their war stories, and that type of thing, and it wasn't like that. And a lot of what they said was what I call "the old days," the old ways. When I came into the system, what they were saying was not the way it was. I mean, they were talking about, you know, bangin' heads, and all this junk, and you know, you don't do that anymore. So, a lot of what they said didn't even apply.

This woman's story alludes to the fact that this system, like those in many states, has undergone dramatic changes in the past thirty years, many of them due to inmate-initiated legal action. Violence is now less routine and its legitimate use more regulated and bureaucratized, and inmate-to-officer ratios have declined significantly. Even in the "old days," however, prison riots were certainly not everyday occurrences, and it is likely that these "war stories" overstate even the violence of that period.

These inflated accounts are part of the construction of a particular kind of occupational masculinity, one that emphasizes the "contingent violence" of the prison. Few male or female officers argue that women have difficulty managing inmates on a routine basis. However, behind this admission for many male officers and supervisors is the constant specter of the prison riot or outbreaks of prison violence, which lends a "what if?" quality to the belief that women can handle the job. Since violence is always a possibility, workers must be prepared to deal with this prospect at any time. It is this contingency that frames resistance to women working in men's prisons. Women correctional officers in these institutions share a status similar to that of women in the military, seen by many as beneficial additions to the armed forces in peacetime but as possible liabilities in the event of war. Resistance to women as correctional officers, particularly in men's prisons, often takes the form of the assertion of "contingent violence"; the belief that violence is always a possibility, coupled with the fear that women, due to their smaller size and lesser physical strength (qualities that are construed as inherently feminine) will be unable to deal with a crisis involving violence should one develop. Training emphasizing the potentially violent aspects of the institution constructs the occupation of the correctional officer almost exclusively in these terms.

Both federal and state officers invariably emphasize that mental endurance and interpersonal communication and negotiation skills are the core requisites for success. Training at the state level, however, simply does not emphasize these qualities, as the experiences of these officers, an African-American man and a white man, illustrate:

> They don't prepare you, they try to prepare you [in training] for the physical part. But that's not what gets to you, it's the mental part. Playing the games with the inmates, they're constantly trying to figure out a way to get over on you.

> It's a whole different type of job. It's not physical, it's just all mental. Just take it, roll it off, and control these inmates. It's almost like a classroom.

The training process contributes to a construction of the occupation as one in which physical toughness and aggressiveness are requirements. This ideology about the prison and the role of the officer is reinforced by cultural representations of prisons as sites of almost unimaginable violence. All this leads to a discourse in which the presence of a *female* correctional officer in a men's facility becomes almost a contradiction in terms.[11]

Gender also shapes one other gap officers perceive between training and their work. In both systems, male and female officers and those who will work in men's and women's prisons are taught from an identical curriculum. "Inmates" and "prisons" are discussed generically, with the apparent intention that officers be prepared to work in any kind of environment. In a gendered culture, however, the generic is masculine. Indeed, officers' accounts reveal that the officer underlying the messages of training is male, and that the "prison" invoked is a men's institution. This is still the most common situation, given that most correctional officers are male, as are the overwhelming number of inmates. However, this generic language, when combined with a notion that training is gender-blind, creates problems for two specific groups of officers.

First, it makes discussions of situations that may be particularly difficult for female officers working in men's facilities seem like an introduction of gender, and thus sexism, into a neutral process (MacKinnon 1987). Research on women's integration into the guard force in men's prisons demonstrates quite clearly that women face challenges not shared by their male colleagues, including harassment by male inmates and resistance, exclusion, and discrimination by male colleagues and supervisors (Jurik 1985, 1988; Owen 1988; Zimmer 1986, 1987). Yet the rhetoric of training, by presuming a male officer who will work in a men's prison, fails to address these issues. This white female officer explains:

> I really feel like . . . they should really have a female officer that comes in there [to training] and tells them what to expect. What you're going to see, what you're going to be exposed to and everything, it's very different than what the males get. You know, I'm talking about fifteen minutes of saying, this is how it's going to be. And I think that may have helped. *Did they talk about this whole issue of being a woman working in a men's institution?* No, they cannot do that. The training has to be asexual, they cannot differentiate, but I wish in a way they had, thirty minutes or something.

This woman's experience reveals that, though the training process is "asexual," in reality it is directed to a scenario in which both officers and inmates are male. The effect is that upon completing training, women may be less prepared for their jobs than their male counterparts.

In invoking the men's prison as generic institution, training also leaves officers who will work in women's prisons ill equipped for the job. As I noted in chapter 2, women's prisons are often quite different from men's institutions. Structurally, ideologically, and procedurally, many bear the legacy of gendered difference that was the cornerstone of the women's reformatory movement. The women's prisons I studied are no exceptions. Two are low-security prisons, one of which does not possess a perimeter fence. The third occupies property that had been a residential school. This facility is very much in the mold of the "cottage plan" favored by reformatory advocates and houses women in small, freestanding dormitories. This design was nowhere in evidence in the men's prisons I studied. Women's prison administrators also frequently have the authority to make gender-specific exceptions to rules that apply in men's prisons (usually, these take the form of allowing women to have cosmetics or certain craft supplies). This practice, combined with the differences in structural design of some women's facilities, can create confusion for new officers. This African-American woman describes her own sense of the disparity between training and her experience in her first days on the unit:

> [In training] they would mention yellow lines, they had yellow lines for the inmates to walk down the center, and I went to [the women's prison] and I was like, where's the yellow line? There's no yellow line? And then the [property] they couldn't have, when I got [here] these women were knitting and crocheting. And I was like, they're not supposed to have that! And the things that they can wear, the knitted caps and gloves, and men don't have those things. They have things here that they sell at the women's commissary, you know, that the men don't have.

This woman's experience reflects the differences that still exist between many men's and women's prisons, differences that draw upon early prison reformers' notions of different standards of incarceration for women.

Similarly, federal officers perceive that the preparation they receive is more explicitly suited to officers working in men's institutions. For this white male officer, the real problem is that the training is directed to working in higher-security facilities:

What's your perception of that training? Did you find it useful? They pretty much train you for the U.S. Penitentiary, but there's not too many U.S. Penitentiaries. So I think that if they could bring it down a notch on the training and the reception of inmates and maybe how they train on those certain subjects. *Was it directed more toward dealing with male inmates or female inmates?* Male.

U.S. Penitentiaries are at the top of the security hierarchy in the Federal Bureau of Prisons. Ten of the bureau's facilities are so designated; all house men.[12] Regardless of the system, however, women offenders tend to be housed in lower-security facilities. This is not because, as popular stereotypes would have it, criminal women are being treated more leniently than their male counterparts. Rather, women are less likely than men to be serving time for violent crimes (men accounted for 96 percent of those serving time for violent offenses in 1999); have shorter criminal histories (28 percent of all women serving time in 1991 were first offenders, compared with 19 percent of men); and are less likely to escape once in custody. Because women inmates constitute such a small part of the prison population (about 6.6 percent), even those serving time for violent offenses (an even more minuscule portion) tend to be housed in low-security institutions. In the prison system as a whole, gender is thus conflated with security level. When one trains officers to work in U.S. Penitentiaries or in high-security institutions, one is, by definition, training them to work with male inmates.

As might be expected, problems can occur when officers prepared for a high-security work environment populated with the "worst of the worst" find themselves instead in a very different prison. As this white woman working in a women's prison notes:

> *Was training useful in terms of preparing for the kinds of things that you have to deal with in this kind of an institution?* No, no. [For working] with the men, yes. With the women, no. And you'll find that a lot with the men, correctional officers, when they come in here, they just can't get adjusted to the camp mentality.

The "camp mentality" is one that realizes that inmates being housed are low-risk and usually nonviolent. As this woman notes, the prison camp environment may prove a particularly tough adjustment for male officers (and, indeed, this is the case for those I interviewed). Training, in its attempt to create ideal-typical officers, constructs a particular kind of occupational masculinity in which the ability to deal with violence, and with violent men, is central. Work with women, in low-security environments, may be eschewed, particularly by men, as having lower status and not befitting a "real man" or a real officer. As one male officer puts it, "I can't stand [working with women inmates]. It just doesn't feel like a prison to me."

Officers are also ill prepared to work with women inmates more generally. There is almost complete unanimity of opinion among those I interviewed who had worked in both men's and women's prisons that female inmates differ from men. Training generally ignores the skills officers believe are crucial for interacting with women, as this white man observes:

> I went to Glynco about six years ago. I enjoyed it. *Did you think it was useful?* To a point it was. *How was it for the kinds of things that you did at the women's facility, or did it cover any of the differences between . . . ?* It covered some of it, but because there are so few women's institutions they don't really get into that. But when you're dealing with a female inmate and male inmate, it's totally different. It is. *What's the difference?* How to handle them. How to one-on-one, interact with them. And, it's just, you just have to change your whole outlook.

There are a number of ways in which COs believe that men and women differ as inmates, and I discuss these in detail in chapter 5. This man's experience clearly underlines the gendering of the generic inmate and the typical prison that occurs during training, however. Though training is intended to be "general," male inmates are the focus.

In addition to leaving officers who will work in women's prisons less prepared, the construction of the typical prison during training has another effect. By omitting any substantial discussion of women's institutions, training creates a situation in which officers are led to see women's facilities both as exceptions to the rule and as much more lenient than men's institutions. Indeed, the latter is a complaint I heard frequently from officers who had worked in both types of institutions. This officer (a white woman) is typical:

> *Did training prepare you for what you do on the job?* I would have to say no, because at the training academy, they teach you on the man's

aspect, not the women's prison. Everything they teach you in preservice had to do with the men's unit. And when you got to a female unit, everything was completely different. *What's different?* Everything. From the rules, to their behavior. Every aspect, everything that you look at is completely different. *Give me an example of a different rule.* OK, let's say like in a female unit, they're allowed to make crocheted blankets, they've got knitting needles in the dorms. Where, at a men's unit, you know, they've got their sheets, they've got their pillows, they've got their mattress, and that's it. They don't have all this little girly stuff everywhere. And, at a men's unit, that's all completely different. You don't have any of that. *Do you think that means it's more lax?* Yeah, I think the women's unit is more lax.

As the doctrine of separate spheres has given way to the ideal of gender equality, training for officers, which now adopts a generic approach, has in reality left men's institutions as the standard. For officers, women's prisons seem less like real prisons, and women inmates appear to be treated much more leniently than their male counterparts; women get "girly stuff," but men get only their bedding.[13] While this comparison is extreme—all inmates are generally allowed to have more than bed linens—it does reveal that officers themselves take men's institutions and the conditions of male inmates as a generic standard. In addition to reinforcing gendered ideas about "typical" officers, inmates, and prisons, constructing women's prisons as more relaxed and comfortable than men's has the effect of obscuring the ways in which some aspects of women's incarceration, while different, may be even more onerous than men's (Belknap 2001; Carlen 1983; Faith 1993).

Conclusion

Correctional work remains among the occupations of last resort. Very few of the officers in my study grew up dreaming about jobs in prisons. The routes through which these individuals, both men and women, come to work behind the walls reveal more in the way of drift than conscious intention. But though both groups are now in the same place, gender, in the form of a deeply segregated labor market, played a fundamental role in shaping their paths. Though they did not set out to be officers, men describe a consistent progression from the military to the paramilitary structure of the officer corps. For those without military experience, the transition from one male-dominated, masculinized occupation to another is relatively smooth. For women, the connection between the skills they acquire in clerical or other female-dominated work and correctional employment is much less obvious. Many are pulled into the occupation by low wages in their local labor markets or by financial adversity after divorce. Unlike their male counterparts, many are happily astonished that they can indeed do the work. Regardless of gender, officers find that the reality of their work contradicts their media-fed preconceptions about prisons and prisoners.

Once hired, officers enter a deeply gendered institution. Their first exposure comes in the form of training. Though intended to be generic, officers' accounts reveal that the underlying assumption at the heart of the curriculum is that the ideal-typical CO is one who can deal with violence, who can "bang heads" if necessary. As the ability to deal with violence is at the core of the image of the officer constructed in training, so, too, is it intimately intertwined with masculinity. Similarly, the institution for which officers are being prepared is implicitly a men's prison; women's institutions are exceptions to the rule. These presumptions invoked in training about the typical officer and the typical prison mean that it serves best only those who fit the requisite image, in this case, men who work in men's prisons.

Training is but one small part of the gendered organizational logic of the prison. Its messages are of short duration, and officers may pick and choose, modifying its dictates in the wake of actual work experience. It is to the day-to-day reality of the work that I now turn. In the next chapter, I examine officers' work with inmates.

5

Work with Inmates

New officers are prepared, by stereotype and training, to expect the worst behavior from inmates. Almost to a person, correctional officers speak of being constantly fearful during their first days on the job that they will be unable to manage recalcitrant inmates, fall victim to assaults, or even be killed in prison riots. Initial concerns usually dissipate, however, in the face of a work environment that bears only a cursory relationship to their preconceived notions or to the prisons depicted by training films. As this white woman, whose first assignment was to a maximum-security men's prison, finds:

> Dealing with inmates and convicts is scary, you know, when you first get there, until you get into it and you realize it's not as bad. I didn't have time to be scared because I was more afraid of what I didn't know. [The cell block I was assigned to] was three stories high, and I was always afraid of getting thrown over the rail, but that didn't happen. But, like I said, once you get your foot in there, you're so busy trying to learn what to do, and how to handle the inmates, you don't have time to be scared.

As her account illustrates, with time, most COs discover that their initial concerns are either inflated or unfounded. Physical violence against officers and mass outbreaks of violence are uncommon. Though inmates are, as one woman put, understandably, sometimes "a little grouchy," with experience officers find, to their surprise, that inmates often share their interests in maintaining order.

But this can present a different kind of problem. In his classic work, *Asylums*, Erving Goffman notes the peculiar difficulties associated with the people work performed by staff in total institutions. Many spend more time with inmates than they do with members of their own families. In some of the prisons I studied, officers are literally locked into dormitories or housing units, isolated from other staff, for their entire shifts. There is often a great deal of communication between officers and inmates in this environment. Inmates certainly speak of their own lives outside of prison, and officers sometimes reciprocate; a CO may "unburden things to an inmate that he would not tell his wife" (Jacobs and Retsky 1975: 17). Proximity has a way of breaking down stereotypes and building relationships; officers may even come to view inmates as "reasonable, responsible creatures who are fitting objects for emotional involvement" (Goffman 1961: 82).

For prison officers, this presents obvious dangers. I heard many cautionary tales of COs who had "gone too far" and become sexually involved with inmates or who were coerced into supplying contraband.[1] But beyond this, sympathetic involvement can be problematic in that it places the officer "into a position to be hurt by what inmates do and what they suffer" (Goffman 1961: 82). For some, this leads to burnout, and ultimately complete detachment; for others, it encourages the construction of unyielding boundaries between themselves and inmates. The most common mechanism for managing the paradox between expectations and experience, however, is the development of a kind of theory of human nature about inmates, a shared perspective that helps to make sense of the duties officers are required to perform and "provides a subtle means of maintaining social distance from inmates and a stereotyped view of them, and justifies the treatment accorded them" (Goffman 1961: 87). An integral part of this ideology is a set of notions about the essential differences between staff and inmates. This set of beliefs helps officers to rationalize the bad behavior of inmates, but it also serves to discount gestures of goodwill on the part of inmates and feelings of empathy that COs may experience. As I noted in chapter 3, research on prison officers reveals that COs adhere to a strong set of subcultural attitudes about inmates. Chief among these is perhaps an overall sense of distrust, as in the advice often conveyed by old-timers to new recruits: "If an inmate tells you what time it is, look at your watch" (quoted in Webb and Morris 1985, 205). That same kind of suspicion is present among those I interviewed.

My interviews reveal a more complex picture, however, one in which commonsense notions about the essential nature of inmates are shaped by the gender and race of both officers and inmates, as well as by deeply gendered and racialized institutional contexts. Theories of inmate human nature are neither gender- nor race-neutral; nor are they echoed by

all officers with equal vehemence. African-American and Hispanic officers, for example, are presented with a unique set of challenges in rationalizing the disproportionate presence of inmates of color within the
prison system. Officers' ideas about inmates are also fundamentally
shaped by notions about gender and reflect the very different institutional contexts in which women and men are confined.

In this chapter, I explore officers' perceptions of inmates and their
views of inmate conduct toward them. Before I proceed, a caveat is necessary. What follows is based on officers' perceptions of how inmates
behave and what inmates think. This obviously privileges the voices of
the officers, and this privileging is made more problematic in the face of
an occupational subculture in which inmates' views are often seriously
devalued. My focus here is obviously on prison workers, and though I
had originally hoped that I might be able to interview inmates about
their perceptions of officers, ultimately, I was only able to speak to a
few informally. Other work has assessed the views of inmates about officers (e.g., Owen 1988; Zimmer 1986), and I will discuss these findings
and their impact on the themes that emerged in my conversations with
officers. It is important to remember, however, that what follows are *officers'* perceptions of the ways inmates think, feel, and behave.

Perceptions of Inmates

"Inmates" as a Group

The bulk of officers' comments about inmates draw on gender distinctions, comparing men in prison to their female counterparts. There
are, however, two themes that invoke views of inmates as a generic, un-
differentiated group. The first is the assertion that though inmates have
made mistakes, they are, essentially, human. The second is the view that
inmates are too privileged.

INMATES ARE HUMAN

At one level, the assertion that inmates are human seems so self-evident as to go unremarked. At another, it flies in the face of stereotypes
of COs as sadistic "screws" and inmates as little more than animals. So
common is this latter notion that a men's prison film released in 2000
was entitled, simply, *Animal Factory*. This kind of cultural iconography,

in which (usually male) inmates are subhuman brutes, is both a reflection of and a catalyst for the public's seemingly unquenchable desire for more and more prisons in which to cage criminals. Some previous research demonstrates that officers subscribe to these ideas as well (e.g., Jacobs and Retsky 1975; Kauffman 1988). In this study, a tiny minority fall into this category. Some COs do refer to inmates as animals or as "the scum of society," and they undoubtedly justify their own or their coworkers' ill-treatment on this basis. These feelings are usually ambivalent, or they are reserved for some categories of inmates and not others. For example, one officer expresses the belief that the system should speed up the pace of executions for women on death row but just a few minutes later admits that she believes it is unfair that battered women who kill in self-defense are sentenced to death. In other cases, officers single out "inmates" for disdain while speaking favorably of "convicts." In this, COs make a distinction between older, "prison-wise" convicts who "do their own time" and make little trouble, and younger, less experienced, more violent "inmates." Officers are certainly not immune to the mind-set that sees inmates as animals, but this belief almost never exists without the simultaneous presence of other, contradictory notions. This kind of multiple consciousness is an inevitable outcome of the counterposition of the intimacy of ongoing contact with the institutional goals of incarceration and dehumanization.

Most officers in my study view inmates as human, and as people who have made mistakes. As Goffman's classic analysis suggests, however, they tend to do so while simultaneously employing rhetorical strategies that maintain distance between themselves and their charges. This white man assigned to a women's prison is a clear example: "A major thing is how you handle yourself. They are human too, I mean they may be inmates but they are human, so you still gotta treat them right." For this CO, "inmate" and "human" are mutually exclusive categories. Even so, one's status as an inmate does not imply the forfeiture of human dignity; as he puts it, "you still gotta treat them right." This white male officer in a men's prison takes a slightly different tack:

Well, when I first hired on, I got a perception from a lot of the other staff . . . I mean, you get a perception like, the inmate's gonna do this, the inmate's gonna do that. But I learned, once I started working here, that they're people too. A lot of them are bad people, but usually when you're dealing with them, they're not. I'm not here to give them a worse time. Just to do my job. *Do you think some people see that as their job, to give them a worse time?* Oh, yeah! Some people really hate inmates. I guess every prison has got people like that. I personally wouldn't have fun coming to work if I'm going to chase a guy down and give him a hard time all day. To me, that's not fun.

This officer sees inmates as "bad people," in that they have committed crimes, but his own experience mitigates a unidimensional negative view. He is clear, however, that some officers do not share this perspective; as he observes, some seem to be out to "give them a worse time." Most COs in my study would probably agree with the observation that "every prison has got people" who thrive on the exercise of arbitrary power. The fact that some object to this behavior suggests that it is not universally accepted, however.

The view of inmates as human, and as having made mistakes, is particularly salient for the African-American COs in my study. The extreme overrepresentation of inmates of color in the American prison system places these officers in a complicated position. During the last twenty years, the proportion of prison officers who are African-American and Hispanic has increased dramatically (though they are still underrepresented as supervisors and administrators). Many of these COs' everyday experiences with racism undoubtedly sensitize them to the reality of discrimination in the criminal justice system (Miller 1996). In the population at large, national surveys consistently demonstrate that African-Americans are more likely than whites to have experienced or to acknowledge the existence of racism by police, in the courts, and in the prison system. Yet the work of COs of color places them in the position of administering the punishments mandated by this very system, upon the bodies of inmates whose skin signifies membership in the same stigmatized group.[2] Alice Walker captures the paradox faced by African-American (and Hispanic) officers in her story about an attempt to visit an African-American inmate in a women's prison. Walker is turned away by the African-American woman at the prison entrance:

We look at each other hard. And I "recognize" her, too. She is very black and her neck is stiff and her countenance has been softened by the blows. All day long, while her children are supported by her earnings here, she sits isolated in this tiny glass entranceway, surrounded by white people who have hired her, as they always have, to do their dirty work for them. It is no accident that she is in this prison, too. (Quoted in Collins 2000: 61)

Similarly, Barbara Omolade argues that the work of black women professionals and semiprofessionals in the modern era is a new form of "mammification"; such women still do the "dirty work" of whites, serving "white superiors while quieting the natives . . . keeping poorer Black women and more angry Black men in check (1994: 55).

Despite this inside/outsider perspective, I have no firsthand evidence that officers of color are more critical of the system than their white counterparts, no direct statements that they believe that black or Hispanic (or even white) inmates are imprisoned unjustly. While in theory the prison could provide fertile ground for raising consciousness and creating identification across the line of prisoner and officer, the structure and function of the institution mitigate this. Norms mandating distance between officers and inmates, and the evaluation of officers in terms of their compliance with these norms, mean that most COs—of whatever race—who take a sympathetic view of inmates often feel compelled to suppress it. This is a process that is likely more difficult for African-American and Hispanic officers, however. Caught in the middle, they share the bond of color and ethnicity with those who disproportionately populate America's prisons, but they wear the uniform of the system that imprisons them. Many undoubtedly feel pressure to demonstrate their loyalty to their white coworkers and supervisors by engaging in strategies of distancing. This may include the apparent adherence to negative stereotypes about inmates that are part of the occupational subculture. George Lamming has called this process of disidentification learning to speak "the language of the overseer":

> The image of the enemy, and the enemy was My People. My people are low-down nigger people. My people don't like to see their people get on. The language of the overseer. The language of the civil servant. The myth had eaten through their consciousness like moths through the pages of ageing documents. Not taking chances with you people, my people. . . . It was the language of the overseer, the language of the government servant. (1983: 26–27)

Learning to speak this language successfully means the denial of one's own racial identity or the active construction and reproduction of other markers of difference. The lack of any indication among these officers that the inmates in their charge are imprisoned unjustly may well be one indication of this process.

Even so, the fact that African-American officers are more likely than whites to subscribe to the idea that inmates are people who have made mistakes suggests that something more complex is going on. These officers do feel some pressure not to express this sentiment. One African-American woman in a men's prison admits to such an opinion only after being assured that no one will identify her with it:

> Most people think that I'm effective because, "Oh, she's probably flirting with them." I don't have to flirt with them! And I wouldn't flirt with them. I wouldn't stoop so low. I know that sounds bad, but in [this system] you're programmed to think they are so beneath you. That's what you're programmed to think. *Is that what you think?* No. To be honest, and it's not going to go anywhere, no. Some of them are pretty decent guys. And some of them are assholes, like little kids who haven't had any home training, and that's basically what I look at it as. And I tell them all the time, "Your mother didn't raise you very well." [They say,] "My mother didn't live with me." I say, "I see your problem right now."

Her comments capture the double consciousness (Du Bois 1989 [1903]) that prison work fosters for many African-American COs. This standpoint takes the form of understanding how the system views inmates (and thus how it expects officers to view them), but it also brings officers' own experiences with racism in the outside world to bear on their assessments. Though the institution "programs" COs to see inmates as beneath them, this officer believes that most of them are probably "decent guys" and that even the "assholes" probably had difficult childhoods.

This same stance is demonstrated by this African-American man who works in a women's prison. He distances himself from the "system" and tries to set a positive example for inmates:

> *Do you enjoy working with inmates?* I do. To me it presents a challenge working with different backgrounds, cultures. What's interesting to me is working with the people I guess at the lowest part of their lives. And trying to somehow make things a little better or just be something positive in their lives. Because I do believe that they're watching us. They're

watching us, and we can be good examples or we can be poor examples. And when you're a poor example and you don't care about your job and you don't care about them, you're nothing but the police or cop or pig. But when they see that you care and you'll do your job and you'll be fair and consistent, they'll refer to you as he's an officer, he's a correctional officer or he's Mr. so and so. *As opposed to what?* Numerous names.

This officer sees representatives of the system—"the police or cop or pig"—as uncaring about both their own work and the inmates. He sets himself apart from this attitude and adopts an approach that sees inmates as people who can change for the better. Perhaps not surprisingly, this orientation toward the positive rehabilitation of inmates is also more commonly expressed by African-American and Hispanic officers in my study.[3]

Those officers who adopt a humanistic, rehabilitative stance toward inmates still employ rhetorical strategies of separation. This African-American woman, who now works in a women's prison, sees inmates as people who have made mistakes. She views connecting with them as one means toward helping them change their lives:

> A lot of them deserve to be here, but you have to look at what your job is. What's my job as an officer? What good would it do if you had a dog, [and] you keep hitting that dog and beating that dog? You treat that dog, you take care of them. With the inmates, the way I look at them is that they made a mistake. Some of these people here have nobody. I'm not gonna go out there and pour out my love to them, but I'm gonna respect them. I tell them, "I don't wanna see you in here. This is no place for nobody. You have family out there. Go out there and take care of your kids. It might be hard, but do it anyway." And if I can help just one inmate get out here and change their life around, that makes me feel good. I don't wanna see nobody up in here. I just look at it like that person made a mistake. They're still human. I still love them. That's the way I see them.

In one way, this officer's views place her on the extreme end of the spectrum. Most COs do not express or acknowledge love for their charges, and even this woman is ambivalent—she will not "pour out [her] love" to inmates, but she "loves" them nonetheless.[4]

At another level, her comparison of inmates to pets places her very much in the mainstream. Most officers who express a humanistic attitude toward inmates also tend to objectify or infantilize them in some ways. This white male officer who works in a men's prison is typical:

> I think you can have a philosophy of communicating instead of doing the, you know, I'm gonna lock you up. If you're able to talk to these people, some of them have the mentality of children, sometimes you have to talk to them as a child, or treat them as a child. And some of them just don't understand because of their educational background or where they came from. And if you take the time to show a little compassion, explain things to them, treat them as a human being, give 'em some respect. You know, I tell these inmates, I say, "You only come into this world with two things, your word and your dignity. You start losing either one of those and you're not much of a man, so you need to try to keep up as much as you can." I really don't care what they did out there. That's not my business, but I do care who I'm dealing with. I look at it that way, and I'll deal with them as a person that way until they give me a reason not to.

This officer prioritizes communication, yet he also believes that one must often talk to inmates as if they are children. In so doing, he plays the role of a father, attempting to model and reconstruct a particular version of appropriate masculinity. The humanistic view is often linked with a transformation of the role of the officer from turnkey or guard to parent. Both men and women speak in these terms, although women are more likely to use the term "mother" to refer to their relationships with inmates.[5]

These comments reveal yet another common theme among officers. Most do not know, and do not see as relevant, the details of the offenses committed by inmates. Indeed, most COs do not have access to case files, though they are obviously aware of the crimes of the small number of "celebrity" inmates whose crimes are the subject of media attention. COs assess inmates largely in terms of their behavior inside prison; if they behave respectfully, they are deemed worthy of at least a minimum level of respect. This reflects the stance of institutional policy as well. Within limits, inmates in most prisons can gain privileges or move to lower-security settings if they exhibit "good" behavior, regardless of what they did while in the free world.

Overall, while officers in my study see inmates as human, they generally do not see them as equals. The norms and practices of the institution in which they work militate strongly against such a view; the rationale for incarceration rests on the judgment that inmates have temporarily forfeited their rights to citizenship and to adulthood. Whether they see themselves as zookeepers or parents, officers fulfill a custodial role. The question raised by critics of the prison and of social control more generally is whether inmates are better off treated as animals or children. Michel Foucault (1979) and others who have drawn on his work argue that paternalistic (or maternalistic) control is more insidious, in that it seeks to transform the souls of inmates rather than simply restrain their bodies. I have considerable sympathy for this view. Women's prisons in particular, which are still influenced by the rehabilitative legacy of the reformatory movement, infantilize inmates through their implicitly family-based regimes of social control (Carlen 1983; Carlen and Tchaikovsky 1985; O'Brien 2001). Even so, I remain unconvinced that inmates are better served by officers who believe that inmates "aren't really like people, most of them are animals" (CO quoted in Kauffman 1988: 119). In reality, both of these standpoints are the product of a system whose functional purpose is control. Through their work, officers become a medium through which this goal is enacted. They make some choices about how to fulfill this role, but they do so only within the limited ambit of the prison disciplinary regime.

INMATES ARE TOO PRIVILEGED

The perception that inmates are not equals is linked to another theme. This is the belief that inmates are too privileged. Officers who take this stance argue that inmates have too much in the way of access to programs, services, and other amenities. This white male officer compares the situation of inmates to his own:

Do they have enough, or too much, in terms of programming? In terms of, say, jobs and training programs and education programs? I think the training, I think it's enough. But, like cable TV, I'm talking about them renting *WrestleMania* with, what's that boxer's name . . . ? That guy that bit off that ear? Tyson! That cost forty dollars at my house, and I couldn't afford it. These guys are locked up, and they're sitting there watching *WrestleMania*, I mean, give me a break. As a matter of fact, sometimes I wonder, after I do my twenty years, go rob a bank, because

I'm gonna be too old to do anything anyway, instead of having my family put me in a rest home, I'll just go here. Three meals a day, utilities paid, kick back. You know, have the federal government pay for it. What would be the difference? Got your weight room, your pool tables, your cable TV, your school, salad bar. I think they should make it a little bit harder in prison, where people don't want to come back. I mean, I would never, I couldn't stand to be locked up, but . . .

This officer jokes that inmates have such an easy life that he would consider incarceration as a retirement plan. Many others in both state and federal systems express similar sentiments. But these comments illustrate considerable ambivalence as well. As with most who make such statements, this officer is quick to note that he himself "couldn't stand to be locked up." COs understand that deprivation of liberty, separate from any institutional perquisites inmates may enjoy, is a formidable punishment.

It is also clear that this officer does not believe that inmates should be completely deprived of privileges. In all the years that I have been studying prisons, I have rarely met COs or administrators who agree with the deeply held popular sentiment that inmates should have nothing but bread, water, and a cell—preferably a dungeonesque one—during their incarceration. Most take a more pragmatic view, seeing access to programs and privileges as a management tool. As one white woman puts it:

I don't think there's too much, because actually the busier they are, the easier it is for us. Some people do have that mentality that they do have too much, but I don't care. The more you give them, the more you can take away when they're bad.

In this context, privileges become incentives to control behavior. In a period in which more and more inmates are being sentenced to longer terms, often without possibility of parole, COs believe that they need more of these tools, rather than fewer. They do, however, take exception to what they describe as extravagance, as in the case of the pay-per-view wrestling match.

Comparing Women and Men as Inmates

By far the most common theme in officers' perceptions of inmates draws on comparisons between men and women. Given that prisons are

TABLE 5.1
Experience with Cross-Gender Supervision, by Sex of Officer

Cross-gender supervision experience?	Male	Female	Total
No	12	16	28
%	27	59	39
Yes	33	11	44
%	73	41	61
Total	45	27	72

sex-segregated—and that officers would seem to have little basis for comparison—this may appear paradoxical. But most of the officers I interviewed do have experience with cross-gender supervision, having either worked in both men's and women's prisons or supervised inmates of the opposite sex who are assigned to periodic work details at their institutions.[6] This is the case for forty-four (61 percent). Experience with cross-gender supervision is more common for the men in my study, as table 5.1 indicates. Of those remaining, seventeen (24 percent) had supervised only male inmates, and eleven (15 percent) had worked only with women. Even among these latter two groups, however, it is not uncommon for officers to compare their experiences to those of other officers they have known who had worked in opposite-sex institutions, or to stories they had heard about them.

The salience of this issue is also due to gender's function as a master status in culture at large. As Erving Goffman writes: "In modern industrial society, as apparently in all others, sex is at the base of a fundamental code in accordance with which social interactions and social structures are built up" (1977: 301). Sex and gender are foundational categories through which we assign meaning to people and to behaviors. Our attributions of sex category and corresponding expectations about gender are fundamental to our interactions with others (Garfinkel 1967; Goffman 1977; Ridgeway 1997; West and Zimmerman 1987; West and Fenstermaker 1995). It is thus not particularly surprising that gender serves as a primary reference point for officers in sorting and explaining their perceptions of the generic category "inmates."

Dichotomous distinctions like gender sort people, but they also rank them. Both men and women COs strongly prefer work in men's prisons (Britton 1999; Pollock-Byrne 1986). Of the seventy-two officers in the current study, only twelve (16 percent) prefer work with women. Though this may seem incongruous—particularly given our images of men's prisons—it makes sense when viewed against a background in which we know that many workers tend to prefer men as coworkers, supervisors, and clients. In the private sphere as well, "son preference" remains strong in the United States and elsewhere. Even some of the most ardent feminists among my students tell me that boys are just "easier to raise" than girls. Among COs, the primary determinant of officers' disdain for work with women lies in negative perceptions of women inmates, views that resonate with stereotypes about femininity in the free world as well.

WOMEN INMATES ARE MORE EMOTIONAL

Both men and women see women inmates as excessively emotional. As these two officers, both white men, put it:

> When I came here they handed me a pair of handcuffs. I couldn't understand why. What they really need to give you is a pack of tissues. Seriously. These handcuffs never come out. You never use them. And all they do is cry. They cry to you. A lot of people don't wanna hear their crying. I'm a sensitive guy. I understand it, you know. It's not gonna sway my decision, but . . . I just think in some ways they're harder to deal with than the men.

> You don't have the violence with the women as opposed to the men. But you've got the emotions. The emotions can be pretty strenuous at times, because to try to talk to a woman who feels like she's at the end of the world and, you know, she's been stepped on and kicked on and crying eyes, and it's just something that takes a little time to get used to working with. You don't see that much with men. They're always taught to be hard and firm and, you know, bottle up feelings. Explode with anger.

Both of these COs contrast the violence of male inmates (upon whom one would need to use handcuffs) to the crying of women (for whom one needs tissues). Paradoxically, they consider the latter to be a greater challenge. These sentiments are noteworthy for another reason: the counterposition of violence and emotion. Both exploding with anger and crying are expressions of emotion. To the extent that men and women do these things, we might justifiably say that both are emotional. Significantly, however, only women inmates are singled out in this way; when you work with women, "you've got the emotions."

Though men often believed that women COs would be better at handling the emotions of women inmates and thus feel more comfortable working with them, women officers also dislike work in women's prisons. This white female CO echoes the sentiments of her male counterparts but offers an additional reservation:

> I would much rather work with the men! I mean, that's awful to say that . . . but it's very true. I'm just not real good at babying, and the females need a lot more attention. They need a lot more coddling, and that's just kind of our gender. That's the way we are. They tend to cry if we go over and talk to them, where you're not going to get that with the men. I just don't deal with that well because I get that sense of mothering coming in to work with the women, and I have to draw the line. I just personally would rather work with the men.

Perhaps even more vehemently than the men, this officer rejects work with women on the grounds of their greater emotionality. Unlike them, however, she cites another, and clearly gendered, source for her resistance, the pressure she feels to "coddle" and to "mother" inmates.

Given the greater cultural latitude granted to women in the open expression of certain kinds of emotion, women inmates probably do cry more than men, or at least cry more openly. But this simple observation begs several important questions. First, why do officers see the emotion that women exhibit as such a significant challenge? Second, why are women's tears the basis for refusing to work with them? And, finally, why would officers rather deal with violence (use their handcuffs) than sobbing (offer a tissue)?

One answer has to do with the kind of training officers receive. Training concentrates heavily on physical self-defense and restraint techniques, and comparatively little attention is paid to counseling and interpersonal skills, particularly for officers at the state level. The training and the job are structured primarily to achieve the goal of custody. Officers may feel more prepared to deal with outright violence than with emotion. Women's emotionality "takes a little time to get used to working with." Men's violence is prepared for and routinized as part of the job. This reaction is linked to training programs' construction of a particular generic inmate, who is the stoic, or even hostile, man—not the crying woman.

Resistance to managing women's emotions also stems from the lower status that accrues to jobs that require this kind of emotional labor. Arlie Hochschild (1983) first drew attention to the often hidden work of managing and utilizing emotions on the job. In her study of bill collectors (most of whom were men) and flight attendants (mostly women), she notes that when men are required to use emotion on the job, it is often in the form of anger and threat. Similarly, the job of correctional officer draws on the purportedly masculine ability to impose discipline and manage physical danger. These qualities are explicitly sought and valued by employers. Women are more likely to be in jobs that require the use of nurturing, charm, and interpersonal skills to deal with others' emotions. Yet because these abilities are perceived by employers as natural to women, they are neither formally cultivated nor highly rewarded. Jobs in which workers perform this kind of emotional labor (like flight attendant, receptionist, social worker, and elementary school teacher) are dominated by women and are often relatively low-paying. When men move into these occupations, it is precisely the tasks involving managing emotions that they are most likely to reject (Pierce 1995; Williams 1989, 1995). When women enter male-dominated occupations, the relatively low-status tasks involving dealing with emotion are delegated to them. Women police officers, for example, often find themselves assigned to deal with "hysterical" victims. Some may resist, as in the case of the woman officer above who refused to "mother" inmates, but in doing so they must overcome the expectations of coworkers, clients, and supervisors that they will take on these roles. In the prison work environment, both men and women understand that the management of emotions (like women inmates' crying) is work that offers relatively little status or reward. Conversely, the management of violence and the imposition of discipline are the central priorities.

In some ways, however, counterposing men's violence to women's emotionality, as these and other officers sometimes do, creates a false distinction. Correctional officers understand that both men and women can be violent. As this white male officer puts it:

> Those female inmates are rough. There's some out there, that if you ever have to go one on one on them, you better be ready to bring your lunch, 'cause they're liable to be there a while, even with a male [officer].

The difference is that men's and women's violence tends to be read through different, and gendered, lenses. Officers make a distinction between "cat fights" and "gang fights" (Britton 1999). This white male officer explains:

> You have to realize that you have different categories of violence. I would say here [in the women's prison] we have like cat fights. In the men's institution, especially in a higher [security] institution, could be extremely violent. Even deadly. But here, no, it's basically cat fights which is good because you don't get anybody seriously hurt.

But this officer's observation only deepens the paradox—if men's institutions are "violent," "even deadly," why do officers prefer them?

One key is the link made by officers between women's greater emotionality and their use of violence. Many COs believe that women are more prone to irrational outbursts than men (i.e., they "go off" more frequently), but that the outcome of male violence is likely to be more serious when it occurs. In women's prisons, violence is almost always read in terms of women's greater propensity to be emotional, while similar violence from men is rationalized in terms of its relationship to legitimate (or at least comprehensible) goals. The unpredictability of women's violence makes it a greater challenge, as this African-American male CO notes:

> A male inmate and a female inmate are two different types of inmates. A male inmate is easier to manage because they're not as emotional as female inmates. And the risk factor in dealing with males is not as serious as it is with females when it comes to a confrontation.

Similarly, this white woman observes:

> Women [inmates] are more emotional. They fly off the handle a lot faster. They don't think, they just react. They just do. The men, some of them do, but most of them think a little bit before they react. So, that's the true difference right there.

For the first CO the emotionality of women's violence makes it *more* dangerous than men's. For the second, the "true difference" between men and women in prison is that women simply "don't think." All these comments are consistent with a large body of literature on perceptions of deviant women and men, which demonstrates that the former are much more likely to be seen as irrational or even mentally ill than the latter (Schur 1984; Morris and Wilczynski 1995).

WOMEN INMATES ARE MANIPULATIVE AND QUESTION AUTHORITY

Like emotionality, a second theme in officers' comments revolves around negative stereotypes associated with femininity. Officers see women as both more manipulative and less obedient than their male counterparts. Many men (and some women) perceive crying as a thinly veiled, and particularly feminine, attempt at manipulation. Others invoke a broader set of traits, seeing women as inherently deceitful. These two white male officers observe:

> Working with male inmates it's more physical. Working with females you need to be on your toes more. You have to be ready. They're gonna try the head games, they're gonna try and get you in that trick bag or whatever.

> You have to be able to handle the women. They try to play games with you, and tricks with you, and I've already had all of that. *In different ways than male inmates, presumably?* Yeah. All kinds of little tricks they try to pull on you. The female thing, they try to get, well, we'll be cuddly up to you to try to get something, befriend you. It's just the female [thing], they try to get over, is what they do.

For these men, trickery and "head games" are "just the female thing." In fact, no officer uses the phrase "head games" to describe the behavior of male inmates. Unlike men, whom COs believe act instrumentally to obtain resources from officers and from the system, women rely on indirect tactics. Handling the latter is considered a more significant challenge.

Officers also perceive that women inmates are simply more intractable than men. Almost two-thirds of the women COs in my study (and about one-third of the men) express the opinion that women are less likely to obey officers' directives immediately or to accept a negative answer to a request. This white female officer, who had recently transferred from a men's to a women's prison, observes:

Female inmates are a little bit different. They ask why. You tell a male inmate something, "Okay, boss, no problem." And he's going to do it. If you ask a female inmate to do something, or you tell them to do something, they turn back and say, "Why?" [laughs] Hello! Knock, knock! [knocking on head] Did I give you an order? Just do it. And if I'm wrong, I'm wrong. If I'm right, I'm right.

This Hispanic man, who now works in a men's prison, echoes these sentiments:

The women whine more. For instance, you could tell a male inmate, "Hey, you're not going to do that." Women, they want an explanation. So, it's real difficult. I don't like [working with the women] myself because of the mind play. I like coming in here, and the inmates know what I'm about, they know where I'm coming from. I don't have to explain myself all the time.

And this woman had also worked with both men and women inmates:

When you tell a male no, they may not like it but they accept it a lot more than what a female does. I hate to say that because I'm female, but females don't take no for an answer at all. They just keep coming back, "But I need this for this, you're not getting it, but I need this . . ." "No!" Where the males, they'll say, "I disagree with you," but they'll move on and go to something else.

Two things stand out about these comments. First, as in the case of women's purportedly higher levels of emotion, officers frame these alleged tendencies in essentialist terms. This is, unfortunately, just how women are—as the officer's "I hate to say that because I'm female" indicates. Concomitantly, men are inherently more able to accept rejection. Working with men means that officers are not required to "explain [themselves] all the time." Second, officers perceive women as needing more than men, in the way of both officer time and system resources. Even after they are rejected, women apparently continue to make demands on the system by "whining" and questioning rules.

Rather than viewing these qualities as inherent female character flaws, however, we can see them as artifacts of the structures and practices of the gendered institutions in which men and women are imprisoned, and of gendered power relationships in the culture as a whole. Women tend to be less violent offenders than men, and they have shorter, less serious prior criminal records. This means that they are typically incarcerated in relatively low-security facilities. In such facilities, whether they house men or women, there is a certain amount of flexibility that is not present in maximum-security prisons. Women's use of what officers see as manipulation and their more open questioning of authority may well be evidence of this atmosphere. As this white woman who works in a low-security women's prison notes:

> Here, it's not that they're females that they have many more advantages than the males [in higher-security prisons]. It's that the security level's a lot lower. So, they get away with a lot more here, and I think that also makes a lot of men more uncomfortable.

This African-American man's comments clearly illustrate this dynamic. He compares his current assignment to a women's prison facility—which has no perimeter fence—with work in a more conventional men's institution:

> If I had a preference, I'd probably work behind the fence [with male inmates]. *And is it because of the security level difference, or because male inmates versus female . . . ?* I think it's basically because of the security level. Things with the women in this facility are not like they are with men in [another medium-security prison]. You know, there's a gray area here. I'd rather work where I know exactly what's what, not have to be second-guessed all the time.

Though the first officer singles this out as a source of discomfort for men, the preference for work in men's facilities is just as strong for women. The problem, from officers' point of view, with work in women's prisons may have much to do with the fact that they are lower-security institutions. Training does not typically prepare officers for work in this kind of facility, in which there are inevitably more shades of gray in the rules and practices governing conduct. Connected to this is training's focus on the development of a custody orientation and the production of COs whose view of the job primarily emphasizes the maintenance of institutional security (rather than the rehabilitation of inmates, for example). The result is that many officers favor conditions, like those in rigidly structured high-security settings, that they perceive will make the accomplishment of that goal easier.[7]

Women's questioning of the system frustrates the goal of institutional control, at least from the perspective of many officers. Men's violence, however, is clearly about control—if not over the institution itself (as in a riot), at least over the conditions of their own lives. Men and women inmates attempt to exercise agency, at least to the extent that the conditions of their incarceration allow. The methods, as officers describe them here, are gendered; men use violence, and women rely on tears and manipulation.

The finding that male COs tend to frame this tendency in terms of manipulation, and female COs in terms of women's essential intractability, may also have to do with gendered norms of interaction that are played out in the prison setting. Women inmates have learned that getting resources from more powerful (heterosexual) men often requires indirect methods, be they tears, or "head games," or "feminine wiles." In fact, women COs worry that men are vulnerable to this kind of deception, as this white woman notes:

> A lot of the females seem to believe that they can get away with more with men. Show them the tears and you'll get your way. "Oh, I got cramps today, I really can't work, you know, give me something easy to do." Or maybe if I flirt with them then they won't make me do that. And the women it's like, "Oh, you got cramps, so what so do I." "Oh, the tears, they're not working." So they tend to try to get their way more with the men.

Echoing the sentiments of many women COs, this officer rejects these tactics as illegitimate. If women inmates do indeed behave in this way (by no means an unproblematic conclusion), these techniques are probably not effective with women officers. Conversely, and again in line with cultural patterns of gendered power inequality, women inmates may feel freer to directly question the authority of female officers.

WOMEN ARE PETTY

A third way officers compare women inmates negatively to men centers on a perception that female inmates are overly concerned with what officers see as trivial issues and problems. This issue is raised much more frequently by male officers (only one woman in my study expresses a similar view). This African-American man is typical:

> When males come to you with problems, they're real problems. It's not like here, where they might come to you and say, "We don't have any toilet tissue in the bathroom," or "So and so was looking at me crazy, I don't like the way she's looking at me." You know, small things that females tend to blow up where males just like push that aside. But when males come to you with problems, it's real big problems. "Somebody's threatening to kill me," "I need to be locked up because five or six people are talking about jumpin' me," or they might come to you and say, "You need to get him out of the building or I'm gonna kill him." Things like that, you know. Here, the worst I've seen here, someone reported that some earrings got stolen out of their locker, that's basically about it. *So, it's more trivial?* Yeah, it's real petty stuff that the ladies come to you with. The guys will come to you with real, legitimate complaints.

Similarly, this white male officer observes:

> In my experience I've found, you know, male inmates won't bicker as much over small things as opposed to women. Women may get into a scuffle over, or a little confrontation over something that male inmates would think would be minute and just go beyond it. For example, the size of a pillow, or what channel the TV's on, something kind of small. Men will always wind up getting along. It's the bigger things that they're involved in, you know, where they have a tendency to be more violent as opposed to the women. So, you know, you've got your male facility where they're worried about where the next packet of drugs is coming from and where they're gonna get their hooch from, and women, you know, they're not too concerned with that, you know. They're just worried about who's gonna sleep with who on *Melrose Place* or something, you know.

Another African-American male officer describes a specific example:

> [The women are] petty, and little things mean a lot more to them, to the female I guess rather as opposed to the male. Like their hobby craft items. They can buy yarn in the commissary. They can make their blan-

kets or whatever. After they make it they're supposed to send that stuff home. They know they're supposed to send it home, but instead they wanna use it and put it on their beds, and they complain about that. "Well, if they don't want us keeping this stuff, why do they sell it," you know? *That sounds like a legitimate question.* I agree to that point, but you know they know that they're gonna have to mail it home and they buy it anyway. *So they can have the yarn, but if they make the blanket they have to send it home?* Yeah, they gotta ship it. And they'll complain about that and complain about that. As for the men, they know if you're gonna buy a hobby craft, you're gonna make something, you know after you make it you gotta send the thing home.

For the first officer, women's purportedly inherent pettiness is a waste of officers' time. Women complain about imaginary slights or minor insults, whereas men have "real, legitimate complaints." The second officer's response is in a similar vein, as he juxtaposes women inmates' concerns about who is sleeping with whom in a prime-time soap opera to men's efforts to secure drugs or alcohol. The final officer expresses a nearly identical sentiment, though he is sympathetic to my (and the inmates') confusion about why possession of the raw materials for crafts (i.e., yarn) is allowed, but finished products are not. Even so, he necessarily adopts a sort of "those are just the rules" posture that the women he supervises apparently cannot help but contest.

Again, this perception that women are petty but that men have real complaints is undoubtedly at least partly an artifact of the security levels at which women are housed. The day-to-day concerns of inmates in maximum-security facilities may well differ from those in low-security prisons, with the former having more reason to worry about violence. Why male officers would be more likely to express this sentiment is less clear. As I note elsewhere (Britton 1997a), whether in men's or in women's prisons, male officers tend to see their unique qualification as being able to deal with violence. It is possible that inmate discontent about issues that do not rise to the level of threats to life and limb is seen by male officers in particular as simply too trivial to demand their attention. Women officers, conversely, do not see their role in working with inmates as drawing on any unique, gendered capacity for dealing with physical violence. They thus may accept a wider range of claims as legitimate.

Officers' perceptions of women inmates as emotional, manipulative, intractable, and petty are not surprising. All these traits are associated with femininity in culture at large (Schur 1984). Emotionality could be seen as a strength, as could women's willingness to admit their needs and see that they are met. Similarly, violence, a trait associated with masculinity, could be evaluated negatively and serve as a reason for a preference for work in women's prisons. Yet in prison as in culture, traits associated with masculinity are viewed more positively than those linked with femininity. Gender is a fundamental category that we apply in interaction with others and through which our perceptions are shaped and filtered (Goffman 1977; Kessler and McKenna 1978). These officers believe that women's pettiness is not something they do, or a behavior that is produced by a particular set of circumstances, or something that only individual women express; it is simply the way women *are*. Similarly, men's stoicism, violence, or willingness to ignore "petty" slights is viewed as inherent in masculine character. The impact of this process of attribution is clear; it forms the basis for officers' near-universal preference for working with male inmates.

But these comments also hint at a much more complex picture. Ideas about gender are never formed or applied in a social vacuum. This happens here in two deeply gendered institutions, the men's and the women's prison. Understanding the role these structures play in shaping ideas about gender can provide substantial insight into how gender is constructed and reproduced at both the individual and the institutional level. In this case, the sorting process begun by the criminal justice system matters. Men commit more crimes and more serious offenses, they have longer prior records, and they constitute the bulk of the incarcerated population. Their needs and their behavior form the substance of our notion of the "typical" inmate. The actual physical structures of men's and women's prisons are also important. Women are more likely to be housed in lower-security settings, a fact that has a host of implications for officers' views of their conduct. Officers' perceptions of women inmates' supposed manipulation, intractability, and pettiness may all be at least partially produced by a custodial environment in which there is much more ambiguity in policies and informal norms than exists in more rigidly structured, high-security environments. Similarly, training policies and practices lead officers to expect a certain kind of inmate, one who is implicitly (if not explicitly) male. Women's emotionality and their "petty" concerns are not part of the training agenda. The interweaving of cultural ideals about what men and women are like, institutional policies in the context of masculinized organizations that sort inmates and reinforce expectations about them, and norms of gendered interaction that reproduce these notions underlie officers' preference for work with male inmates and their corresponding disdain for supervising women.

Racial Differences among Inmates

Prisons are one of the most racialized institutions in American society. Given this, it is perhaps surprising that I collected very few comments from officers about their perceptions of racial differences between inmates. One or two white officers expressed only thinly veiled racist attitudes, and another handful identified particular racial groups of inmates (usually African-Americans or Hispanics) as the primary troublemakers in their institutions. The overwhelming majority of COs, echoing currently socially appropriate discourse, profess a race-blind attitude. Those who acknowledge racism and discrimination, like this white male officer who works in a men's prison, often see it as a thing of the past:

> [In this community], there's very few blacks here. That tends to make people uncomfortable, and that can carry over in their job. I think for the most part that, you probably have some old guard people that, I don't want to say are racist, but just not fond of other races. Not being blatant race-haters, or anything like that, but just as soon not to deal with anybody from other races. And you know, I think some people tend to let that show. And you can't do that, because inmates can pick up on that.

His reference to the surrounding community reflects a fundamental fact about the American prison system. Because prisons require relatively large tracts of land, most institutions are located in predominantly white-populated rural areas and draw their officer corps from the surrounding population base. This particular town has a long and notorious history of racism; in fact, many African-American officers to whom I spoke at this prison do not feel comfortable living in the community and so commute from surrounding towns. This history, in exaggerated form, has become folklore among officers and inmates—one CO who often transports inmates to jobs and appointments in the community even jokes of threatening African-American inmates with leaving them behind if they misbehave.

Some officers, particularly African-American and Hispanic COs, do make oblique references to racism and discrimination directed at inmates by their coworkers and supervisors. Most often, they do so in the context of their experiences in other institutions or other systems. This Hispanic male officer describes a men's prison where he previously worked:

> [That prison was] much more violent, very racist. The inmates were 46 percent black. So, all of the black inmates stuck together over here, the Hispanic inmates were together over there, and the white inmates were together over there. I think there was four Hispanic officers, or five Hispanic staff. Four or five black staff. But the majority of the inmates were black, so a lot of the white staff did not know how to interact with the black people because there were no black people from the area the prison was in. *So, it was mostly black male inmates, and white male staff?* Yeah, so there was a lot of conflict there.

This officer gives whites the benefit of the doubt, attributing discrimination and racial tension to the fact that whites may simply not know how to "deal with" black and Hispanic inmates. From this perspective, racism is an outgrowth of cultural illiteracy.

Many African-American and Hispanic officers echo the race-blind attitude of their white colleagues. This African-American woman, who works in a women's prison, observes:

> This is not the setting for racial. When I see an inmate, I see an inmate. I don't see black, white, or Hispanic. If he or she comes to me, I don't care what color they are. I'm gonna talk to them. I'm gonna help them because they're people. That's the way I was raised. Even when I had black inmates coming to me trying to get into this racial stuff, I said, "I don't wanna hear it." That's not me. That's not what I'm about. My job here is about everybody. If you can't help everybody here, you don't need to be in this type of work. That's just the way I feel.

Though inmates of color see her as a potential ally, this officer is quick to disabuse them of this notion. For her, the job is "about everybody." In her claim that "this is not the setting for racial," I got the sense, however, that she is at pains to set herself apart from some officers (and inmates) who express racist attitudes or draw on racialized rhetoric to elicit support. This woman's observation, and the few comments I heard in which officers did express prejudiced attitudes about African-American or Hispanic inmates, suggest that discriminatory actions that contradict race-blind rhetoric clearly take place.

Beyond this general race blindness, there are two ways that racial difference between inmates is addressed. The first, which considers race in the context of gender, is the observation that racial tension between inmates is much more common in men's prisons than in women's. This African-American male CO, who now works in a women's prison, notes:

> In the men's prisons everywhere I've worked the men segregate themselves. You'll have the blacks eat in one corner. You'll have your Hispanics eat in another place. You'll have whites eat in another place. Motorcycle gangs eating in a group. And then the guys that aren't involved with anybody, you know, they don't sit with anybody. Every day they sit in the same place. I've seen inmates run off other inmates for sitting in those particular places. *What about here?* I haven't seen it. Women, they sit wherever they want pretty much. *So there's not the kind of racial tension that there is in men's prisons?* Right. I've seen the mixing.

This view is strikingly consistent across officers I interviewed and fits with other research which finds that racial segregation, race-based gangs, and racially motivated violence are less common in women's prisons. Most officers who worked in both kinds of institutions take this difference for granted; those who interrogate it attribute it to men's purportedly greater propensity for violence.

The second common theme takes the form of a multiculturalist discourse that interprets the behaviors of inmates as by-products of specific cultural backgrounds. The federal prison system in particular incorporates a cultural diversity component into its ongoing training. Officers are provided with opportunities to learn Spanish, and they describe a curriculum in which they are taught about the histories and tendencies of various racial and ethnic groups of inmates. As this white male CO in a men's prison observes:

> It's a challenge because you've got 'em from all walks of life, from all cultures, and that's what makes it interesting. You know, learning Spanish,

and being able to converse in different languages, and learning the customs and all that. Learning how you need to deal with different ethnic
groups differently. All inmates need to be treated the same, but within
certain parameters, you might want to approach it in a different way.
*When you say you should approach them differently, can you give me an
example?* Well, a lot of that is inmate by inmate, just knowing the inmate.
For example, like if a Hispanic inmate, their blood pressure seems to get
up and they'll talk real loud, but they might not be mad. That's just the
way they talk. You know, and certain customs are you get up closer to the
person, and other ones, that's too close.

In addition to providing training, the federal system is typically more
accommodating of the religious and cultural practices of inmates of diverse cultures than are state systems. This has perhaps led to a heightened consciousness of cultural diversity among federal officers and has
undoubtedly accelerated a trend toward reframing racial differences as
cultural ones. Whether, as some critics have suggested, this discourse of
"culturalism" (Collins 2000; Ferguson 2000) may simply be racism in
disguise, I cannot say. Unquestionably, such a curriculum has the potential to reify "race," transforming it from a social category to the essential nature of groups so marked. I was unable to determine what sort of
effect this curriculum had on white officers. Most speak of it in positive
terms as a tool for understanding inmates. When they do not, they reject it altogether as one more example of what they see as the system's
overemphasis on "political correctness" and diversity.

Perceptions of Inmate Conduct toward Officers

This section focuses on officers' views of inmates' behavior towards
them and on their perceptions of the most significant challenges they
face in their work with inmates. These are obviously connected to officers' notions about inmates' "essential natures," and much of the material to follow will translate assumptions about character into rationales
for action. As previously, these perspectives should be taken as partial
accounts of prison life. The most obvious limitation lies in the exclusion
of the voices of inmates. As I have also demonstrated, officers' visions
are constricted by the absence of a structural frame of reference, one
that recognizes the role of the institution in shaping behavior. On the

whole, officers believe that inmates are entirely responsible for their actions. Though psychologists or sociologists may offer various versions of determinism as explanations for what inmates do, as Goffman notes, staff can ill afford this kind of reasoning. In administrative philosophy, prisons are about forcing inmates to direct themselves in manageable ways, and "for this to be promoted, both desired and undesired conduct must be defined as springing from the personal will and character of the individual inmate himself, and defined as something he can himself do something about" (1961: 87). Officers only rarely invoke the conditions of incarceration itself to account for inmate behavior.[8]

Just as some of the themes in my interviews capture officers' views of inmates as a group, so, too, is there a kind of generalized harassment that occurs regardless of the race or sex of the officer and in both men's and women's prisons. The ubiquity of this behavior probably indicates that it is an outgrowth of the conditions of incarceration, though its degree or prevalence may be influenced by institutional context and take on different levels of salience for particular groups of officers. Almost to a person, officers speak of an "initiation period," during their early days on the job, and talk about the challenges in learning the unwritten rules of discretion that are the keys to maintaining the prison's negotiated order. Though most officers' initial fears center around violence, with experience, they almost invariably find that low-level harassment is a much more persistent challenge (Webb and Morris 1985). Inmates sometimes verbally bait officers, throw objects and destroy property, or attempt to con them into bringing in various forms of contraband. These themes are relatively generic; as Goffman's (1961) account suggests, there are clearly some ways in which "officer" becomes a master status, outweighing or at least obscuring differences by gender, race, and institutional context. There are others in which this is not the case, however. COs perceive that male inmates treat women differently than their male coworkers, though there are some disagreements about the form this takes. Similarly, officers believe that men are treated differently by female inmates. In both instances, these patterns of difference reflect and perpetuate gendered difference and, ultimately, inequality.

An Officer and a Lady: Women COs, Men's Prisons

Two themes run through officers' comments about male inmates' treatment of women and encompass two seemingly opposing points of view. In one account, women officers are welcomed by male inmates and are treated with more respect than their male coworkers, while in the other women are harassed more by inmates and are less able to establish authority. Underlying both themes, however, are gendered ideals about women's appropriate behavior and assumptions about the kind of authority they can command.

Some COs argue that male inmates actually prefer female officers over male COs, and most studies find that the majority do indeed at least favor the presence of women (Kissel and Katsampes 1980; Owen 1988; Pollock-Byrne 1986; Szockyj 1989; Zimmer 1986) in men's prisons. There are several reasons for this preference, at least from the perspective of COs. First, officers believe that male inmates simply enjoy the sight of women in an environment otherwise devoid of ongoing contact with the opposite sex. This officer, a white man assigned to a men's prison, relates his experience:

> I had an inmate come up to me last week, "You know what, boss, I think female officers make better officers." I said, "Why is that?" He told me, the reason is because these inmates are, you know, their wives are out there, and they're never around women. They like women. They like to be woken up in the morning, "Say, hey, you need to go to work," by a woman. They like the sight of them.

Similarly, this African-American officer in a men's prison believes that male inmates crave social, though not necessarily sexual, contact with women:

> With male officers, they're more chummy, you know, they're more, joking attitude. But with female officers they're more protective. We had a little fight in food service about a year ago, and I was standing next to one of the female officers and a couple of the inmates that were in the housing unit that she was in the day before, you know, we were standing there next to 'em, the fight broke out. And I told her, you go secure the doors. And the two inmates said, "Don't worry about her, man, we got her. If anybody comes to the door, we'll make sure that they don't get in." So, they're more protective of females than they are of males. I think it's simply because of being in prison, and not having females around, just the simple contact of being able to walk up and say hello, they don't want to lose that. So, if there are females around, they tend

to be more protective and trying to make it so that their day is easier so that they will stay and not leave. It's not that they want sexual contact, it's that they need that contact with the opposite sex, but not exactly sexual contact.

These observations raise a number of interesting issues. First, they invoke a naturalized notion of desire common to both public and institutional discourse about male inmates—male inmates "haven't seen a woman in a while" and thus welcome the opportunity for any kind of interaction. For women officers, this is double-edged. It creates a space for them, but it does so in a way that can have the effect of invoking their vulnerability as potential victims.[9] Male officers, supervisors, and administrators who express resistance to women's presence in men's prisons often make the leap from heterosocial contact to heterosexual assault and worry that female COs will be willing or unwilling victims of seduction by male inmates, or that they will let their sexuality be used against them in more subtle ways.

Second, this preference is contingent on women officers' "doing femininity" by accepting the protection of men, be they coworkers or inmates. In the preceding account, this happens in two ways. First, the male officer removes his coworker from the fight by telling her to secure the doors. Second, the inmates promise to assist her by keeping other inmates out. The former occurs with some frequency to women COs (and to women in many male-dominated occupations). The latter is arguably more problematic. Many women report this kind of protective behavior from inmates; some, like those in Lynn Zimmer's (1986) "inventive" role, actively seek out such assistance; others resist it (Owen 1988). In either event, women officers are in a double bind. If they accept the protection of inmates, they risk creating the perception that they are unable to do their jobs effectively. Given that their role is already sexualized, accepting such protection can, and often does, lead to rumors that women officers are sexually involved with male inmates. Yet if they reject protection, they may create animosity and expose themselves to future danger. This protection may also be more available to some female officers than others. Comments about being protected by inmates came much more frequently from white women officers than from African-American women, suggesting that the racialized femininity of white women may, as in U.S. culture at large, make them seem more worthy of protection.

What this obscures is that male COs also receive similar kinds of assistance from inmates. The small number of officers in any prison means that a certain amount of cooperation between inmates and officers is necessary to maintain order; as a white male CO puts it, "I get to go home every day only because the inmates let me." This African-American woman describes assistance as a fact of life:

> When I worked at the [men's prison] after 9:00 they took my keys from me. You're locked in a unit from 9:00 P.M. to 6:00 A.M. You can't take the keys in the units because the inmates might take the keys and get out. In this unit I got a hundred-something male inmates, rapists, murderers, whatever. Who do you think I gotta depend on if somebody if one of these inmates wants to attack me? I gotta depend on another inmate. Hopefully they'll talk that inmate out of hurting me or [help me] if I get sick and pass out. We make watch call [call in to central control by radio at specified intervals], but still anything can happen between that time and somebody getting there. So that's when you have to use your head. You can't go in that unit being nasty to these people because you're gonna have to depend on them at one time or another to help you. That's the way I think. I've never had any serious problem. Nobody's ever threatened to hit me. Not saying that it won't happen, but I never had any problem like that. I've been doing it almost eight years.

Any officer under these conditions would need to rely, at least to some degree, on the cooperation of inmates. While male officers also depend on help and even protection (Webb and Morris 1985), such acts may simply be less visible and are certainly less likely to be interpreted through a gendered and sexualized frame.

Women officers may also be welcomed because of their purportedly greater ability to reduce violence within men's prisons. Female COs in particular believe that they exert a positive influence in men's prisons by calming tension and defusing violence. This white woman observes:

> I think women even out the temperament of the unit. If you had strictly male on male, you don't have someone there that can be a peacemaker, to make things a little more rational. And I think you see, when you're working together with male and female, that women will have more of a calming effect, that they keep the violence from happening.

And this African-American man concurs:

> To my experience there are positives in having female officers at a male institution. There's a lot of times when you will have certain inmates who are violent, angry, and you're trying to deal with them and you can't just calm them down. A female can come up and calm them down, and you no longer have that volatile situation. I've seen it done time and time again. I don't know if it's a mother figure, but it's just something about some of the females that can do that to a man. Another man, you know, the inmate feels I am a threat to him and, you know, who am I to tell him what to do and how to do it. So there are definite advantages.

For the first CO, women are inherently better than men at being peacemakers. For the second, it is women's representation of mother figures that makes them inherently less threatening than men. This kind of reasoning is often used to justify the presence of women in men's institutions; the potential "calming influence" of women in these facilities was identified in one of the earliest studies of women correctional officers as one of the primary benefits to the institution (Kissel and Katsampes 1980). This influence is predicated on gendered characteristics; women are less likely to be physically aggressive with male inmates, and their femininity "softens" the rough atmosphere of a men's institution. While both conceptions do create a space for women, they so in narrow ways. Women COs are welcomed to the extent that they do not contradict the prevailing gender ideology that frames them as weaker and more nurturing than men.

The fact that women COs are welcomed in men's prisons does not mean that they do not face challenges, however. Perhaps the most consistent obstacle that women officers must overcome in men's prisons involves exercising authority. Though all officers struggle with this initially, prevailing patterns of gendered power inequality mean that male inmates are generally unaccustomed (at least as adults) to accepting women in positions of power over them (Jenne and Kersting 1998). This means that women have to work harder than their male counterparts to establish themselves as legitimate authority figures. The experience of this African-American woman officer underlines this point:

> Well, with the women they feel that, you know, you think you're doing something, telling a man what to do. So, they give us a harder time. They

resent us basically, for telling them what to do, because they think, if I was out there in the world, you wouldn't be telling me what to do. So, you really get tired of that, because they give you such a hard time.

This white man agrees:

There's some inmates that just get plain mad that a woman tells them what to do. And you can see the anger, you know, where if I was working the same post, telling them the same thing, it'd be, okay. You know, I've seen that quite a bit.

Women's roles as COs are in some ways a reversal of the "natural order," in which women are generally subordinate to men. This creates an additional challenge for women, who, if they are to be successful in the job, must devise methods for asserting their authority in the face of resistance.

Female COs must also deal with flirting and sexual overtures from male inmates. As anyone who has ever visited a maximum-security men's institution can attest, some inmates engage in verbal sexual harassment and other less serious kinds of sexual banter directed at both men and women. Female officers report that they experience this much more frequently than their male counterparts (who generally corroborate this assertion). This white woman's story illustrates this point:

The inmates play games. Especially male inmates with female staff, you know, they're like, oh, your hair looks nice, your eyes are pretty. You know, they just do that stupid bull stuff that they do so well. I think that when I first walked in the door, and an inmate said I was pretty, or had pretty eyes, I just didn't know what to do, I was flustered. I was like, ah . . . I don't know what to do.

Women officers are often unprepared to deal with this kind of banter by their training, which tends to be framed in gender-neutral terms (Britton 1997a). Most women COs see this harassment as just another part of the inmate "con games" with which all officers have to deal. In this case, "cons" take on a gendered form. The danger in succumbing is obvious; in all the facilities I visited, I heard accounts of women who had lost their jobs after becoming involved (or having been perceived to be involved) with male inmates. Even if female officers do not become entangled in such relationships, the mere fact that they are subject to sexual banter often leads to suspicion and rumors among male inmates, supervisors, and staff.

Women eventually develop techniques for dealing with these overtures. The most common strategy is one of maintaining very high privacy boundaries. Female COs indicate that they take great care never to become overly friendly with inmates. This white woman explains:

> I think that a lot of the reason I haven't had problems is that I don't say anything to them. If they ask me a question, I answer it, and I shut up, and I leave it right there. Because they try to make conversation, and I'll tell them, "You know, I don't feel like talking." And they'll say, "Oh, she thinks she's cute, she's stuck up."

In a variation on this theme, others adopt what they describe as a "hard" or a strictly rule-based approach to the job (Owen 1988; Zimmer 1986). Both of these techniques are methods of managing gender in interaction by attempting to minimize its significance. While it can be effective, the adoption of such a strategy is also potentially problematic. The job of the correctional officer requires considerable flexibility, and at least some discretion in enforcing institutional rules is expected of officers (Blau, Light, and Chamlin 1986; Cheek and Miller 1983; Jacobs 1977; Lombardo 1981; Sykes 1958). Women who are forced into a rigid application of the rules are unable to show the discretion and judgment that supervisors expect in dealing with inmates. This produces a paradox for women, who may feel more protected by adhering to a strictly rule-based approach to the job, but who at the same time may be hindered in their chances for advancement.

Finally, women are subjected to a specific kind of sexual harassment that their male counterparts do not experience: open masturbation by male inmates. Since total institutions, unlike Weber's ideal-typical organization, straddle the divide between public and private, they are forced to deal in some way with normally private aspects of members' behavior, including sexuality (Hearn and Parkin 1987). Prisons typically manage sexuality in a repressive manner, forbidding almost all forms of sexual activity. Limited sexual behavior may be tolerated as long as it is not coercive, and this has been the case particularly in women's prisons (Giallombardo 1966; Owen 1998; Pollock-Byrne 1986).

Given that prisons are places of very limited privacy, it is difficult for inmates to engage in any private sexual behavior, and it is likely that officers will witness even acts that are meant to be concealed. However, female officers I interviewed discuss open masturbation by male inmates as a form of intentional harassment to which male officers are not subjected. These white female officers describe their frustration with the situation:

> There's a lot of sexual misconduct down there in the building, especially toward, directed toward female officers. I hate to talk ugly like that, but you see just about anything down there. *Sexual misconduct from the inmates to the female COs?* Yeah. What's the correct word for that? A lot of masturbating.

> On a daily basis, when I make my rounds, there's a couple of particular inmates that will masturbate every time I go down range in front of the cells. Every time. *Is it your sense that that gets directed at female officers more?* Oh, yeah. A male officer has never written an incident report on it.

In fact, very few male officers mentioned witnessing inmate masturbation when they were assigned to a post in a living area, and most said they had never seen it happen until a female officer called them over to point it out (Britton 1997a).

Female officers are left very much on their own in learning how to deal with inmate masturbation. Some use institutional rules, writing disciplinary cases against those whose behavior is particularly persistent. But most do not see this as a productive use of their time and employ more informal strategies, as do these two white women:

> The male inmates, they like to test you a lot, I mean, a whole lot. We've had a few where, if there's a female officer walking the cat walk, which is up and above the dorms, you'll have a lot of inmates who will, oh, search for something in their pants. And they will especially when there's a female officer up there because they know that you're scanning the dorms. And if you happen to stop and look, you're like, "Oh, man, not again." I have one in particular, I called him over to the steps and said, "Did you find what you're looking for? If you didn't find it, maybe you should go back and look again." And they get embarrassed, if you

embarrass a male inmate, nine times out of ten he's not going to come back on you with anything.

Rather than write sex cases up, you can embarrass [the inmate] in such a way in front of his peers such that the next time that you're on the cell block, he'll be under his covers. And I did that quite frequently, and it got to where when I got on the block, I didn't have that problem. [laughs] It worked for me.

Visible masturbation by male inmates could be read as a strategy for re-asserting the "natural" gendered hierarchy implicit in heterosexuality, one in which men are active and aggressive, and women are passive and compliant. In reacting assertively and publicly, these women turn the usual arrangement on its head, catching inmates off guard and embar-rassing them in such a way that they keep their sexual activities within informally established boundaries (i.e., they stay "under the covers"). Most of the women who work in men's prisons use this kind of strategy and find that it works satisfactorily (though how many leave as a result of their frustration in dealing with this behavior I cannot say). Even so, the very fact that women must be exposed to this behavior serves as one of the two primary grounds (the other is their presumed inability to deal with physical violence) that male officers and supervisors who oppose women's presence give for their position. In this, they invoke a protec-tionist model of masculinity, arguing that there are some things to which women simply should not be exposed.

At first glance, this account of the challenges women officers face in men's prisons contradicts much of what precedes it. Women COs prefer work in men's prisons and report that male inmates give them more re-spect and (for good or ill) protection from violence. Some officers even assert that women can command *more* obedience from male inmates. Two factors help to resolve this paradox. First, to the extent that women command more obedience, they do so in line with gendered ideals about feminine protection and masculine deference. Prevailing patterns of gen-der socialization dictate a certain masculine chivalry; women are to be protected from other men, and assistance with gender-typed tasks (such as changing a tire or taking out the garbage or opening a jar) is to be provided upon request. This does not represent an inversion of gen-dered power, however, but rather visibly underlines difference. These expectations structure interactions in prison as well. This white woman's observation illustrates this point:

> When an inmate is getting in trouble for something, getting disciplined or told what to do, he'll pay attention to what a male officer tells him quicker than he will a female officer. Because men aren't supposed to listen to what women tell them to do. And I think that male officers get a little more respect. We have a lot harder time in dealing with [inmates]. But when we want them to do something for us, they tend to jump to it a lot quicker than they would a male. *Why do you think that is?* I don't know, I guess because when your mother tells you to do something, you go try to do it. If you ask them to do something to help you [they will], but as far as fussing at them, they're going to listen to the men.

There are obvious limits to the exercise of any gendered advantage by women officers. Whatever respect they may receive is discounted by other norms that constrain the kind of power that women may routinely exercise over men. Though women COs may request and receive masculine deference, in response they have more difficulty commanding obedience.

The "benefits" of femininity may extend to some groups of women officers more than others. In American culture generally, ideals of "true womanhood" are racialized. Under the cloak of the mythology of the pure, delicate, dependent woman of myth has always been the body of a white (middle-class, native-born) woman. African-American women have never enjoyed the chivalrous protection of white men, and African-American men have been systematically denied the resources that would have enabled them to provide it. Historically, African-American men have also been subject to the power of white women in ways that white men have not. In the context of the prison, white women may well be the primary beneficiaries of male inmates' deference. This white woman CO in a men's prison speculates:

> I think that white females have a much easier time dealing with black inmates than black female officers. Because I think that in society, there's a hierarchy where white males are at the top, and then probably white females are pretty close to black males, but black women are always at the bottom. I think that black males have a little more respect for us. Black women have a lot harder time here than the white women, because black men have a harder time, like taking orders and respecting them.

It is true that white women COs in my study are much more likely than their counterparts of color to report the respect and protection of male inmates. This may explain why the scant research on the topic (e.g., Britton 1997b) indicates that white women are particularly satisfied with their work in prisons; African-American women report much lower levels of satisfaction. In prison, as in culture, race attenuates even the dubious rewards that accrue to femininity.

Finally, the apparent paradox between women's preference for work in men's prisons and their accounts of the challenges they face may also be explained by the fact that the particular obstacles women must over-come in dealing with male inmates are simply not the most salient fac-tors in shaping their overall perception of their work. Such behavior, though extreme in content, is not so different in form from the harass-ment women experience from men in the free world on a routine basis. For example, though a substantial number of women mention witness-ing masturbation, I did not get the sense from any of them that they experience high levels of distress in dealing with this behavior. This African-American woman is typical:

> As far as the inmates go, with the jacking off, well, I'm thirty-five years old, so there's nothing that I haven't seen. So, as you would do a child, "You know better than this, you do this at home," that's basically what you give them. And then, they're so embarrassed, "Okay, Miss [name], I won't do it anymore, I'm sorry."

Some women COs, particularly those in the federal system, believe that the policies in place at their institutions are sufficient to deter and/or punish this behavior. Others, like this officer, are confident in their abil-ity to utilize informal strategies. Regardless, the difficulties women face in asserting authority and dealing with sexual banter and harassment from male inmates do not, on the whole, lead them to abandon their preference for work in men's prisons.

An Officer and a Gentleman: Men COs, Women's Prisons

Except for a brief interruption during the reformatory era, men have always worked in women's prisons. When employed in small numbers, their primary role was to serve as enforcers, providing physical force (or the threat of force) as a last resort in controlling recalcitrant inmates. As explicitly gender-neutral hiring and assignment policies have become the norm, men now constitute almost half of officers in women's prisons. Ongoing court battles have resulted in formal restrictions in their duties, however. In one of the women's prisons I studied, men are not allowed to pat-search women inmates, and so are less likely to be assigned to inmate housing units. In practical terms, this means that the men in my study assigned to women's prisons have less routine contact in close quarters with inmates than do women who work in men's prisons. Even so, the scant evidence collected by other researchers (Owen 1998; Zupan 1992a) indicates that women inmates have generally welcomed the presence of men.[10]

The primary way that officers in women's prisons believe the treatment of male officers differs is in terms of the obedience they can command. This white woman observes:

> I think the men have a little more control over the females than the women, because the female inmates will mouth a lot more to the women than they will to the men, and try the female officers more than they will the male officers.

This Hispanic man's experience underlines this point:

> The men inmates give me a hard time for me being a man, but to the females they're going to be nicer. I think that with females, they try to be nicer to the men, and mean with the women. That's what I noticed.

As the second officer's comment suggests, this seems like a complement to the experience of women COs in men's prisons; women defer to male COs because they are men, as male inmates defer to female COs because they are women.

As West and Zimmerman (1987) observe, however, "doing gender" is always asymmetrical: for men, affirming masculinity means affirming dominance; for women, emphasizing femininity usually means perpetuating subordination. For men, the advantages that accrue to gender in the context of the women's prison derive primarily from the power that accompanies masculinity. In a pattern that harkens back to their days as enforcers, men command respect through intimidation. This white woman explicitly links respect and fear:

Is it your sense that inmates treat male and female officers differently?
Absolutely. Male officers intimidate them, just the sight of being a man.
They show more respect to the men.

Similarly, this white male officer believes that the presence of a male CO
is enough to defuse a potentially violent situation:

> Just the presence of a guy changes the whole [situation]. Because in-
> mates know, hey, he will do that. He will use whatever force, and he
> can do it. A lot of times, we get females, supervisors even, that will
> threaten force and inmates will laugh at them. And a lot of times,
> just the presence of a man in that same situation, it's just different. It's
> intimidating.

This second officer claims later in the interview that male officers are
less likely than women to need to resort to physical violence in restrain-
ing inmates. As the first CO's observation suggests, simply "the sight of
being a man," with its concomitant evocation of strength, is sufficient.

There is a parallel here: COs perceive that men in women's prisons
decrease violence in these institutions, just as women becalm the environment in men's facilities. A very different set of gendered characteristics lies beneath these outcomes, however. Male officers "intimidate"
inmates, but as a result inmates are calmed, and there is less need to resort to physical violence. This intimidation need not be intentional, as
this man suggests:

> I get it all the time, because of my size. Inmates will say, "God, where'd
> they get that big man from? Jeez, he's a mountain!" And I get that
> tossed at me more than anything else. Usually when that happens, it's
> the inmate who's very diminutive, and their entire lives, anyone that
> was bigger than them intimidated them, so . . . It's really funny, some-
> times, the comments they make.

This officer is indeed quite large and could undoubtedly seem threatening. As Connell (1987) suggests, however, it is in the nature of hegemonic masculinity that all men, whatever their physical stature, may lay
claim to the attributes deemed essentially masculine in a particular context. This explains why "just the presence of a man" matters, apart

from any individual male officer's actual size or physical ability. The calming influence said to be exerted by cross-gender officers presents a case in which the same end result is interpreted differently according to the gender of the officer, relies on a different set of gendered traits in each case (i.e., masculine strength versus nurturing femininity), and reproduces a different relationship to power. Women emphasize their seeming weakness to appear less threatening; men evoke—intentionally or not—intimidation through their potential for violence.

As do their women counterparts in men's prisons, some men report being subjected to sexual banter, flirting, and innuendo. This African-American man describes his discomfort:

> I'm no Romeo, but I guess in here all the men are Romeos, and all the eyes are on you. It's very uncomfortable. I can appreciate women now that work in a male institution. *Do you get a little talked about?* Oh, yeah, all the time. You know, you'll be walking by and you'll hear your name just being called. I don't entertain anything.

Officers rarely report witnessing masturbation by women inmates. Instead, women are perceived to harass male officers by exposing themselves. This white male CO recounts a recent incident:

> Well, it's just like, one officer the other day, there was a bunch of women laying out in their bras and underwear. And, uh, they're not supposed to do that. They could've been doing that just to see how he'd react, or you know, what he'd do.

Several men officers discussed seeing women inmates totally or partially nude, and they believe that such displays are provided for their benefit. Institutional rules require that women in dormitories be fully clothed, but violations of these rules are apparently frequent. Though opposite-sex officers are not usually assigned to posts—like showers—that require routine supervision of unclothed inmates, both men and women COs in men's and women's prisons report viewing inmates in various states of undress. Women in men's prisons rarely mention feeling uncomfortable doing this; male COs in women's prisons find it much more disconcerting.

The reason lies in male officers' persistent fear that they will be falsely accused of engaging in sexual relations—consensual or nonconsensual—with female inmates. This is by far the most common theme mentioned by men who work in women's prisons. Many COs report knowing of verified incidents in which male officers had become sexually involved with female inmates. Most, however, believe the majority of women's claims of such acts to be baseless, and they worry that the system will take the side of the inmate if an allegation is made. For this white man, the fear of false allegations is the basis for his preference for working with male inmates:

> I would rather work with male inmates, a hundred percent. *Why?* To my knowledge, we haven't had problems with males having sex or whatever with the female inmates, but if one said something happened, then, and I've seen this several times in here, they tend to believe the female right off the bat. So, say you shook her room down and you took a bunch of stuff from her, and then she and her friends are going to concoct a story on you, you're not innocent until proven guilty, you're on the street, pending investigation. I just don't need that.

Women officers largely take the side of their male coworkers, arguing that the system does not provide them with sufficient protection, as in the case of this white woman:

> You can't rely on an inmate. That's what they're in here for. They're lying, but the administration is the first one to believe an inmate. And I've seen an instance before where two women were caught in bed before by two male officers. So to try and get out of trouble these two inmates said that the officers sat there and watched them. These two officers and another inmate said that it didn't happen, and they still went on for months. An investigation based on that. An inmate can just walk up there and say, "Oh, well, I saw [officer] doing this, this, and this," totally making it up, but they have to investigate it. Even if an inmate says something and it's not true, they never find evidence to support it, there's still always in the backs of people's minds there's, you know, they did it, they just didn't get caught.

More than half of all the federal officers in my study expressed some level of concern about the possibility that false allegations would be made and that the system would take the word of the inmate over that of the officer. It is difficult to overstate officers' anxiety regarding this issue.

This topic was less salient for state officers, which may provide a clue to its prevalence among federal COs. The federal system has been more proactive than the state system in incorporating material on officer sexual misconduct in its training curriculum. This may well be related to the fact that some recent high-profile lawsuits involving the sexual assault of women inmates by male officers have originated in federal prisons. It may also be part of the generally more progressive and extensive training offered to federal officers. Regardless, one effect of this curriculum has apparently been the creation of a climate of fear. This white male CO observes:

> When they train new officers, they tend to put scare tactics into male officers about working with females. And that intimidates a lot of the male officers when they come here. And some of the male officers think, well, gee, I can't do nothing, because they're gonna file on me for sexual harassment or they're going to file on me for this, that and the other. The biggest problem with male officers working here is the training, because they scare 'em.

A "better safe than sorry" philosophy in training, combined with the somewhat greater level of seriousness with which inmate complaints are treated in the federal system, creates the perception among male officers that they are always potentially vulnerable to false allegations of sexual misconduct, and that the system will do little to protect them.[11]

Though women officers in men's prisons can also be accused of sexual impropriety, they mentioned nothing like the pervasive fear that I observed among male COs in women's prisons. What explains this difference? One factor is simply that there are more substantiated allegations of sexual misconduct among male officers than among women. A General Accounting Office report from 1999 reveals that between 1995 and 1998, a total of 92 charges of sexual misconduct made by female inmates in California, Texas, the District of Columbia, and the Federal Bureau of Prisons were substantiated and resulted in disciplinary action; in almost all cases, the offenders were male officers (General Accounting Office 1999). This constitutes only 18 percent of the total of 506 allegations reported in these jurisdictions, however. Most of the remaining 82 percent were not sustained due to lack of physical or medical evidence, proof that might understandably be difficult for inmates to produce. Even so, the fact that there were 414 "unsubstantiated" allegations is undoubtedly enough to cause concern among COs and to fuel officers' worries that inmates make such claims solely for the sake of manipulating staff. No similar statistics are available regarding staff sexual misconduct in men's prisons, but my own informal search of media sources turned up only a handful of cases of sexual assault involving male officers and male inmates; the few accounts regarding female COs almost were invariably instances in which women had become involved in "consensual" relationships with male inmates and had been terminated from their jobs as a result. These allegations may be the most feared because they are the most credible, given existing evidence. Such concerns are amplified by stereotypes that frame women inmates as devious, manipulative, and willing to use whatever uniquely "feminine" tools they have at their disposal—tears, flirting, or, in this instance, false allegations—to "get over" on the system.

Challenges in Work with Inmates: Managing Violence and Sex

Finally, two areas emerge from officers' comments as being among the most important challenges in working with inmates: violence and sexuality. These themes resonate with popular conceptions. Portrayals of prisons are awash in violence and rarely omit a hint, if not an actual depiction, of sexual assault; it almost goes without saying that the prisons in question are men's institutions, and the assaultive prisoners are male. Officer comments reflect these commonly held notions in some ways and contradict them in others. Correctional officers are concerned about violence, but they cite just as much of it in women's prisons as in men's. And in terms of sexuality, officers find dealing with women's sexuality a much more consistent challenge than managing that of male inmates. These themes take form in two very different environments in which architectural structures, interactions between inmates and staff, and ideas about inmates' (and officers') "essential" natures come together to construct and reproduce seemingly generic, but in reality gendered, notions about real prisons and typical inmates.

Physical Violence

Most prisons bear little resemblance to the anarchic battlegrounds of popular imagination. Neither inmate assaults on other inmates nor assaults on staff members are everyday occurrences. According to the most recent data available, during 1995 federal and state prisons experienced an average of twenty-two assaults of inmates by other inmates (the median number of assaults was six; 23 percent of facilities reported none) and twelve assaults of staff by inmates (the median number was two; 37 percent reported none).[12] Though these data probably undercount minor altercations, the fact remains that serious violence is far from common in most prisons. Even so, violence and the fear of it are important factors in shaping the day-to-day work of correctional officers. Training, through its presentation of worst-case scenarios, aims to inculcate hypervigilance, and experienced officers pass this value down to new recruits during their first days on the job. Technology augments this posture. COs in many systems now wear body alarms that allow them to sound an alert at the first sign of trouble; some of these devices even signal the central control room automatically if the officer wearing it goes down. Both high-tech and low-tech vigilance are taken for granted, as this white man assigned to a men's prison notes:

> Everybody's scared. If you're not, something's wrong with you. You got to always play the "what if" game, in any situation you're in at work. You're always thinking, what would I do, trying to keep yourself on your toes. What I'm saying is, don't forget where you're at.

I heard this last phrase repeatedly during my interviews and have since seen it and heard it uttered many times in correctional training materials and seminars. It invokes contingent violence, serving as a shorthand reminder that, no matter how comfortable you may feel, you must always be "on your toes," alert for the possibility that violence may break out. In the final analysis, many officers believe that even though they may befriend inmates or at least develop good working relationships with them, should violence break out, inmates will stick together. As this African-American woman officer in a men's prison puts it:

> [The inmates] know just who they can get over on. I just don't like to play with them. Like they say, when the lights go out, you're going to be the first one he's going to try to stab. I don't care, you don't have no friends in here. You might think they are, but when something really goes down, you find out you don't have any friends.

In its norms and dictates regarding violence the occupational subculture is framed very much in terms of a distinction between us and them. In one of the systems I studied, this contrast is often expressed through the medium of the color of uniforms. Inmates wear white; officers wear gray. COs sometimes describe particular inmates with the caveat that, no matter how helpful or trustworthy they may seem, they are still "wearing white."

INMATE ASSAULTS ON INMATES

Assaults on inmates are much more common than assaults on staff. This is at least partly because of the sanctions attached to the latter: inmates who assault officers may face felony charges, but those involved in altercations with other inmates (those that do not result in death or serious injury) are more likely to face some institutional sanction, such as loss of privileges or "good time" or a stay in segregation. Overall, officers in my study express much less concern about inmate-on-inmate violence than assaults on staff; the former poses less danger to COs except in the extremely unlikely event that it escalates to a riot. The attitude of officers toward such assaults is that they are sometimes inevitable, and dealing with the consequences is part of the job. This white male CO in a men's prison exemplifies this perspective:

> *Have you had many incidents of violence, be they inmate on inmate or inmate on staff, in the last six months or so?* I was around for one within the last six months. I was working on the day shift, and a body alarm went off in the food service, and I was the first one to get over there. It was just an inmate-on-inmate assault. Nothing major. Both of 'em had stopped, you could see the officers coming across the compound, they had stopped by the time we got over there, so . . . *So there was nothing to it by the time you got there?* Yeah, just a little bit of blood, and both of 'em were still standing.

This officer's framing of the fight as "just an inmate-on-inmate assault" captures the routine way many describe these incidents. Fights are neither everyday events in most prisons nor do they appear to create excessive concern among COs. This is true for both men and women. Those I interviewed in state prisons are somewhat more likely than their federal counterparts to relate stories of inmate violence. This fits with the national picture; inmate assaults are more common in state than in federal institutions, in part because federal facilities typically hold inmates who have been convicted of less serious crimes. Federal facilities are also governed by a standardized set of security procedures, are often of more recent construction, and utilize more advanced security technology than their state counterparts.

Officers in women's prisons are just as likely as those in men's to relate incidents of inmate on inmate assaults. This situation also reflects national data.[13] The primary difference lies in the way officers characterize these assaults. Mirroring their attitudes about women inmates' character more generally, COs see fights among women inmates as petty, labeling them "cat fights." This white man describes the difference between men's violence and women's "cat fighting":

> *When you say women get into cat fights, what are they fighting about?*
> Could fight about anything. Girlfriends, things like that. You stole this, or you said this to other people about me. *And when the men are fighting, what are they fighting about?* Could be fighting about anything. Could be fighting about drugs, and stuff like that.

Officers use the phrase "cat fight" only to refer to altercations between women. Such a fight, according to COs (and in common parlance), is provoked by something "petty" and involves screaming, hair pulling, scratching, and other "unfair," "unmasculine" techniques. A real fight, by definition, one in which the participants are men, is "extremely violent, even deadly," and has what officers see as a legitimate instrumental basis.

Officers often say they prefer dealing with the latter. The threat of serious inmate violence is one of the defining characteristics of a "real"—men's—prison. At one of the women's prisons I studied, the segregation unit consists of two glassed-in rooms with bunk beds. When I asked a male officer about them, he laughed derisively and wanted to know if I had ever seen a real segregation unit. The only reason these cells were ever used, he said, was for cat fights. Similarly, this African-American man hopes to transfer out of the women's prison in which he currently works:

> Believe me, I'm not into the action where you gotta fight every day and gas people every day. I've been through all that. I just wanna go some-

where a little higher up. Where you'll have something to do every now and then. I think a person stays here too long, he can really lose touch with what an institution is.

It is the *lack* of serious inmate-on-inmate violence that marks women's prisons as something less than real prisons. Both men and women COs see women's prisons in this way, which confirms that the generic "prison," the essence of "what an institution is," incarcerates men. The few officers who prefer work in women's prisons often do so because they make an explicit choice to avoid the violence in men's prisons.

INMATE-ON-STAFF ASSAULTS

Few things create instant solidarity among officers like an attack on one of their number (Kauffman 1988). A handful of the officers I interviewed had been victims of inmate assaults, though the consequences of those incidents, which included a stabbing with an ink pen, and slapping, hitting, grabbing, and shoving by individual inmates, were relatively minor. A few COs reported receiving threats on their lives. Officers related perhaps a dozen anecdotes of assaults at their institutions or at others, attacks on other COs that involved being slapped, knocked down, scalded with hot soup, hit with a glass jar full of liquid, beaten with a shoe and an ash can, burned with a curling iron, and struck from behind with a bucket. There was also one account of a rape of a female officer by a male inmate. Almost all these cases involved moderate to severe injury; no officer described witnessing a fatal attack.

As in the case of inmate assaults on other inmates, officers in my study who work in women's prisons are just as likely as those in men's facilities to relate accounts of inmate assaults on staff. Again, this mirrors nationally collected data, which indicate that the number of staff assaults in women's prisons does not differ significantly from that in men's prisons.[14] Officers recount serious attacks in both men's and women's prisons. These stories, from a white male CO in a men's prison and a Hispanic woman in a women's prison, are typical:

A couple of months ago we had an inmate, I would say, try to kill a staff. It was with a bucket, he hit him over the back with it. The staff and the inmate were wrestling, and then another inmate came in and rescued the staff, and everybody else just ganged in.

We had an officer on our shift, she was sitting at the table, and there's this window that goes into the bedroom area. She was a hard-core officer, I mean, she would write them up for every little thing. She was not afraid of them, she just got right in their face, and I thought she agitated needlessly, sometimes. But, anyway, one of the inmates filled a plastic pitcher full of water, and when she wasn't looking, they threw it at her through the window, and she had to have, like, eight stitches. Luckily she had a radio, and she was able to call for help. Something like that happens, it's like that line between white and gray, it just becomes big and wide.

As a result of the first case, the inmate faced felony charges and was sentenced to serve additional time. I have no information on the outcome of the second example, though similar incidents are handled through institutional sanctions, usually time in segregation. There are two especially noteworthy—and somewhat contradictory—strands in these accounts. In the first, an inmate intervenes on behalf of a staff member, an event that underscores the fact that relationships between officers and inmates are not always based in mutual antagonism. In the second, though the CO is critical of the other officer's behavior, she is clear that violence draws COs together—at such moments, the "line between white and gray, it just becomes big and wide."

The threat of sexual assault has been a central feature of both legal and popular discourse framing men's prisons as inappropriate places for women to work. None of the women I interviewed had been sexually assaulted, and fewer than a half dozen women talked about being fearful of being raped by an inmate. No officer provided an account of a sexual assault at any of the facilities in which they worked, but this African-American woman CO relates a story of an assault at another facility:

[An inmate] raped this woman in the day room. He got mad because she changed the [television] channel, and he beat her up. They say he took something out, I want to say it was a shoe, they say he had his shoe, they say he just started hitting her with it. I've heard so many stories about that.

A white woman speaks of living with the fear of sexual assault:

You've always got that in the back of your mind because you never know what one of them can do, or what one of them will do, because they all can do it. If you're on a [cell] block up on the third floor of a block, you're on a [walkway] about three feet wide with forty inmates walking up and down it. The officer in the [control room] can't see you down there. They could throw you in one of the cells and do whatever they wanted to and be through with you before anyone could come up there and help you. There is always that chance. You've just got to keep that in the back of your mind and not worry about it.

This topic came up only rarely. It may be that this concern is simply not omnipresent for female officers. In fact, many feel safer in the relatively supervised milieu of the prison, where other officers are constantly present, than in the more uncontrolled environment outside. As one white woman puts it, "I feel safer here than I do at [a convenience store] at three o'clock in the morning in downtown [large city]." This attitude is not uncommon among female COs and contradicts commonly accepted notions about men's prisons. Women often deconstruct the notion of the men's prison as a site of unimaginable violence, finding greater reason for fear in the free world.

THE PARADOX OF WOMEN'S VIOLENCE AND THE MEANING OF "ASSAULT"

There are no significant differences between men's and women's prisons, either in my study or in the most recent national census of prisons, in the rates of inmate assaults on other inmates or on staff. This stands in stark contradiction to notions about women, and women's institutions, as somehow kinder and gentler than their male counterparts. It may be simply that we have been wrong about women, perpetuating a "deceptive distinction" (Epstein 1988) between men's and women's essential natures that obscures women's potential for violence. Indeed, many officers in women's prisons are quick to point out that women can be just as dangerous as men. The stories I heard of women inmates who had beaten officers, stabbed them with ink pens, beaten them with trash buckets, or thrown hot coffee or pitchers of water at them certainly undermine the assumption that women in prison are passive and nonviolent.

Other information calls this apparent equality into question, however. On measures such as staff and inmate fatalities resulting from assaults, women's prisons are clearly safer. In 1995, women's prisons reported no deaths in either category; in men's state and federal prisons, fourteen staff and seventy-four inmates died as a result of assaults. My interviews, as well as other research, also demonstrate that women inmates are much less likely than men to possess contraband such as "shanks" (handmade knives) or guns. This white woman confirms the absence of such weapons in the women's institution in which she works:

> *In men's institutions you see things like toothbrushes turned into knives or something like that. You don't see anything like that here?* No. Here if we [need to] have weapons for training purposes, we have to make them ourselves.

As anyone who has ever toured a men's prison can attest, one of the staples of such a visit is the display of the collection of contraband collected from inmates. Such items usually include shanks fashioned from a variety of materials, such as razor blades melted into toothbrush handles. This exhibition is intended to underline the true danger of the institution and the inmates, as well as the vigilance of the staff. I have never seen such an exhibit during a visit to a women's prison.

The picture conveyed by the data on rates of assaults may well be an artifact of the masculinized regime of control in operation at prisons in general, regardless of whether they house men or women. Emile Durkheim, in his famous discussion of the normality of crime, argues that acts collectively defined as "criminal" or "deviant" exist in all societies. Because of this apparent universality, he argues, the social reaction in which acts are so labeled must be very important to the functioning of all healthy societies. Among other things, in defining behavior as deviant or criminal, we set the boundaries of those acts that are acceptable while at the same time identifying ourselves as members of a law-abiding collectivity. It is for this reason that crime and deviance will always be with us, no matter how virtuous we may be:

> Imagine a society of saints, a perfect cloister of exemplary individuals. Crimes properly so called, will there be unknown; but faults which appear venial to the layman will create there the same scandal that the ordinary offence does in ordinary consciousness. If, then, this society has the power to judge and punish, it will define these acts as criminal and will treat them as such (Durkheim 1950 [1895]: 68–69).

Simply put, what Durkheim suggests is the operation of a sort of functional "sliding scale" of deviance definition—in a society of extreme conformity, the most minute divergence from the norm will be defined as criminal. Without such criminal "others," it is impossible to define the boundaries of the law and morality that bind individuals together. More so than society as a whole, prisons rely for the justification of their very existence on sharpening the lines between right and wrong, between the criminal and the noncriminal. Regardless of the security level or the "objective" amount of violence in a particular prison, inmate character and behavior must serve as the raison d'être of incarceration.

In general, women are imprisoned for less serious crimes than men, are less likely to be recidivists, and tend to be housed in lower-security facilities. Though women inmates may not constitute a "society of saints," they are, on the whole, less violent than men on most measures. The apparent equality of men's and women's rates of assaults may be at least partially accounted for by the very sort of sliding scale of deviance that Durkheim envisioned. In a study of Texas inmates, Dorothy McClellan (1994) finds that women are more likely to be cited for minor rule infractions, and much more likely to be severely punished for them. Similarly, this African-American male CO in a women's prison observes that acts which would never draw attention in a men's prison are the subject of considerable scrutiny in the women's prison to which he is now assigned:

> Here, it seems like the little things they blow up out of proportion. Maybe it's little things here because nothing really happens here. They tend to take the little things and harp on them and keep harping on them. It's just little things to where in other facilities like maximum security they have other things to worry about like killings. . . . *What is an example of a petty rule?* Like matchsticks on the concrete. Some people, if they see one matchstick they start yelling, "Why is this here?" "Get them out of here." In a maximum-security facility they have a thousand matchsticks on the ground, but as long as you're not fighting and killing each other or you're obeying the rules, you're not in there with any kind of drugs or anything like that, what's wrong with a matchstick being on the ground?

Dropping a matchstick may well become a serious offense in an environment in which "nothing really happens." By extension, acts that would probably not merit the definition of "assault" in a men's prison may well be so labeled in a women's institution, as this white female CO observes:

Have you had any violent incidents or assaults in the last six months or so in this facility between inmates or between inmates and officers? Inmates, yeah. They had a little scratching fight a while back. When we're talking fight we're not talking about a real fight, but more of pushing each other. One person did get scratched. There was a staff assault when someone got milk poured on them. I'm serious.

Some critics contend that the regime of control in women's prisons, in which hypersurveillance transforms what seem to be relatively minor infractions into major violations, amounts to infantilization, or treating women like children (Belknap 2001; Carlen 1983; Fox 1975; Leonard 1983; O'Brien 2001). My study provides some support for this view. It also reveals that the logic of incarceration itself, at the heart of which is a sorting process in which the label "criminal" is affixed, is both self-perpetuating and based in masculinized ideas about who criminals are and the kind of environment that holds them. Prisons, in a generic sense, contain "bad" people, of unspecified gender, who, by definition, have the potential to harm others. Regardless of actual inmates' behavior, the mechanisms of prison surveillance and control operate to reproduce this notion. Statistical data indicating equality in counts of "assaults" in men's and women's prisons are not numerical representations of predefined behavior. Rather, they are the outcome of the application of a sliding scale of deviance definition in two very different, and gendered, contexts.[15]

Sexuality

The fact that officers are called upon to manage the sexuality of inmates is one of the key features that differentiates the prison from more typical work environments. Prisons are total institutions; like the military and the monastery, they encompass the entire lives of their residents. Because of this, the job of the CO involves a considerable amount of body work, from performing body cavity and strip searches, to shower supervision, to the enforcement of organizational rules regarding sexual behavior. Through policy, prisons typically deal with sexuality in a repressive manner, forbidding almost all forms of sexual activity. Sex between inmates and staff is usually grounds for disciplinary action or dismissal; in many states, staff may also be held criminally liable. Masturbation and sex between inmates are handled differently, however. In everyday practice, officers, supervisors; and administrators tolerate limited noncoercive sexual behavior, as long as such conduct respects norms around privacy.

Officers in men's prisons rarely broach the topic of sexuality among male inmates. This is an unexpected finding. The rape of men by other men is one of the most enduring public images associated with incarceration; both comic and tragic stories about (men's) prison life turn on this event.[16] Men's prison architecture itself often makes homosexuality strikingly visible through the segregation of "known" gay inmates in special sections of the institutions. For instance, the state prison I studied has what officers call a "gay block." This white male officer describes inmates housed in this area:

Most of the homosexuals on the [unit] are all on that one block. That's safekeeping. *Why the segregation?* Most of them ask for it. They shower by themselves so we can watch them. They're just weak, easy prey for the other ones. But not all the homosexuals are there. We usually watch out for them. . . . If he and his boyfriend decide to go to chapel together, or there's anywhere they can find a place together, they will. [We just] watch out for them.

As this officer's comment indicates, the dominant image of homosexuality in men's prisons conflates gender and sexuality, framing homosexuality as gender inversion. In a universally accepted strict dichotomy, one partner, the receiver in oral or anal sex, is seen as "weak" or, in prison jargon, a "punk." In a context in which masculinity is conflated with physical strength, homosexual inmates are perceived as "not men" (Coggeshall 1991; Tewksbury 1989a, 1989b; Wooden and Parker 1982). Homosexual male inmates are often described in terms that suggest inversion: as having high voices and feminine mannerisms and expressing a preference for certain typically "feminine" pursuits.[17] The "dominant" partner in such interactions is almost never described in these terms.

While one woman did speak of witnessing the rape of a male inmate, the handful of other stories I heard involved either prostitution or consensual relationships.[18] This white woman relates her experience:

Of course, sometimes you catch the inmates having sex with each other. *And then what do you do?* Well, after you finish laughing at them, and embarrassing them, and talking shit to them, you usually separate them, if they're stuck together . . . [laughs] . . . and you write them up, give them a disciplinary case. That's all you can do to them.

As her reaction shows, this woman clearly sees sexual behavior between inmates as trivial. This attitude is not at all uncommon; with the exception of those who mention rape, officers who raise the subject of sex between men inmates always do so in a manner that suggests that it is not a particularly important concern.[19]

In contrast, sexual interaction between inmates is a central issue for officers at women's prisons. Despite the absence of questions on my interview schedule specifically addressing the topic, approximately two-thirds of the COs in these institutions discussed lesbian relationships between inmates (and between inmates and staff). Women's prisons are sexualized in a way that men's prisons are not. This reflects the preoccupations of both popular culture and academic research. Cultural representations of men's and women's prisons differ primarily in that fictional portrayals of men's prisons revolve almost exclusively around violence, whereas portrayals of women's prisons revolve around sexuality. This is the case in the academic literature as well. While prison violence has been a central concern of men's prison researchers, even a cursory examination of the literature on the women's prison reveals the ubiquity of the topic of lesbian relationships. Almost all the early studies of women's prisons deal with the topic of homosexuality (Giallombardo 1966; Ward and Kassebaum 1965; Pollock-Byrne 1986). Early accounts place relationships between women squarely in the realm of deviant behavior, wholly due to the unnatural (i.e., sex-segregated) conditions of incarceration. The following observation is characteristic:

> The newly arrived female prisoner is placed in a situation in which any source of relieving the pains of imprisonment holds great attraction. . . . Despite efforts of the staff to cope with the problem, there remains for many women only the comfort and help that can come from a close association with another individual. And the persons who are the quickest, most available, and most aggressive in offering information and solace are homosexual. (Ward and Kassebaum 1971: 53)

Both popular and academic representations of the prison have relied on the stereotype of the predatory lesbian, who seeks and "turns out" vulnerable, newly arrived inmates. This view takes heteronormativity as its reference point and frames lesbian relationships as deviance to be explained and repressed by the institution.

It is possible to read these relationships as resistance. From this perspective, female inmates attempt to subvert the repression of their imprisonment by constructing their own families and, indeed, entire communities, in which primary emotional relationships are central. This standpoint, which is less objectifying than other perspectives and more cognizant of women's agency, sees sexuality and sexual identity as mutable and socially constructed, but it is largely missing from academic research on the women's prison. COs' perceptions of these relationships are much more in line with the former view than the latter.

Officers describe sexual relationships between women in very different terms than do COs in men's prisons. Language suggesting gender inversion is rare. COs often draw on family imagery in describing women's connections to one another, as in the case of this white male officer:

> The gangs, where the men have gangs, women don't have them. Women have social cliques, they have homosexual groups where this is my boyfriend, or this is my husband, these are our kids. And that's how they hang together.

Similarly, this African-American man who had previously worked in a women's prison observes:

> Women, they group together for social needs, you know, they have family structures. Like, some one of 'em might be a mother to the daughters, and they'll call each other mom, daughter. With men, the gangs, they're totally different. It's all about power. It's all about power, I'm head, and I lead, and we go beat up these guys and that's that. But, it's not that way with women.

These officers' comments describe what researchers have called "pseudofamilies" or "prison families" (Burkhart 1973; Giallombardo 1966; Heffernan 1972; O'Brien 2001). Ethnographic research supports their observations; structures of this kind have been reported only in women's prisons.[20] These COs attribute these familial relationships to their belief that inmates have different styles of interaction, and that intimate, openly affectionate relationships are important to women, whereas power is important to men.

Officers generally agree that relationships between women are consensual. As one woman puts it, "On the women's unit, if a woman wants to go with another woman, she's the one to say yes. They don't force it." Officers who had worked with both male and female inmates describe a greater depth of intimacy in relationships between women. Sex between men is more commonly described as instrumentally oriented (e.g., intended to satisfy a biological need, without emotional connections), and perhaps this is part of what makes sex between men seem less problematic. Sex between female inmates is more likely to be depicted in the context of an intimate, emotional relationship, and officers commonly conflate intimacy and sexuality in talking about homosexuality among female inmates. This white woman offers an explanation for why women become "prison gay":

> Women, when you're growing up, you always combed each other's hair, you always hugged each other, or whatever. And women need that bonding with somebody, you know, that attention. They need to feel like they're wanted. And when they come onto the unit, even if they weren't homosexual in the free world, they soon would be.

This officer's conception of sexual identity is fluid, in that she sees normal female gender socialization as conducive to the kinds of relationships she observes among female inmates. Combing hair, hugging, and bonding segue seamlessly into homosexuality in the prison context.

This material raises a very important question, however. If COs agree that relationships between women are consensual and based on genuine emotional connection, then why is this theme so salient for officers in women's prisons? One reason may be the sheer visibility of women's relationships. Lacking a strong taboo on doing so, women are freer to openly and physically express affection. In one women's prison I toured, inmates walked down sidewalks holding hands, and several pairs of women had their arms around one another. This level of open physical display between women would be unusual in the free world, but it seemed hardly worthy of comment in the institutional setting. At the women's prisons in this study, displays of this kind are less common, no doubt because of more punitive institutional policies. These rules can be difficult to enforce, however, as this white female officer's experience demonstrates:

> You're sitting in [the recreation room], and they can't be lying in each other's laps, they can't be lying [together] on the floor. They've got to have space between them. You're supposed to be able to see the wall. I walk around, and it's, "Get some space." And I'm thinking, if I have to come around and tell these women to get some space again, they're all going home. I mean, I'm just going to kick them out. You either just kick them out or you just write them up.

The open expression of affection between women in prison, *whether or not it is accompanied by a sexual relationship*, means that officers in women's institutions are forced to deal with this behavior in one way or another. Some are quite matter-of-fact; this officer sees enforcing such policies simply as part of her job and holds little personal animosity toward the inmates themselves over their relationships.

Most officers are less positive. Some are straightforwardly heterosexist, as in the case of this white female officer:

> The homosexuality [was one of the hardest things to get used to]. I was never exposed to any of that before I went to work here. *And what makes it hard to deal with?* I guess because it's such a way of life with them. It doesn't matter to them. There's no respect. There's no dignity, there's nothing. And I have never known these type people before. Never. It just doesn't matter what they do, what they say, when they say it, where they do it. It doesn't matter. It's very sickening.

This officer has a deep personal aversion to relationships between inmates and sees them as a sign that the women involved have little respect, either for themselves or for others. Many COs in women's prisons express similar, though perhaps less extreme, sentiments. At best, mirroring much of the classic academic literature, they see lesbian relationships as a response to the pains of incarceration. Women become "prison gay" and then resume "normal" heterosexuality upon release.

Conclusion

In his classic work *Asylums*, Erving Goffman (1961) writes that through their daily work, staff in total institutions like the prison participate in the construction and maintenance of an "institutional perspective" about their client population, one that serves the functional purpose of rationalizing the divide between "us" and "them." My study reveals that a contextualized theory of human nature is a key part of the everyday working knowledge of the correctional officer. The conditions of incarceration, which ironically sometimes foster more intimacy among officers and inmates than that which sometimes exists with their friends and families, produce a contradictory set of notions, however. Inmates are human, but not equal; they are too privileged, but not undeserving of rights.

This study also demonstrates in a myriad of ways that Goffman's elegant formulation imposes an artificial consensus. The extreme overrepresentation of offenders of color means that many African-American and Hispanic officers find it more difficult to impose the rhetorical divide at the heart of this ideology, often taking a more humanistic and rehabilitative view than their white counterparts. Ideas about "them" are both generic and gendered. Stereotypes about women's emotionality, manipulation, and pettiness combine to form the basis for officers' preference for work with men, who through the influence of structure, training, and shared assumptions, become the apparently generic, but in reality gendered, inmate.

Officers share some challenges that derive from the conditions of incarceration itself and the kinds of interaction that emerge from it, such as surviving an initiation period and dealing with everyday, low-level harassment. While doing their jobs, however, officers are also doing gender. In the men's prison, notions about women's essential nature underlie their struggle to establish authority and influence the kinds of sexualized harassment to which they are subject. Men draw on the connection between masculinity and physical force to exert power as enforcers in women's prisons, and it is the nexus between masculinized sex and violence that places them at the center of charges of sexual impropriety. Doing time is also about doing gender. Men's violence is expected; women's violence takes on added significance in institutions that are not "real prisons." In the same way that women officers become signifiers for the sexual in men's prisons, so too do women inmates' relationships with one another become a central preoccupation for the officers who find themselves behind bars with them.

While work with inmates is arguably the center of most officers' day-to-day existence, this is not the whole story. Relationships with coworkers, supervisors, and administrators are, for many, even more important factors in shaping their perceptions of, and satisfaction with, their work. It is to this topic that I now turn.

6

The Rest of the Job

Coworkers, Supervisors, and Satisfaction

The fact that inmates are an involuntary population is what defines the prison as a total institution, and it makes the job of the correctional officer nearly unique in the realm of occupations. Many other features place it squarely in the mainstream, however. The organization in which officers do their jobs is bureaucratically structured along conventional lines, and COs' day-to-day work responsibilities—for example, completing reports and other paperwork, managing the movement of people from place to place, enforcing rules and solving "client" problems—do not differ greatly from those of other service workers. It is these most conventional aspects of the job that officers find most problematic. As this African-American woman in a men's prison observes:

> The inmate stress I can take because they're there, and not by choice. And I can understand them being a little grouchy, and not happy with their situation. But for the supervisor to create more than 90 percent of the stress, or the COs, no.

This finding is not atypical (see, e.g., Jurik and Halemba 1984; Schulz, Greeley, and Brown 1995). In almost any occupation involving people work, workers discover that the primary source of stress is usually not the unruly client or rude customer, whose behavior can be understood or at least rationalized as part of the job, but inflexible and illogical work rules, inept colleagues, or incompetent and unsupportive supervisors.

This chapter returns to the more conventional terrain of the sociology of work and organizations and examines these aspects of the work of the correctional officer. In terms of the composition of their frontline workforce, men's and women's prisons have been, throughout much of their histories, sex segregated organizations. Men's prisons are largely staffed by male officers, and women's institutions have been dominated by women. The story of the integration of men's and women's prisons reflects much of what we already know about the asymmetrical experiences of men and women who enter occupations dominated by the other sex. Far from being generic "tokens" who face resistance due to their rarity (Kanter 1977), men are advantaged in women's domains such as elementary school teaching, social work, and nursing. They are welcomed by coworkers, advance to supervisory positions more quickly, and earn higher salaries than equally qualified female counterparts. Women in male-dominated occupations have not fared as well, facing resistance from coworkers and supervisors who see women as unsuited for masculinized tasks that range from policing (Appier 1998; Martin 1980; Miller 1999; Prokos and Padavic 2002), to management (Kanter 1977; Sheppard 1989; Martin 2001), to cooking fast food (Leidner 1991, 1993). Women in male-dominated occupations generally make less and are less likely to be in supervisory positions than equally qualified male coworkers.

The same is true in prison work. Nationally, men hold most top positions, constituting the majority of administrators in both men's and women's prisons. As of 1995, 46 percent of men's prisons had no female administrators at all, while only 18 percent of women's prisons had no male administrators.[1] All but one of the top administrators in the prisons I studied is a man. All the correctional supervisors in the two men's facilities are men; neither has a female supervisor in a custody position (though women had previously been in supervisory roles at one). The opposite is true in the women's prisons in the study; in one, the majority of supervisors are women, though men are overrepresented; in the others, the majority of supervisors are men.

Thus men are more likely to be in powerful positions whether a prison houses women or men, or, to return to the more general picture, whether an occupation is male- or female-dominated. The same is true about race—it is not just men but white men who occupy most positions of power in organizations. This is certainly the case in the current study. But there are other ways that we can see gender and race at work in organizations. Interactions with coworkers and supervisors draw upon and reinforce stereotypes, as do formally and informally sanctioned policies and practices. All these elements come together to shape perceptions of the job, to encourage the adoption of some forms of gendered identities at work and discourage others.

Men's Prisons

Early research on the integration of the officer corps in men's prisons uncovered significant resistance among the white male "old guard" to the presence of women and minority men. In some cases, supervisors and coworkers sabotaged new officers, setting them up for failure by refusing to train them adequately or attempting to induce them to resign through covert and overt harassment (Jurik 1985; Martin and Jurik 1996; Owen 1988; Zimmer 1986, 1987; Zupan 1992b). I collected few stories of this kind; such incidents are almost always conveyed as historical artifacts, or as the actions and attitudes of a few recalcitrant veterans, as this white male officer notes:

> There was resistance, I have to be real honest with you. For many many years the type of work we do was looked at as man's work. When women started coming into men's prisons, I saw a lot of the old-timers, a lot of guys who started out as a correctional officer back in nineteen whatever-the-hell-it-was, and there were no women, basically, unless they were a secretary. And the comments that they made, just, well, she doesn't belong in here. She has no business in here.

This officer, who has more than a dozen years of experience, was starting his career just as the first wave of women came to work in men's institutions. His comments illustrate the ideological positioning of work in men's prisons as appropriate only for men; women belong at home, or if they must work in prisons, they should hold only clerical positions. From his perspective, such notions are a thing of the past, products of the prejudices of unenlightened "old-timers." Like many of his male counterparts, this officer expresses no resistance to women's work in men's prisons. Another African-American male CO puts it this way: "I don't believe in excluding women from this type of thing because it's a job and they can do it just as well as I can do it." Most men in this category take a liberal position that advocates equality in employment, arguing that while some individuals are not suited for the job, women as a category should not be excluded.

But while the kind of blatant resistance the first officer describes may be less common now, these attitudes have not disappeared entirely. A handful of men in my study argue very directly that women should not be allowed to work in men's prisons. A white male correctional supervisor told me straightforwardly that women "don't belong here. They belong in a women's institution. I wouldn't have them at all." Still another white male officer agrees:

> I know that women are going to be working here, because you can't discriminate. Honestly, if I had a penitentiary to run, I wouldn't hire, if I didn't have to, I wouldn't hire them in a men's institution. Because I don't think it's good for business. Security, the sexual harassment that they go through from inmates. I don't think it's a very dignified job for a woman to do. *What is a dignified job for a woman?* Not working in a men's prison.

Male officers who express this sentiment directly are in a distinct minority, and they are concentrated at the state men's prison I studied. This may in part be due to the fact that federal officers are, on the whole, more educated. But these comments hint at two sources of resistance to women's presence even among men whose attitudes are more guarded or conditional. The first, and most salient, concern has to do with security, translated in this context as women's ability to deal with violence. The second issue gets at the notion of "dignity," citing sexual harassment and enticement as reasons that the environment of the men's prison is inappropriate for women.

Contingent Violence

In their early days on the job, all officers must prove themselves, not only to inmates, but also to coworkers and supervisors. In a men's prison, the key to accomplishing this is demonstrating the ability to handle violence. This white male officer provides a particularly vivid example:

> It was one of my first days at [a men's prison], and I was a brand-new officer. I tried to talk to this supervisor, trying to ask questions. You know, "Can I ask you a question?", and he snapped around and pointed his finger and says, "Don't you talk to me unless you have blood on your shift first!" And walked away! And I didn't really know what he meant. Then I found out later on that you had to prove yourself. That means that you had to show people that you're willing to be

just as equal as they are, and protect them, and deal with inmates that way. So, until you're willing to get in there and mix it up, you're not an equal. That was a culture shock. I just wanted to ask him a question, you know!

Though his criterion—"blood on your shirt"—is extreme, for this man's supervisor, as well as for many officers in my study, proving oneself in a men's prison is understood to coincide with showing that one is willing and able to "mix it up" physically with inmates. Doing this is what it means to have the status of officer and to be respected by supervisors and peers.

Men and women must demonstrate this ability if they are to be accepted. But women face barriers that men do not. The first is an ideological equation between masculinity and physical strength that is at the heart of the occupational culture in men's prisons (and in culture at large). Even the most equality-minded of men mitigate their acceptance of women with an assertion of contingent violence—they argue that women handle the job well under normal circumstances but are not as able to deal with inmate violence. The same African-American male officer who above expresses his support for female officers says later:

> I think, of course, if we were in a fight situation or anything like that, that's the only thing I feel where I would be at an advantage more so than they would, but everything else, as far as mentally and such, they can do the same thing I can do.

This white man expresses a similar sentiment:

> I'm not sure if, in a male prison, if most men would feel comfortable knowing that the person that's gonna come to their aid is a female instead of a male.

Here the ability to use physical means to control violence is asserted as an inherent requirement of the job, one that sets the limits of what women are able to contribute.

This kind of categorical assertion relies fundamentally on essentialist notions about masculinity and femininity. These ideas are key components in the prevailing form of occupational masculinity that holds that men, strictly by virtue of being male, are better able to deal with inmate violence than women. The status concomitant with this form of hegemonic masculinity (Connell 1987) can then be claimed by all men in the organization, no matter what their actual physical stature may be. This white male officer is very young and slightly built, but he still feels that women should not be allowed to fill positions requiring inmate contact:

> I think [women] should be assigned to [guard towers and control rooms] . . . inside [control rooms], outside, not with inmates, because if something happened, you know, they're just going to be the first to go, if something came down on the [cell] block. I don't care who, how big the female officer is, I'm going to be able to take care of myself a lot better than they are. You know, that's sexist, but it's realistic.

The fact that this officer has no reservations about making this claim indicates the status available to him through the institutional construction of masculinity. From his viewpoint, it is simply a statement of reality that by definition no woman would be as able to handle violent inmates as he. The possibility that his own physical stature might contradict his assertion indicates the seamlessness of the connection between masculinity and physical strength.

This hegemonic form of occupational masculinity is premised on a notion of femininity that is essentially a negative version of the characteristics attributed to men. Women as a group are excluded a priori from having the characteristics of physical strength and aggressiveness. This white woman describes how this works in practice:

> There was an argument the other day between officers, and one of the men said, "I don't like women in corrections, I feel like if something happens, I'm stuck in this prison when I'm with a female." And the lady officer that he was talking to could make two of me, she could take care of business if something happened! You know, I believe you'd be safe working with her!

Even when female officers meet the requirements of physical size and strength, they are excluded from the status that these characteristics provide for men. This white woman's experience underlines the disjuncture between femininity and the essential requirements of being an "officer":

I do think there's this mentality that a lot of male officers, not really a lot, but some of them, think that females have no business working in this environment. And you might hear comments like from another male officer, "Well, you're good for a female officer." But if I would go to a black officer and say, "Well, you know, for a black officer, you're not bad." I mean, that would be terrible because they'd say you're racist, and what do you mean by that, and if you go to a Hispanic guy, and you say, "You know, for a Puerto Rican, you're pretty good," that would be a big insult. But people say things like that to females all the time, and it's just accepted.

Apparently, the presumption among many male coworkers is that women are not cut out for the job. When women perform adequately, they are still seen through their master status as women—they are "good for a female officer."

The second barrier women face derives from supervisory policies and practices and patterns of interaction with coworkers that draw on and reinforce stereotypes about women's alleged inability to deal with physical violence. On any given day, a CO might be assigned to a variety of posts. The most common posting is in an inmate housing unit, usually a dormitory or a cell block. Other typical assignments involve supervision of inmates in the showers, cafeteria (universally referred to as the "chow hall"), "yard" or "compound," administrative segregation units, visiting rooms, work details within or outside the prison, control room, perimeter control towers, and mobile patrols, or involve working as "roving" officers, performing duties as required by supervisors. I have arranged these roughly in order of the amount of close contact they require with inmates—housing unit officers typically have the most contact, those in towers or on patrols, the least. There is considerable consensus among officers regarding the most preferred assignments. Because they allow for little freedom of movement or variety, housing unit postings rank near the bottom of the list. Compound or roving positions are among the least restrictive; they are among the most sought after. Roving and control room positions are also attractive because of the access they provide to administrators and their centrality in the prison's communication network.

As of this writing, women in both systems are formally restricted only from strip- or cavity-searching male inmates. They are not necessarily barred from posts that require these tasks; in the event that an officer deems that a search is necessary, she requests that a male officer perform this duty. In the state system, women are generally also prohibited from supervising male inmates in the showers. In the federal system, officers bid for posts quarterly, which are then awarded on the basis of seniority. The state has a nominally random rotation system in which supervisors have wide discretion in assigning of officers.

In both systems, I collected some evidence that women's assignments are shaped by supervisors' presumptions that women are less able than men to deal with inmate violence. This practice is much more common at the state level, however. Assignment policies in the federal system are more formalized and bureaucratized, and it is thus more difficult for supervisors' personal preferences to undermine the system through the systematic sex segregation of assignments. The discretion allowed to state prison supervisors means that processes of ascription based on ideas about gender can play a much greater role. This white male CO offers an example of the ways in which seemingly gender-neutral assignment policies at the state men's prison are subverted by gender stereotypes:

> The way the system works is that there's no female officer or male officer, it's just officer. But then, it is different, as in, if you're working outside dorms, they won't put two, there's nothing in writing, but they're not going to put two female officers out there.

Assignments to dormitories outside the main building are perceived as more dangerous because officers there are somewhat isolated. Even inside the main facility, however, women's assignments are sometimes restricted to noncontact positions (such as perimeter security tower positions, control rooms, or positions that require clerical work). This African-American male officer observes:

> Most women here, they have a position where they can possibly type if needed, or work in a control [room] where they're answering the phones, or work beside the supervisors, like the lieutenant or whatever, while the male officers have to work [cell] blocks more.

This Hispanic male officer's experience corroborates this pattern:

Where do you usually work? Building security. The majority of times, close custody. Where, females are usually put in a situation where they're in the control [room], out of the way . . . well, where they can't get hurt. Or, even if they're working roving [between cell blocks or dormitories], they put them where there's someone else they can depend on. They don't put them in close custody.

These comments indicate that perceptions of assignments in men's prisons tend to be dichotomized into "safe" and "unsafe" positions, with the former defined as those with less inmate contact, or less contact with inmates classified as potentially violent. By definition, "unsafe" positions are inappropriate for women.[2]

Male coworkers extend this supervisory practice by acting informally to protect women. This white female officer describes a situation she encountered:

Once there was this huge fight, and one of the inmates was an ex-policeman, so it was a very bad fight. And every time I tried to go in the day room, I kept getting spun around on the stairs [by male officers]. And finally, the lieutenant comes in, I had just barely gotten into the day room, and I said, "I'm so sorry, they kept pushing me off the stairs." And he said, "I don't ever want you in there, I don't expect you to go in there, your place is out here."

This account mirrors those of women in many male-dominated occupations (Williams 1989). By behaving in this way, men do gender by conforming to norms that define them as women's natural protectors. In the process, they also reassert the claim to the unique ability to deal with physical violence. For male COs, staking out this terrain cements the bond between masculinity and occupation.

This connection between masculinity and the work of the officer may account both for the resentment of female officers and for their protection. Psychoanalytic feminists (e.g., Chodorow 1978) argue that masculinity in American culture is defined both as an achieved status and as a negative version of femininity—that is, if "even a girl can do it," a task holds little value for proving masculinity. Many women do indeed perceive that men are threatened by their presence because it undermines the essential masculinity of the work. These white women officers explain:

The men started here, we invaded their territory, and they tend to feel threatened. I've had some try and get in my face about it. *They feel threatened because . . . ?* Some men, I guess they really have this problem of a female possibly outdoing them. When you walk the halls, you don't ever know, an inmate pops you, and a female just happens to be there, and the adrenaline pumps and she pulls him off, how's that going to make him feel, you know? You never know when something like that could happen.

Unfortunately, this line of work does attract a lot of people that get their power and prestige [from their job]. I think that's one reason why men have a problem with women in this job because they get their masculinity from this job just like being a cop. And a female that can do the same job in a penitentiary, man, that's terribly threatening. They say, "Hey, I work the penitentiary, high security," and girls work in it. It's very threatening to them.

This shifts the focus of the resentment and the protection to the potential for embarrassment. If women are kept out, or are prevented from doing tasks that might demonstrate their equality, then the job retains its value as a proving ground for masculinity (Britton and Williams 1996; Williams 1989, 1995).

For women, the situation is considerably more ambivalent. Some happily accept "safe" postings. This white woman exemplifies this attitude:

It's real funny, they're real protective of me. I have one lieutenant, he said, "I'm never going to put you anywhere where I think you're going to be hurt." Okay, and he would never say that to a guy. "I'll never assign you where I think you'll be in danger." And, I think that's *so sweet*! I think it's so sexist, but I mean, I appreciate it!

This officer has a visceral reaction to the sexism implied by this practice but simultaneously embraces what she perceives as its chivalrous intention. Many women are in fact appreciative of the protection of their supervisors and coworkers, and in this way they are similar to officers described by Zimmer (1986) as adopting a "modified" strategy in approaching the job, one in which female officers rely on male protection and seek out safe job assignments.

This approach is one way of claiming a gendered identity at work.

Women are expected to be weaker than men and to accept protection gratefully. The problem is that accepting protection also marks women as less capable in an environment in which the willingness and ability to deal with violence are core components of what it means to be an officer. This white woman describes this double bind:

> I think the males here to a great extent, if you're having difficulty dealing with an inmate, they're just your instant big brothers. They will take care of it. But you don't want that to happen . . . because then you lose control of the situation. Then you have to say, "I was not able to resolve this and I had to turn it over."

This officer identifies her male coworkers not simply as brothers but as big brothers. The notion of fraternity has been used in the workplace to signify a relationship of equality in which workers share conditions and characteristics, as in "the Brotherhood of Teamsters." This is not the imagery invoked here; rather, this woman relies on a notion of hierarchy, in which women are unequal and in need of protection. Though women are expected to accept this gratefully, it also identifies them as weak in an environment in which strength is considered a job requisite.

Such shielding of female officers can also be conducive to resentment by male officers. Women's assignment to protected roles often leads to speculation that they use their sexuality to obtain such assignments. This African-American man describes the rumors that circulated about female officers at another men's unit from which he transferred:

> And that unit, [women] were limited also, a lot more, that's the main, they were mainly the turnkey [officer] instead of a block officer where you have to deal directly with the inmate in a closed environment. *Do you think there's ever any resentment that women get posted to those positions?* Oh, yeah, every day, every day. And that's when you get the rumors and such, you know.

Housing unit postings require a significant amount of contact with inmates, and for most COs such postings are among the least preferred. The practice of not assigning women to these positions gives the appearance that they are receiving preferential treatment. As this officer's speculation illustrates, in an environment in which difference between men and women is framed in terms of the sexual, organizational practices that privilege women will also be perceived in this way. As this CO's reference to the "rumors and such" makes clear, in a context in which men are "officers" and women are "female officers," differences in assignments or treatment are likely to be framed in terms of sexuality.

Still other women actively reject the protection of supervisors and coworkers. This white woman was one of the first female officers in a men's prison to which she was formerly assigned. Her account illustrates the lengths to which women must go to disrupt gendered assignment practices and to undermine assumptions about their capabilities:

> I think the men do get their identity from their job, and I think that they were resentful. When I was in [another men's prison] women didn't go for the forced cell moves.[3] So, you're getting paid the same money, but you didn't work certain housing units, or all they had you for was a token figurehead. I'm not saying that I changed things, but I insisted . . . I remember on one of the forced cell moves they wanted me to run the [video]camera, and I asked the lieutenant if I could be in on the forced cell move, I would really like to do it. I've been bounced before, it's not like I get any thrill from being bounced around, but I just felt that if I get paid the same money as the men, I have to do the same job no matter what it is. My experience is that if you are willing to carry your weight, they will accept you.

This strategy has all the hallmarks of a liberal feminist approach—one in which women do not challenge the hegemonic definition of the officer but instead try to demonstrate that they can meet its requisites. Though this woman and others who emphasize this approach generally believe that they have proven themselves in the face of resistance, enacting this method may be easier for some than others. Doing this successfully to some extent involves unlearning gendered socialization. These women reject the protection of male coworkers and supervisors and are willing to place themselves in violent situations. Women who emphasize this approach often walk a fine line; if they perform "just like a man," their femininity is open to question, yet if they fail to do so, they appear to concede the truth of men's assertions that women just don't belong in men's prisons.

Before moving on, a caveat is in order. While most men and many women officers believe that masculinity is a job requisite for dealing with male inmates, they are very clear that hypermasculinity is not. COs view the "macho" officer extremely negatively and see this posture as potentially dangerous. These COs, sometimes called "badge heavy" or "John Wayne" types, are almost invariably male and are described as likely to yell or "get in the faces of inmates" when reprimanding them or issuing orders. This African-American male CO describes the macho officer:

> Yeah, you get a lot of them here with ego trips. Maybe when they were younger, maybe they were bullied a lot and never could do much about it. Whereas now you're in here and you can totally control this guy. I mean, he has to stand there and listen to everything you say. And he has to accept it. And I think it builds your ego after a while, seeing that, I have total control over your life. *Are those good officers?* No. They're headed for a bad fall. Because they're going to finally meet somebody that's not going to take it. And then, you have to deal with that.

The macho posture is one in which officers abuse their power and incite inmates to the point of violence, and then use the rules to render them powerless to retaliate. COs generally agree that this is an ineffective and inherently dangerous strategy, one that endangers all officers.

Sexuality—Dignity and Seduction

The second source of resistance to women's presence revolves around gendered notions about sexuality. There are two primary modes through which this is expressed. In the first, male officers and supervisors argue that women should not be exposed to sexual harassment and masturbation by male inmates. This African-American woman describes the objections of her male coworkers:

> A lot of the men that work here, they'll quickly tell you that they wouldn't let their wives work here, because they feel it's not a place where women should be. Because one thing they're always talking about is inmates masturbating . . . so, the warden said he wouldn't have his wife working here, to have to go through that.

This white man also frames his comments in terms of how he would feel if his wife worked in a men's prison:

My wife was going to apply here, and we decided that she shouldn't. That was four years ago. And, you know, that was the best choice we ever made. Because I know how those inmates are. *Why wouldn't you want your wife working with you here?* I wouldn't want anyone looking at my wife. I mean, you know, if you're an officer and you stand around here, you see how some of these inmates look at females once in a while. And there's nothing they've done to get in trouble, but if I saw someone look at my wife that way, I'm not the kinda person that would handle it right.

This is another version of the kind of protection described earlier, and such attitudes are fairly common among men in my study. There is a higher level of social acceptability to attitudes of chivalry when they concern wives or other women in one's family, and men may feel more comfortable expressing concerns about women officers in this thinly veiled way.[4]

Because I dealt with this issue at length in chapter 5, I will not belabor it here. Suffice it to say that women officers themselves often find dealing with these behaviors much less problematic than their relationships with male coworkers and supervisors. This African-American woman underlines this point:

Well, I'd had friends that worked at [other prisons] and the biggest complaint everyone had was the supervisors, not the inmates, the supervisors. And they are the biggest problem. But as far as the inmates go, with the jacking off, and all this, well, I'm thirty-nine years old, so there's nothing that I haven't seen.

This officer identifies inmate sexual behavior as a minor irritation compared with her interactions with supervisors. In a pattern similar to that observed in other occupations (Dellinger and Williams 2002), women officers do not define the behavior of male inmates as sexual harassment, as they see dealing with it as part of the job. Male COs' discomfort around this issue may reflect more about the prerogatives of heterosexual masculinity than their female colleagues' concerns for dignity.

The second avenue through which sexuality becomes a source of resistance focuses on concerns that women officers will be seduced by male inmates. In the prison occupational subculture, one of the core normative distinctions is between "strong" and "weak" officers, which is contingent on, but not entirely contained by, notions about gender difference. Men or women COs can be weak, but this term takes on different meanings depending on the gender of the officer. Men (and sometimes women) are "weak" when they are inconsistent, give in to inmate demands, or bring contraband into the prison. For women in particular, however, the primary way in which they are viewed as potentially weak is in terms of their (hetero)sexuality. This is a discourse in which heterosexual desire is naturalized. One supervisor expressed his belief that "sex is the oldest game in town," and that male inmates are naturally going to try to sexually exploit women, be they officers or other staff. This African-American man expresses strong reservations about women's interactions with inmates:

> I have more of a problem with a woman talking to an inmate than a man talking to an inmate because I know a lot of times what the male inmates will talk to the women about, compared to what the male inmates will talk to the men about. I mean, [a male officer] may say, "This football game was great," or this and that. But, the women, [inmates] tend to say, "Boy, you sure smell good today," and [the women say], "Oh, thank you." And, "Boy, your clothes are sure pressed today." Or, "What'd you do last night?" It tends to be more of a pick-up with the women than with the men. *And that's going to be natural.* (Emphasis mine)

The implication is that inmates will inevitably attempt to solicit female officers sexually, and that women will find it difficult to resist due to "natural" heterosexual attraction. As another officer put it, attraction between men and women, "even when the men are inmates," is just the "nature of the beast." This view of sexual desire as constant and irresistible means that female officers are always positioned as potentially weaker on the basis of their sexuality, regardless of whether they ever become involved with an inmate.

Even if female officers do not display this kind of favoritism, they are often perceived to have done so. Almost any contact between female officers and inmates may be viewed by coworkers and other inmates through a lens of sexuality (Fox 1982). This African-American male officer describes his perception of his female coworkers' conversations with inmates:

*Do you think if a male officer is talking to an inmate, and a female offi-
cer is talking to an inmate, sort of the same kind of interaction, do you
think that the perceptions of those interactions are going to be different?* Well, yes, now I know they will. But I guess, women tend to get
more relaxed, from what I've experienced. I've experienced times where
the women have talked to inmates in more of a direct way, and then
sort of gotten relaxed and sort of looked starry-eyed.

Even in the case of hypothetical identical interactions, this officer reaf-
firms the potential weakness of female officers in the face of "natural"
heterosexual desire. The importance of this construction is heightened
by the fact that as in most total institutions, rumor is a fact of life in the
prison, and rumors about sex often achieve greater currency than any
others. These women officers, one African-American and one white, describe how the process works:

The women are tougher on the inmates than men are. . . . They have to
be, because if we aren't, we'd be accused of favoritism, even going so
far as sleeping with the inmates. A male and a female can do the same
exact thing as far as being nice to an inmate, and they'll say, "Well,
what is she doing?" And then if that same male goes back and does
that, nothing's said. *You think rumors follow female officers around a
lot more?* Yes. Yes.

The one bad thing about being a female here is you get a lot of rumors
about you, and a lot of people believe those rumors. And those rumors
have held me back. *And is it your sense that it follows female officers?*
Oh, definitely, and you get one new female, a rumor would be around
about her the next day. *And who spreads these rumors?* Oh, everybody,
everybody. *And are they rumors about female staff with inmates, or female staff with other staff, or female staff with supervisors?* Everything.
Everything!

This heightened visibility is not unlike that described more than two
decades ago by Rosabeth Moss Kanter (1977) in her discussion of "tokens" in corporate environments. In this case, however, the process is
gendered and sexualized. Women's actions are seen through the lens of
cultural and ideological constructions of femininity that mark women
as more sexual and as more vulnerable to seduction than men.[5]

This current of suspicion about the conduct of female officers not only restricts the strategies available to them in dealing with inmates but also circumscribes their interactions with coworkers and supervisors. Fearing that their motives will be misperceived, women COs often feel compelled to maintain very high privacy boundaries and eschew opportunities for socializing informally with (male) coworkers and supervisors. This has intrinsic disadvantages, in that women may not be able to form the kinds of interpersonal bonds with coworkers that men do. It undoubtedly also has negative material effects. As I will discuss in more detail later, in all the prisons I studied, officers indicate that informal contacts, either within the institution itself or at higher levels of administration, still play a crucial role in securing advancement opportunities. Because their informal interactions are often perceived through the lens of sexuality, however, women do not feel as free to exploit these kinds of contacts as do their male counterparts. The result, undoubtedly, is that women are simply not as well placed in the informal networks that link officers to advancement opportunities.

Women's Prisons

Men's experiences in fully integrating positions in women's prisons have been very different than those of women in men's institutions. By and large, they have been welcomed by female coworkers and supervisors and have been subject to none of the blatant harassment that faced pioneer women officers. Gender has played an equally important role in shaping the conditions of their work, however. As in the case of women, ideas about violence and sexuality are the primary forces that set the boundaries of men's role in women's prisons. Unlike women in men's prisons, men generally benefit from policies and practices that link gender, violence, and sexuality.

Violence—Men as Enforcers

The ideological connection between masculinity and physical strength fundamental to occupational masculinity in men's prisons is equally prevalent in women's institutions. Both male and female officers see men's specialized role as dealing with violent women inmates. This white woman and African-American man underline this view:

> On a female unit, you need mainly the men there for the . . . well, the manpower. You know, when it comes down to it, they're stronger than we are, and you've got to have those men there.

> I think that one advantage for me being here in a female institution with female inmates and a lot of female staff is brute strength.

These comments reveal the essentialism at the core of the prison's hegemonic occupational masculinity. In both men's and women's prisons, to be a male officer is, by definition, to be stronger than a woman and better able to deal with inmate violence. The actual size and strength of individual male officers are beside the point. This essential connection between masculinity and physical strength makes men necessary to the operation of a women's prison: "You've got to have those men there." This is in marked contrast to the much more problematic role of women in the men's prison, where no officer claims that "you've got to have those women there."

This link shapes policy and practice such that men are more likely than women to be called upon to deal with inmate violence. This pattern is much more pronounced at the state women's prison I studied, which again may be an artifact of the much greater discretion given to supervisors there. Both men and women officers at that facility agree that male COs are more frequently called on for situations involving "use of force." "Use of force" is the technical designation for incidents in which officers use physical force against inmates, usually during an altercation between inmates or because an inmate (in the jargon used by officers) "goes off;" or, less commonly, in the event of an assault against an officer. In all these instances, men are more likely to be involved. These two women, white and Hispanic, agree that supervisors are more likely to use men in these situations:

> If they can arrange for a man to do it [handle a use of force], they will. If it's a use of force that they can plan, they're going to take their stronger officers, and they will utilize the men. Because, if you see five burly men coming at you, the inmates are going to back down quicker than if there

were five women, regardless of their size. The female inmates are more intimidated by the men, and the male sizes, than they are by the females.

*When you have a use of force, are male officers more likely to get in-
volved?* Yes. Yes. They always want the males in there. [During a recent
incident] there were two men that were holding [the inmate] down, a
woman was holding her legs, and the lieutenant looked at me, and she
said: "I need another male, where is there another male? Where is there
another male?" So they sent another officer to go relieve that male officer in the dorm, and he came and took over for the woman that was
involved.

This white male officer agrees:

Do you think [female supervisors] come to you because you're a man?
In some situations, [like] use of force. Usually when we're going in and
we're having to fight one, it's pretty much going to be guys. We put the
females in every now and then, [but just as] tokens.

These comments make it quite clear that women supervisors also subscribe to the notion that men, by definition, are more able to deal with
violence. Men are more intimidating "regardless of their size," and for
the female lieutenant, any male is preferable to a woman CO. If women
are involved in such incidents at all, it is as "tokens."

Women officers are ambivalent about this practice. Some, like the
woman quoted at the beginning of this section, agree that men are better able to use physical force; she conflates this ability with masculinity,
labeling it "manpower." Others resent this practice on the grounds of
equality. These women do not necessarily want to use force, but they
object to their exclusion on the basis of fairness. In no case do male officers express open resentment that they are more likely to be called
upon to deal with these situations. In fact, they see dealing with violence as a fundamental part of their role in the institution. This white
male officer supports calling on men:

If they're available, they generally tend to have a majority of male officers for a use of force. I think that is so, generally, men can intimidate
them, where they may not have to use force. Plus if they do have to use

force, they may be stronger, they can do it in a manner to which a female might have to do it harder to accomplish that.

As this comment indicates, claims of this kind are often buttressed by the intimidation rationale discussed earlier; male COs, due to their physical presence, may be able to prevent violence. This officer does not minimize the potential for violence by female inmates, nor does any other CO. In this instance, the essential connection between masculinity and strength is maintained; the strength of women inmates does not undermine the stereotype that men are stronger than women.

For some male officers, there almost seems to be a sense of anticipation about incidents of violence. In a women's institution, the use of physical force is one of the only ways that male officers achieve validation for stereotypical masculine qualities and are able to maintain clear lines of gender difference. This white man's attitude about use of force is indicative of this perspective:

> I kind of look at it as tension reduction. You know, we need a good one every now and then.

This white woman officer underlines this point as well:

> [In] use of force, that's where the men really get macho. If they can, they'll have a five-man team. But on this five-man team, it's a five-person team, there might be three women. But they'll put a man on point. And they act real macho. They're not supposed to, but they do. And officers are just normal people, our job is different, and when your ego is at stake, that male still comes through. Even though the inmates are at a disadvantage, they still get this macho feeling about it. It's weird.

As this second CO indicates, female officers tend to view this issue in terms of the masculinity of male officers and describe this attitude as macho. Male officers are more likely to see the use of violence as an inherent part of their role in women's institutions; in many cases, they cite it as the primary reason for their presence. In emphasizing their difference from women, men gain status in the female-dominated environment of the women's prison; indeed, they become essential to the functioning of the institution.

Sexuality—Men as Predators

The second way that gender shapes the work experiences of men in women's prisons lies in the connection between masculinity and aggressive and uncontrollable sexuality. The asymmetry in the access of men and women to positions in inmate housing units and in pat-searching inmates of the opposite sex is fundamentally based on fears surrounding the potential sexual exploitation of women inmates by male officers. International standards set forth in the United Nations Standard Minimum Rules for the Treatment of Prisoners provide that women prisoners should be attended and supervised only by women officers; there is no similar restriction for men. In a number of critical reports, Amnesty International (1999a, 1999b) and Human Rights Watch (1996, 1998) support their calls for U.S. compliance with these rules by recounting dozens of egregious cases of sexual assault, forced prostitution, sexual molestation, and other forms of coercive sexual activity. Only secondarily is women's presumed greater need for privacy cited as a reason that male officers should be barred from women's prisons.

The assumption of predatory sexuality has material effects on policy and practice in women's prisons. The state system has gone through a number of policy iterations for which the rationale has been the protection of inmate privacy. This male officer with long experience describes changes over the years:

> When I first came out here, most of the men were roving officers, just out moving around. We had curtains in the dormitories, and the curtains had to be pulled. Male officers [would observe the dorms from outside], but they could see in the showers, so they put up this little curtain on the sides so the men couldn't gawk at [inmates] in the showers. Then they took down all the curtains at one time in the dorms. But that didn't last too long because the guys are walking around gawking in the windows, and now they've got the curtains back up. [At that time male officers] had to announce themselves every time they went into a dorm. I do it still as a courtesy, and a habit. It's not required. I could understand it as far as being courteous, but it gives up anything you had as far as catching them doing anything.

As his experience illustrates, prison administrators (and the courts) have taken steps to protect inmate privacy in women's institutions in a way that would seem almost inconceivable in a men's facility. Dormitories have curtains in all the windows; individual showers are in each dormitory and cell block and are covered by curtains as well. This is in marked contrast to the "gang showers" in most men's prisons, where large numbers of inmates shower together, without benefit of stalls or curtains. One of the most extreme examples of a policy designed to protect the privacy of female inmates is related by a woman who had worked in another of the state's institutions:

> When we have a [forced] cell move, sometimes these inmates are naked. [In a unit where I previously worked] the [male officer] was supposed to get a sheet and put it right over his face, and walk into the cell like that with a sheet. Now you tell me how he's going to see the inmate? *Whose rule is that?* The warden who was there at the time said that [it] was because the men aren't supposed to see the tits of the woman, but we're supposed to see everything else on the men. It was so silly.

This is an atypical example (this policy was later changed), but it is suggestive of a larger dynamic in which administrators and courts have made the protection of female inmates a primary concern. Male COs in the state system routinely announce themselves; during my time at the unit, I observed that as I entered a dormitory with a male officer, the female officer on duty consistently called out, "Man in the dorm, ladies!" The contradiction between surveillance and this kind of advance notification is obvious.

The most important way concerns about male sexuality continue to structure policy in women's prisons lies in restrictions on pat-searching of female inmates by male officers. The two systems I studied handle this issue in different ways. In the federal system, officers are currently assigned without regard to gender and can staff all posts. Pat-searching of women inmates by male officers is routinely allowed, with one modification—officers must search the chest area of women's bodies with the backs of their hands, rather than their palms. This African-American man explains:

> You have to use the back of your hand, I guess if you use the palm they will feel like you are violating them or getting a cheap thrill or whatever. *So, all officers do it that way? Both male and female?* Right. *Do they do that in men's facilities too?* No, I didn't see that. I've seen

female officers shake down male inmates the same way as male officers did and we did them with palms. I don't know why. Maybe females feel more violated if a male officer or anybody fondles them like that to where the male might care but he wouldn't verbally say it.

This officer's sentiments have much in common with those of his co-workers. It is clear that he has not bought into the rationale offered by the system for the practice—the notion that women inmates feel more violated by pat-searching than men. The legal basis for restricting men from pat-searching women—but not the converse—is women's disproportionate experience with sexual abuse at the hands of men. In response to a doctrine based on the recognition of gendered difference, he reimposes his own notion of equality—male inmates "might care" but "wouldn't verbally say it." Concomitant with stereotypes of women inmates as manipulative, most officers also distrust the motives of women who complain about pat-searching, seeing it as one more attempt to manipulate the system.[6]

The state system deals with this issue differently. At the time I was at this prison, male officers were completely prohibited from performing pat searches of female inmates. According to officers, the ban was imposed after women inmates filed a lawsuit in which they claimed that they had been abused or molested by men, and that having men's hands on their bodies, particularly in the breast and genital areas, traumatized them by reminding them of their earlier abuse. At this prison, men began to be assigned to dormitories during the early 1990s. For a brief period, male officers pat-searched female inmates returning to dormitories, as required by policy. During the time I was there, male COs were assigned to minimum-custody dormitories but were not allowed to search female inmates. If a male officer posted to a minimum-custody dormitory decides that an inmate needs to be searched, he calls for a woman officer to perform the search. This situation is the subject of intense debate and resentment, particularly among female officers.

The source of this resentment lies in the accommodations that are made. Because men are not allowed to pat-search, they are less likely to be assigned to dormitories and more likely to be given roving duties. The latter position is one of the most desirable because these officers have much greater mobility and are in closer contact with supervisors. Because men cannot search, women officers are more likely to be assigned to dormitories. This officer describes the sentiments of many women:

> Well, it is kind of hard, you know, when you go in there and you sit with these thirty-four inmates all day, every day, and they have the men assigned outside, where they get to go in and eat chow and run all over the place. They're just sort of free to go wherever they want. It's pretty unfair.

Rather than penalizing men, restrictions often lead to female officers being assigned the least desirable duties. Women are tied down in inmate housing units; men are assigned to high-mobility posts. At this prison, this situation led to the filing of a joint grievance by a man and a woman officer, but ultimately to no avail.

In the face of an ideology that links masculinity and uncontrollable sexuality, and policy and practice based on that connection, male COs face a considerable identity challenge. To accept prevailing institutional discourse appears to be a concession that they are inherently dangerous to their women charges. Few men in my study confront this issue very directly. This may well be because on the whole they benefit from the accommodations that are made to protect women inmates.

The handful of critical responses by men to the state's ban on pat-searching are instructive, however. These two officers, one African-American and one white, disagree strongly with the policy:

> *So, you're not pat-searching [in minimum custody dorms] at all now?*
> No, and it's a major breach of security and it's unsafe for the officers. If a man works a dorm, that means a female inmate could bring anything in. It's not that I want to, believe me, I don't even want to pat-search female inmates, but it's your job, and it's something that needs to be done. Either way you look at it, it's dangerous if you don't do it, it's kind of like you're darned if you do, and you're darned if you don't do it.

> You know, as a male, I have no interest in touching a female inmate to pat-search her. I really don't like that at all. I don't want to put my hands on them unless I've got to. Because they're inmates. You don't know where they've been. But if it becomes part of my job to do it, in the case of me being assigned to a dormitory to work and I've got

inmates turning in and out of that dormitory, for me not to have the skill, the ability to pat-search this individual coming in for contraband, I'm not being able to effectively do my job.

Both of these men deal with the implicit assumptions embodied in policy by changing the focus to security, concern about which they see as central to the role of the officer, in a generic sense. If they cannot search inmates, then they cannot "do the job."[7] They also go to extreme lengths to distance themselves from the system's presumption that they desire inmates sexually; the first officer assures me that he would never *want* to search inmates, and the second CO expresses his disgust because "you don't know where [inmates have] been." This same distancing strategy may well be embodied in men's persistent fear of false allegations. One white man explicitly links searching with this prospect:

The problem I have with pat-searching female inmates, especially when I'm not being observed by another officer, is the fact that accusations can be made, and I'm not sure how far or how wide my department will protect me from those accusations.

In a psychoanalytic vein, one could see the persistent fear of false allegations as a projection of men's desire onto the bodies of women inmates. This would be an especially powerful strategy for denying agency. Other kinds of negative stereotyping of women inmates may also serve the purpose of making sexual desire for them seem a contradiction in terms. In this connection, it is worth reiterating that women COs generally participate in this process, colluding in perpetuating these ideas and empathizing with male coworkers' fears that they will be "set up" by manipulative women inmates. Unlike women officers in women's prisons, who are always to some degree suspect, both men and women collaborate in a discourse that views men as victims of female inmates' con games.

Evaluation and Opportunity

Though officers in this study work in either men's or women's prisons, they are all part of the same administrative structures. State and federal COs are evaluated and promoted in accordance with standards and policies set out by their respective correctional systems. As in the case of hiring, available promotions are not listed separately for men's and women's prisons; rather, officers may apply for specific positions that are available at particular institutions. Evaluation and promotion are thus system-level issues, and it makes sense to consider officers' experiences across types of institutions.

These processes have become increasingly formalized over the past few decades. State and federal officers are evaluated several times yearly using a standard set of criteria, and promotions are based largely on these evaluations and a rating system. On the whole, officers in my study are relatively optimistic about their own opportunities to advance. Correctional officers believe expansion in the state and federal prison systems creates a wealth of opportunities for experienced officers; as one woman puts it, "If you're willing to transfer, the sky's the limit." This sentiment finds support in the projection that the job of correctional officer will be one of the fastest growing occupations during the next decade (U.S. Department of Labor 2001a). Officers' relative optimism does not necessarily mean they believe that evaluations and promotions are fairly and equitably awarded, however.

Though nominally merit-based, these processes leave considerable space for the interference of more subjective concerns. Evaluations, which take the form of a graduated set of ratings, may be influenced by supervisor bias, for example, in ranking officers as merely "acceptable" or as "outstanding." This white woman relates an incident in which she believes that her evaluations were influenced by favoritism:

> We get quarterly evaluations. They give us log entries and at the end of the year you add that all up and determine what you're rated as. They have "outstanding," "exceeds [expectations]," "fully successful," and "minimally sat[isfactory]." But it's all so relative. An example of that is when I was in [another institution]. I pissed this captain off so my evaluation turned all "fully successfuls". Then he forgave me, and they were all "outstanding." It doesn't mean anything.

These evaluations in turn affect officers' rankings for promotion. Because many officers may have similar ratings or numbers of points, in both systems, supervisors and administrators also rely on a personal network of contacts at their own and other institutions to help form their impressions of potential candidates for promotion. This white man believes that informal connections to supervisors are crucial in providing access to promotions:

> I'd rather work with inmates than some of the staff! [laughs] You know how they say it's a stressful job, it's not from the inmates. You can lock an inmate up and forget about it. It's the staff that's constantly, you gotta come see everyday. We gotta lot of favoritism here, and you know, it gets old once in a while. Like you want a job, but someone else will get it because he goes and drinks a beer with the lieutenant or something. And, you know, I don't see how they get away with doing it, but it happens.

This gap between policy and practice creates the one area of almost complete consensus among COs in my study—their belief in the importance of informal relationships with supervisors and administrators in influencing rewards and opportunities. In this, they are not so different from the majority of American workers, who invariably tell researchers that in order to advance, what matters is "not what you know, but who you know." A wealth of empirical research indeed reflects their suspicions, demonstrating the enduring importance of personal networks in hiring and promotion (Granovetter 1995).

These sentiments are typical of most officers, regardless of race or gender. While the objections may be generic, however, the effects of these practices are not. I focus here on the ways that race and gender affect officers' access to rewards and powerful positions. This occurs through explicit policies, such as facially gender-neutral rules that require transfers for promotion. Indirect avenues, such as the persistent association of masculinity with physical strength, affect women's opportunities as well. Direct mechanisms, such as outright racism and sexual harassment, also contribute to a structure in which white men still enjoy disproportionate access to power. Efforts by the systems to change this, in the form of affirmative action programs, are increasingly a source of resentment among white officers in both systems, who often label them "reverse discrimination."

Informal Networks, Policy, and Ideology

In prisons as in other occupations, connections are important for advancement. Ties with powerful, well-connected people can smooth the way for promotion; bad relationships or poor visibility can make the prospect all but impossible. This is true in both of the systems I studied, though the mechanisms through which these contacts work are somewhat different. At the federal level, officers compete with other COs nationwide for positions available through lateral transfers and promotion. System rules generally require those who are promoted to transfer to other institutions. This has the effect of giving supervisors a wide variety of experience, but also prevents the building of a power base at any one prison. Those in the federal system routinely divide career employees into "homesteaders," officers or other staff from the local area who do not want to leave, and those one administrator describes as "movers and shakers," people who are ambitious and willing to move out and up. Networks in the federal system are built on personal ties at particular institutions but are also likely to involve more far-flung contacts, forged between officers and administrators at previous postings and including "friends of friends" at those institutions. At the state level, officers are more likely to be "homesteaders" (though they do not use this term), with most drawn from the local communities in which prisons are situated. There are no formal requirements for transfer upon promotion in this system, though opportunities are greatest at newly built institutions, which may be a considerable distance from officers' current postings. Networks at this level are more likely to be based on face-to-face ties at particular institutions, though having contacts at other prisons can be helpful if an officer seeks a transfer.

Officers in both systems understand the importance of having connections to powerful, well-connected people. This white man underlines the importance of having a sponsor:

> *So, is it your sense if you wanted to move up, you could?* I don't think so. I don't have a daddy. And you do need a daddy to go somewhere. Like right now, I'm trying to get to [another institution], a promotion, but I need that person to call for me to get the stuff started, and I don't have anybody to call for me. But, say you had like an assistant warden or a big lieutenant, and he called someone and he said, "Hey, this guy's good." You're gone.

Like many other officers in his system, this CO calls such advocates "daddies"; they are not mentors, gender unspecified, but clearly male.

He believes that his chances for promotion are essentially nil because he lacks a relationship with a powerful man.

Such relationships and networks are often built through informal means, by socializing with supervisors or administrators, or through participation in institutional social events, such as parties or softball or bowling leagues. Such contacts, particularly those outside the institution, tend to be sex-segregated, as this African-American woman indicates:

> Most of the time those people that do socialize, they're the ones that get the better jobs. *And is it groups of men that socialize together?* Yes, basically. You have a few women that socialize. *And you think the people that socialize are the people that get promoted?* Well, the ones that socialize very well with the supervisors. That helps a lot. I'm not saying all of them do, but it does help. It helps a whole lot.

Most of the women officers I interviewed report that they only infrequently see their coworkers and supervisors outside of the prison. Male officers do sometimes socialize, but they describe these activities as sex-segregated, because "not many women show up."

The importance of informal ties leads to a situation in which opportunities are restricted in terms of both gender and race. Women are affected by this process in two ways. First, they may be unable to form and maintain the necessary social contacts because of their child care and family responsibilities, as this African-American woman's experience demonstrates:

> It's not what you know in [the Department of Corrections], it's who you know. *And some folks are more likely to know people than other folks.* Oh, yeah, because I don't play golf. I have a small child, so, getting around to the parties, and just being there all the time, I don't have the time. I'm thirty-nine years old; my child will soon be four.

This officer points to a number of factors that explain why women have less access to the informal networks that can lead to promotion. Such contacts may be more difficult to make because of family responsibilities, which still weigh more heavily on men than women.

Women may also simply lack the skills or interest to take part in the activities through which these bonds are formed. The most common activities officers mention engaging in together or with supervisors are golf, fishing, and "beer drinking." The first two are hobbies that boys are still more likely to learn than girls, and that men more often pursue as adults. The latter often presents unexpected dangers. For women in men's prisons, already viewed in terms of their sexuality and potential for seduction, drinking with male coworkers and supervisors can heighten this perception (see also Pierce 1995). This African-American female CO describes her experience with socializing outside the workplace:

> It's too much mess here, and if you don't want your business brought here, it's best you keep your visiting and your business to yourself. So I do that . . . I socialize with very few people that work here. I don't see socializing with them anymore, they'll come on back, and especially men, and they saw me and my boyfriend and the baby, they were saying something about what I had on, and made all this mess about what I had on, and just this was tight, and that was tight. So, that's why I don't fool with them, it's best not to.

This connection may be especially salient in structuring assumptions about African-American women. The hypersexualized "jezebel" or "hoochie" is a central representational image of African-American women, one that pervades American popular culture (Collins 2000). Other women officers in the men's prisons in this study describe a similar wariness about socializing, while simultaneously acknowledging that these contacts are helpful if promotions are to be gained.

Race also matters in creating or restricting access to informal ties. These African-American men, while rejecting the idea that race is important, both nonetheless underline its significance:

> Socializing matters. It's just, you know, whoever you click with, it's like a natural bond. If you're in, you're in. If you don't get along, you're gonna, no one's gonna take you under their wing, no one's gonna take care of you. That makes it harder on the next person who's not into what you guys are into, be it baseball or golf, or whatever, or fund-raising for this place, or taking part in activities in [the local community].

> I think sometimes if they've known you, like some of the rank has known the COs from around town, or whatever, and so they kind of grew up, you knew my daughter, you know things like that. Or, well, did you go to the fishin' tournament last week, and you know, that's

going to happen, I understand that. That's not if I like it or not, but that's going to happen. I can't do anything about that. *And your sense is that that kind of informal socializing, outside here, still breaks down on the basis of race?* Right, right. . . . See, because I am not a fisherman, and the primary [reason you] go fishing may not be black or white, but the white supervisors go fishing with the white COs, or something like that.

Both of these men describe contacts on the basis of affinity rather than race, but the result is the same. Informal social contacts for most Americans are racially segregated. Though I may not choose a fishing or golf buddy explicitly on the basis of race, she or he is very likely to be racially similar to me—"the white supervisors go fishing with the white COs." The link to inequality lies in the relative payoff of these networks. Given that white male officers hold most positions of power in these institutions, and given that informal socializing is still racially segregated, the resulting system is one in which informal contacts with those in power are available more frequently to white COs.

Gendered Organizational Logic—Policy and Opportunity

Gendered organizational logic is a policy or practice that appears gender-neutral on its face but reproduces and sustains gender inequality. An example, as I note in chapter 1, might be height or weight requirements for an occupation that exclude a disproportionate number of women, but not men. A policy which mandates that promoted workers must transfer works in a less obvious but similar way. This rule, explicit in the federal system and implicit at the state level, creates greater obstacles for women than men. These two white women illustrate this point:

> *Are you interested in moving up? Do you want to promote?* I want to promote, but I find that I really don't want to move away from this area, and with the federal system they really encourage a lot of movement and mobility. When you get to a certain point, if you keep moving up you will have to move. And so, I'm not really in a big hurry. I am interested in other positions, but I feel like I don't really want to move, so I haven't really been very aggressive in moving up. *You have a family in the area?* Right.

Would it be difficult for you to move from here? Yeah, my folks are elderly, and so I would not even be interested in going, God forbid, if anything happened to them, but until something did. They're elderly, and they both have bad health, so I'm not looking to go anywhere for a while. *So that would be part of it, too, why you would stay?* Yeah, yeah.

The first officer has a husband and children; the second is the primary caretaker for her parents. Neither sees transfer as a possibility. This finding mirrors those of studies of workers in a variety of occupations, which indicate that couples are more likely to relocate for the husband's work, and that married men are much more likely than married women to report that they would move for the prospect of better job opportunities elsewhere (e.g., Bielby and Bielby 1992; Shihadeh 1991). The effect of requiring transfers for promotion may be particularly strong in the federal system, in which officers sometimes have to move across the country to advance.

This is a particularly clear example of gendered organizational logic in action; transfer policies discriminate not in their intention but in their effect. The long hours and extra duties required of supervisors may also create higher barriers for women than men. Women who eschew promotion entirely often speak of the constraints imposed by domestic and family responsibilities. These white women reject the option of advancement for this reason:

I love what I do, God, I've worked every profession that you could think of, but I love it. I love what I do. But it takes too much time away from my family. But if I was career-minded, I would definitely already have been trying to go up for rank.

Are you interested in moving up in rank? No. *Why not?* Sergeants have got weirder schedules. I work Monday through Friday. I got my weekends off, I know when I have to come to work. I work from 7:30 to 4:30, I get an hour for lunch, I couldn't ask for a better schedule. And with these two kids, I want to be here, I don't want to have to work nights, or something, be away from the house. I want to be here with them.

The first officer explicitly counterposes a career—which would involve seeking advancement—to family, prioritizing the latter. The second woman, who has accumulated enough seniority to be able to work the hours she needs for her family, sees promotion as a loss. Some men also reject promotion due to family obligations, but given women's primary responsibilities in this domain, this rationale is still more common among women in my study.

Ideology—Masculinity and Violence

In both men's and women's prisons, men gain by emphasizing their "essential" difference from women; the discourse that links masculinity and strength has the effect of making men seem more capable and better candidates for promotion. This is accentuated in men's prisons, in which men occupy all the supervisory positions at the institutions in my study. In one facility, most of the recent promotions had gone to men officers who worked in the administrative segregation unit of the prison, where the most assaultive inmates are housed. This underscores the importance of physical aggressiveness and strength in the promotion process, as this white woman notes:

> Now, for a male, your choice would be to go to [administrative segregation] and be promoted from there . . . they want you to have that, be subjected to violence enough that you know what to do in crisis. But definitely, your promotion chances are higher on [administrative segregation]. The worse the place, there's more chance for promotion.

Proof that one is capable of dealing with violent inmates is key to establishing competence, and fitness for promotion.[8] Some women also work with these inmates, but these positions have thus far been a more efficient path to promotion for male officers. The more women are in protected roles, the less viable they are as candidates for promotion.

Because the connection between masculinity and physical strength and aggressiveness is naturalized in occupational discourse, women are seen as essentially less qualified for promotion. This white woman officer, who believes that men are much more likely to be promoted than women, speculates about why:

> Ah, the only thing that I can see, or think of, men are basically stronger than women, okay, unless we're body builders. When something really

bad happens, I think they feel safer. That's the only thing I can see . . . but it just doesn't happen, the women are not promoted like the men. There are other ways to achieve rank, but they don't seem to be through custody.

Indeed, the three women who had achieved rank at this prison pursued these alternate routes. Two are lieutenants, and one is a sergeant; all work in administrative positions. None works inside the main building of the institution with the general inmate population.

Direct Discrimination—Sexual Harassment and Racism

Informal ties, gender-neutral policies, and ideological definitions of the ideal worker are all examples of what one might call indirect discrimination. They are policies and practices that discriminate in their effect rather than in their intention. This section focuses on practices that are meant to discriminate, or that are legally recognized as doing so. One such practice is sexual harassment. The law makes a distinction between two kinds of sexual harassment, commonly called "quid pro quo" and poisoned environment. The former is the classic (and rarer) case, a scenario in which an employee is promised a raise, promotion, or some other reward for having sex with a supervisor. The latter occurs when an employee's work environment is made "toxic" by sexual overtures, innuendo, and banter. I collected two accounts of the former, which involved rumors of a female officer at another institution sleeping with a male supervisor to obtain a promotion. Stories involving poisoned environment harassment are more common, but those who tell them are ambivalent, unsure about whether they have "really" been harassed or whether something they did provoked the behavior, and they are almost always unwilling to utilize the protections provided by formal policies against harassment. A clear example is an African-American woman who relates an account of having been constantly "chased around the desk" by a male lieutenant at another men's prison. When I asked her if she had complained about his sexual harassment, she told me that she had simply "gotten in his face" and "told him to back off." She continues: "You just have to give them a chance to back off, and they will. I take care of my stuff on my own." This officer is satisfied with the way she handled the situation and claims that the harasser was dissuaded. It is clear that she believes that all women faced with such behavior should deal with it individually. Interestingly enough, she also says that she is certain this supervisor's behavior did not affect her own evaluations or opportunity to advance. Had she believed that it had done so, she would have filed a formal complaint.

Stories of outright harassment are rare among officers in my study. More common are experiences like the one described by this African-American woman, who works in a men's prison:

> They make little, snide little comments. You've got one that will always say, you know, "Miss [name], put your hand here." And I'm like, "No, Phil, I know you, I'm not going to put my hand there." And you look down, and he'll have his finger in his pocket poking out, so that represents his penis.

Like the woman chased around the desk, women officers often perceive that the best way to deal with such comments was just to go along so as not to be seen as a troublemaker.

This puts women in a double bind; those who do not take offense openly or resort to formal procedures may be more likely to be subject to this kind of behavior. As one woman puts it, "If you're in that relaxed group where they know little things won't bother you, and you won't take offense to it, or you won't write them up on charges, then, yeah, they'll make little comments like that." On the other hand, if officers "rock the boat," they may lose favored assignments or be negatively sanctioned in other ways. The prospect of retaliation by supervisors is identified by officers as a prime motivator for not making their discontent visible through the formal procedure provided by the system (see also McMahon 1999). As one officer puts it, "This is a very military-run place, and you don't want to get on their shit list."

Explicit policies that discriminate against workers on the basis of race are now prohibited by law. Even so, prisons are deeply racialized institutions; violence between inmates is often racially motivated, and inmates segregate themselves on the basis of race and refer to one another using a wide variety of racial epithets. Any prison ethnography provides evidence of these patterns, particularly in men's prisons, as do my own observations. System policies prohibit officers from treating inmates differently on the basis of race and also bar the use of racist terminology (or epithets of any kind) to refer to inmates. In the state system I studied, this kind of language is prohibited by policy, but it apparently is not uncommon in practice. This African-American woman worries that this reflects prejudices about officers as well:

> When you hear a supervisor call an inmate that nigger, and you're standing right there, what is that telling you? If he'll say that about him, even though he's an inmate, he'll say that about you too. They'll justify them saying nigger because they are inmates, but that is no justification. Not for saying that word, not around me. I get offended. They feel like we should just kind of look over that. Or, that wetback, you know. To me, those are all signs that you are racist in your own way. Kind of undercover, that's what we call it. [laughs] *Undercover racism?* I hate that. I'd rather for you to be up-front with me, and say, "Hey, I don't like you because you're black." I don't like anyone grinning in my face, and then go back and say, "I really don't like that nigger." *And you think there's a lot of that undercover . . . ?* Yeah, there is.

Given the nature of the language involved, it is incredible that this officer labels this behavior "undercover" racism. That she is able to do so speaks to the power of the dichotomy between "us" and "them" ("even though he's an inmate") that is one of the basic components of the officer subculture (Britton 1997a; Owen 1988; Zimmer 1986). Though her preference for racism of the up-front variety seems paradoxical, this mirrors the findings of a number of studies of African-Americans (Blauner 1989; Feagin and Sikes 1994; Feagin, Vera, and Imani 1996; Gwaltney 1980). Blatant racism is often easier to confront and ultimately more honest than the kind of duplicity in which whites are "grinning" one moment and racist the next.

Officers themselves also report more direct experiences of discrimination on the basis of race, though this often happens covertly. I heard very few accounts of this kind; all come from African-American women at state facilities. This CO vents her frustration at dealing with racist supervisors:

> Some of the old supervisors came from the old school, so no matter how you talk or how you act, in their book, you're still a wetback if you're Hispanic. If you're black, you're still a nigger. And they carry on these little conversations behind closed doors in the office. So, their favorite little [roving officers] get to hear all of this, so they don't keep

quiet, they'll come back out and say, "Oh, you know, sarge called so-and-so this and that."

In this case, the racism of supervisors is amplified by being carried on the constant current of rumor that pervades the prison. Such supervisors apparently behave in socially acceptable ways in the presence of COs themselves. This woman's qualifier, "no matter how you talk or how you act," also supports the dichotomy set out by the first officer; there presumably are inmates who might, by virtue of their behavior, merit these descriptors.

These two African-American officers believe that racial discrimination is the reason that they failed to receive assignments and promotions. This woman, who has a bachelor's degree, lost a promotion to a (well-connected) white woman with a high school general equivalency degree (GED):

> I was told at one [interview], they said, "Well, when you went into the interview, you were at the top of the list." I said, "What happened?" *Yeah, that's a good question. What happened?* I don't know. I filed a grievance, [and] they said they were right in their choice because even though I do have education, that's not the basis for [the position] because it only calls for a GED. This person with a GED, [she was a supervisor's] sister. And the grievance went [through all these steps], they said the same thing, so I left it alone.

This woman lost a position she enjoyed, one in which she had accumulated considerable experience:

> I was working in [a workshop] for three years. I complained to [a previous warden] about our supply officer, and, well, I did it a little more vocally than I should have because I was upset when I wrote him. The supply officer was talking to me lower than the worst of the inmates, and this was just out of the blue for no reason whatsoever. He was holding my supplies and stuff, telling me it wasn't in, yet telling the inmates it was there but I was too lazy to pick it up. So, I wrote the warden complaining about him. His solution was to take me out of the [workshop]. And I was racially discriminated against. The warden and the supply officer were both white. And there were two white female officers that were working in the central office, neither one of them ever did work [in custody]. They gave one my position, and the other one

they made a sergeant. *They set you up it sounds like. . . .* Yes. *And is it your sense that that's fairly widespread, or an isolated incident?* No, I'm sure it's widespread. With the black officer, see after that happened, no one there would speak up and say anything because they saw the way the warden was.

The first officer pursued grievance procedures but was apparently told that her claim had no merit, since a bachelor's degree was not required for the position she sought. The second woman's experience speaks to the chilling effect of racism by those in power on its victims' willingness to complain—after this incident, no black officer would "speak up." These accounts also point to the racial privilege enjoyed by white women, who were the beneficiaries of the discrimination in both cases.

Identification of blatant racism and discrimination by supervisors is unique to African-American officers; no white COs mention racism directed at officers or inmates. This is true even though I pressed a number of officers on this point. This man's response is typical:

I've never been able to pick out a racist person very well. But, I mean, I have a lot of black friends and stuff here, and they know all the racist people. Me, being white, I'm like, "Who are they?" I don't know who they are! *So, not that you see it.* Not that I see it, but then, you know, I've never been prone to being a racist.

For this CO, the adage "it takes one to know one" obviously holds. He believes that since he is not a racist, he is also unable to identify racism. His ignorance of the subject places him very much in the mainstream in white America, a context in which blacks and whites regularly and markedly disagree in public opinion polls about the prevalence of racism and discrimination.

This officer works in the federal system, which suggests that though the accounts thus far come exclusively from state officers, racism is not absent at this level. When asked about the opportunities he perceives for himself, this African-American male CO observes:

People get the wrong idea if they see you and they expect you to act a certain kind of way based on a stereotype or a culture. When you exhibit something else, then they become intimidated, and then they label it as arrogance or know-it-all or a jerk or anything like that based on their inability to accept you that you're not what they think you are. Consequently, sometimes that holds you up.

Though this man believes that eventually "it will all work out" and he will be able to advance, his experience reveals that stereotypes about African-American officers present obstacles in the federal system. However, given that federal COs are more educated and that the system itself provides training and promulgates policies with diversity in mind, the racial climate is probably better in most federal institutions than in the state system I studied.

It is interesting that the most blatant incidents of racism in my study are all related by African-American women. This does not mean, of course, that African-American men or Hispanic officers are not affected —the prevalence of the term "wetback" is a clear indicator of the latter. But it may be that gender and racial dynamics in prisons, as in many masculinized institutions, combine to make minority women the most likely victims of discrimination. In an analysis of data collected from 2,979 correctional officers and supervisors in the federal system (Britton 1997b), I found that African-American officers are less satisfied with their work than any other racial group. African-American women, in particular, experience the highest levels of job-related stress; for African-American men, this appears to be mediated by the high levels of efficacy they feel in working with inmates (who themselves are disproportionately African-American men).[9] In this case, as in other masculinized and male-dominated workplaces, African-American women officers find themselves at the intersection of gendered and racialized disadvantage.

A Discourse of "Reverse Racism"—Affirmative Action

Affirmative action policies that aim to promote diversity among staff are in place in both the federal system and the state system I studied. The Bureau of Prisons has a network of committees that oversee its affirmative action program, from the central office in Washington, D.C., in regional offices, and at individual institutions. The federal system also makes a visible commitment to diversity; in one federal prison I visited, a placard in the hallway of the administration building prominently announced recognition of "Asian and Pacific Islander Month." The state's version of affirmative action takes the form of policy more than specific programs; it exists as a directive, but without the same bureaucratic system to ensure its implementation.

On the topic of hiring and promotion, one of the most persistent themes in my interviews with officers is affirmative action. About one-third of the white officers in my study are dissatisfied with such policies; this number is split equally between state and federal COs.[10] Officers express two sets of concerns about affirmative action. First, they believe that such policies lead to the hiring and promotion of unqualified staff. One white male officer put the effects of affirmative action on the system in terms of the adage "You don't make the weak strong by making the strong weaker," indicating his fear that the ability of competent officers to do their jobs is being undermined by the system's wholesale attempt to promote minority COs. This white male officer agrees:

> On affirmative action, I'm all for, hey, if you're qualified, come and work, I don't care who, you could be purple, if you're qualified, come on and join us. But we've had people here who have slipped through the cracks, so to speak, and they have no business working here, and they're white, black, Hispanics, they shouldn't be here. But, based on "quotas," they put 'em in here.

Like many Americans, this officer believes that affirmative action programs employ quotas that require hiring a certain number of women, African-Americans, or Hispanics. This form of affirmative action is generally illegal (Reskin 1998) and is not practiced by either the federal or the state system I studied.[11] The enduring belief in the "quota" system is testament to the power of mythology and rumor in the discourse over affirmative action.[12]

For this officer, as for many like him, the overt focus of discontent about the policy in practice is on qualifications, rather than race or gender per se. Officers who express this sentiment almost always claim to know of a woman or minority man officer who, by virtue of experience or qualifications, deserves to be hired or promoted. I asked a few such COs whether unqualified white men are ever hired or promoted. The few who answered admit that this does happen but is due to the "good old boy" system, which fails to generate such vociferous condemnation.

The second set of concerns about affirmative action policies center on COs' observations that rather than reduce racism, such programs may actually generate hostility.[13] Though she believes affirmative action creates greater opportunities for women and minority men, this white woman rejects it nonetheless:

> *Is [this system] a good system in terms of moving up for women, do you think?* Yeah. *And by race as well?* By minorities, yeah. Very affirmative action conscious. *And what's the perception of that?* Not good. Not good at all. Affirmative action is not the way to go. It only creates for people like the white male, it only creates a bigger not really hatred, well hatred is kinda harsh, but it just creates a mentality that this person only got the job because they're female or this person only got the job because they're black.

Similarly, this white woman believes that qualified white men are being passed over to meet affirmative action goals:

> I have a friend, her brother applied at [the Department of Corrections], and he still hasn't heard anything. I told her they have a certain quota to meet and that's why he probably hasn't heard. You know, they're getting lot of people in here now that are not qualified because of that.

These comments are interesting for a number of reasons. Earlier in her interview, the first officer says that she sees increasing opportunities as a laudable goal, but here she rejects affirmative action as a way to achieve it. In so doing, she evokes the inescapable paradox posed by such policies—explicitly emphasizing race or gender (or other traits) in hiring leads to a perception among both majority and minority group members that individuals with those preferred characteristics have gotten jobs or promotions "only" for that reason. As an unmarked category, white men are presumed to have succeeded solely on the basis of their qualifications. As the second officer's comments also indicate, white men who are not hired or promoted have immediate recourse to affirmative action (even if its effect is only rumored) as a rationale. It is also worth noting that these sentiments are expressed by white women, a group that has been one of the main beneficiaries of affirmative action programs. Research finds that white women are generally more supportive of affirmative action programs than white men, and this is the case in my study as well. White women who oppose such policies may do so on the basis of collective, rather than individual, interest, however, if they perceive that their husband, brother, or other white male family member is negatively affected. For white women, racial privilege sometimes erodes the effect of gendered self-interest.

Several aspects of this discourse around affirmative action are incongruous. First, these beliefs coexist quite harmoniously with an almost universal notion that the most important route to promotion is through informal ties to those in positions of power. Several officers who express concern with affirmative action also state emphatically that those who are likely to be promoted have to "know somebody." No white officer perceives that women and minority men have greater access to informal contacts; as has already been discussed, these kinds of ties are much more available to white officers, given that informal socializing is still segregated along racial lines.

This creates an apparent contradiction, which could be explained in two ways. It seems clear that the promotion system is widely perceived as arbitrary, and these two beliefs may be expressions of officers' feelings that there is little they can do to influence the process. In this case, the coexisting beliefs that affirmative action is the most efficient route to promotion, and that informal contacts are crucial are external attributions (i.e., race or "knowing someone" is the way to get promoted) of an arbitrary result. This belief may also represent an acceptable gloss on the racism of the officers involved. The public debate over affirmative action has been a powerful forum for the rearticulation of racial privilege (Omi and Winant 1986; cf. Lynch 1991); this issue was a centerpiece of David Duke's successful (and unsuccessful) campaigns for public office, in which he carried the majority of the white vote in Louisiana. The prevalence of this discourse around affirmative action may be part of an attempt to reassert white male racial privilege, which they see being eroded by government and its policies (Daniels 1997; Omi and Winant 1986).

Second, the existence of these beliefs is also curious given the small number of women and minority men in positions of power in these institutions. I often questioned officers who expressed dissatisfaction with affirmative action on this point. Their responses typically take the form of distancing such as, "We haven't had a promotion here in a while, but I'm sure the next one will be a minority," or "It's happening in other prisons in the system." It may be that women and minority male supervisors are more visible given their small numbers, which heightens the fear of white male officers that they will not be promoted. In this environment, almost any woman or minority man who is promoted may be seen as undeserving, and the discourse functions to undercut the competence of these officers.

African-American and Hispanic COs are less sanguine than their white coworkers about the prospects of minority officers in both systems.[14] This African-American woman is one of the only officers to openly support affirmative action:

> I've talked to people who are against affirmative action, but like for the [Department of Corrections], look at it! They won't even give a minority a chance. To me, that's when affirmative action should really kick in. I don't know, we have some people, like for example, there's a secretary that works in administration that said that black people are the ignorant-est people, they are just dogs, man. I'm serious! When I heard that she said that, it just really blew me away.

Though she is in favor of such policies, this woman believes that they nonetheless have little effect on overcoming obstacles to advancement, a perception that is underlined by her own ongoing experiences of racism at work.

Perceptions of the Job

Relationships with inmates, coworkers, and supervisors, as well as individual expectations, combine to structure COs' perceptions of and happiness with the job itself. Many COs choose the work for reasons such as salaries and benefits, and those factors contribute most to their enjoyment of the work. Extrinsic factors such as required shift work and overtime also lie at the root of dissatisfaction for some officers. Such requirements may be particularly difficult for women officers.

Intrinsic factors are also important. The single factor that officers cite most often as giving them a sense of satisfaction with their work is having a positive effect on inmates' lives. Officers feel that they do this through the example of their own conduct, in the context of personal interactions in which they provide advice about how to do time productively, or in conversations about inmates' lives and what brought them to prison. This white man links his ability to promote change with his core identity as a correctional officer:

It's funny, people say to me, "You're a prison guard," when I meet them on the street. That's offensive to me. I say, "You know, I'm not a guard. That guy works in [a department store] or something watching the clothes. The title is correctional worker." I find a lot of enjoyment from the job because I get the ability to work with so many different people from so many vastly different backgrounds. At the same time you can kinda help them, you know. It's a wonderful feeling when one of them calls back and says, "Hey, I got this job and my life back in order now, and it has a lot to do with all of the stuff you instilled in me." That's really a good feeling. You know that you've helped somebody.

Similarly, this Hispanic man hopes to promote change through his work:

For you, what's the most enjoyable aspect of your job? I would probably say, help make a difference in a person. I actually had that experience; former inmates have come back to me, "Man, you really helped me out, and I'll never forget you," and stuff like that. I even had an inmate that, he left to another institution, and he got me by surprise, he gave me a hug, and I was, like, "Oh my god!" [laughs] His intention was, like, saying thank you to me, but I was kinda, he did catch me off guard a little bit.

This kind of rehabilitation orientation is somewhat more prominent among African-American and Hispanic officers in my sample than among whites, and is also more common among those with more education. Regardless, it is obvious that this sense of personal efficacy in their work with inmates is a key source of satisfaction for many, who might best be described as *correctional* officers. At this particular historical moment, this kind of approach to the job conflicts quite sharply with the general orientation of the American correctional system, which has, at least officially, abandoned a doctrine of rehabilitation in favor of the rhetoric of custody and deterrence. Those in my study who see their function as little more than custody maintenance, those who are correctional *officers*, are among the least satisfied.[15]

Another source of satisfaction for officers is the sheer variety offered by the job. Though the job is structured by routine, COs deal with a diverse population and usually work multiple posts. This African-American man likes the excitement of uncertainty:

What do you like most about the job? It's a challenge. Every day going into work you never know, you know, what you're gonna be faced with that day. My wife, she goes to work and she knows what she's gonna be doing, she knows what has to be done, and I don't. I don't know if someone's gonna go crazy that particular day or try to escape or whatever. It's different.

Similarly, this white woman loves the variety in the work, so much so that she hopes to advance to the top of the institutional ladder:

I like it here. I love my position. It's just endless, what I learn here. There's never a routine day. You can make your to-do list in the morning, and you may not get to any of it! [laughs] But someday, I do want to move up. I do want to be a lieutenant someday. I'd love to be a captain someday. [in a whisper] I'd like to be a warden someday.

This first officer's comment gets at a fundamental issue in the sex segregation of work; male-dominated jobs are indeed those in which workers are more likely to perform a variety of tasks, and to work in settings characterized by uncertainty.

That this may be a particularly important source of job satisfaction for men is underlined by the fact that one of the most commonly cited sources of dissatisfaction with the work (after relationships with co-workers and supervisors) is boredom. All the officers who express this sentiment are men. This white CO's comments capture what it means to be bored for these men:

I like where I work. And obviously, [administration's] doing a good job, you know, fights are down to minimal. Staff safety has never really been a big issue, so obviously they're doing something right. So, I mean, it's not coming to work fearing for my life every day, but then, sometimes it gets a little dull, you know, routine. *You're a little bored?* Yeah. But I guess that's a good thing.

These men are all in institutions that they perceive as safe, but many have worked in what they describe as more exciting and more dangerous settings and express nostalgia for the kind of adrenaline rush that comes from dealing with violence. Such men strongly eschew work in women's prisons, where "nothing real ever happens." Their orientation to the work exemplifies the hegemonically masculine definition of the officer as someone whose key responsibilities revolve around the control of men's violence.

The second officer, who would "like to be a warden someday," is representative of a small number of women in the sample who express satisfaction with the work because they feel a sense of accomplishment in defying the strictures of gendered expectations about what they can do. Such women typically work in men's prisons. This African-American officer moved into a custody position after having been a secretary for many years:

> I have pushed myself to do things that I never thought I would be able to do before. You know, working with weapons, inmates. I never thought I could do that, but I can. That's why I don't think there's anything anybody could put before me that I don't think I could do if I put my mind to it. I could do it. It has proven to me that I can do anything I want because years ago if you would have told me I could work with inmates I would have laughed in your face. I was so scared. Now I'm a different person. I know I'm a different person.

These women have indeed overcome considerable obstacles in the process of becoming officers. During the course of this research, I heard stories of women who had become sergeants, lieutenants, and, indeed, even wardens in men's prisons. As their relative rarity suggests, however, this does not mean that the barriers have collapsed for women in corrections.

Though my presentation makes it appear as if officers may be sorted neatly into the categories of "satisfied" or "dissatisfied," this is, of course, an oversimplification. As with most workers, COs are happy with some aspects of their work, unhappy with others. This kind of ambivalence is likely in any job that involves complex webs of relationships and uncertain expectations; on any given day, I may be extremely satisfied with my contacts with students but be in conflict with my colleagues or university administration. But there is a particular kind of ambivalence among officers in my study that derives from the gendered and racialized structure of the institution itself. For women, and women of color especially, the experiences of gaining new opportunities and accomplishing what had previously seemed impossible tasks coexist uneasily with barriers imposed by race and gender. This kind of dissonance creates what W. E. B. Du Bois (1989 [1903]) calls "double consciousness"; steeped in American ideals, members of oppressed groups (Du Bois focuses on African-Americans) believe strongly in ideals of equality of opportunity and justice, but their day-to-day reality makes them deeply pessimistic that these ideals will ever be achieved. The whisper of the white woman, whose ambition to become warden is a goal too lofty to be spoken of aloud, speaks to this kind of conflict. The African-American woman, who believes that "there's [nothing] anybody could put before me that I don't think I could do," is also deeply disconcerted by racial problems in her institution.

Two interviews in particular demonstrate this kind of double consciousness in striking detail. On numerous occasions in our conversation, this woman, who works in a men's prison, expressed sentiments similar to the following: "I come and do what I'm supposed to do, but I'll tell you, I'll tell the captain I don't like it. I'll tell anybody I don't like it. . . . I just think women shouldn't be working in here." She seems unequivocal in her dislike of the job, even extending her own dissatisfaction to the assertion that women should not be in the institution at all. In fact, she made this point so many times that I almost did not ask her whether she was interested in remaining in the system or advancing. When I did, she answered this way:

> *I hesitate to ask you this question. I think I know what your answer would be. If you didn't perceive that the system was biased in terms of promotions, would you be more interested in moving up or staying around?* Well, I still would stay in custody. It's not that I don't have any interest in moving up. Well, yes, I would. *You think you would, if you perceived that the system weren't biased.* Yes, because even though I know that I still go for interviews. And it's kind of hard to walk into an interview and not have an attitude. Because you've heard, a lot of them, they say, you waste your time going up, because they already know who they're going to put in that position.

This next officer also illustrates this apparent contradiction in attitudes. Early in the interview, she expresses this view of the job: "At first, I was kind of scared, but now I just like the job very much." Near the end, her attitude exhibits the following apparent reversal:

> *So, do you like the job?* No, I really don't have anything good to say about the job. It's a very stressful job. Sometimes I'm depressed because

they don't treat everybody the same. They're very unfair. I have more problems dealing with the supervisors than I do with the inmates. The inmates I can handle, but the supervisors gossiping, talking about other officers, to me, I just feel that that's not necessary. I think that they should stick to the [Department of Corrections] and that's it.

For this officer, as for many others, one of the most important sources of dissatisfaction is her relationship with supervisors, whom she considers unprofessional and unfair in their treatment of officers. The difference here is that this feeling coexists with the knowledge that she and others like her face systematic—not individualized—discrimination on the basis of race and gender. When she observes, "Sometimes I'm depressed because they don't treat everybody the same," she references group-level processes of inequality. Similarly, the first CO "doesn't think women should be working here" but at the same time interviews for promotions, though she believes the system is biased. The complex set of apparent contradictions embodied in these beliefs provide a vivid demonstration of double consciousness in action. These women believe strongly in rewards based on equal opportunity and merit, but they also experience the disjuncture between these ideals and their own reality.

Conclusion

In her classic study *Men and Women of the Corporation*, Rosabeth Moss Kanter (1977) introduced the notion of the "token" worker as a way to explain the situation of women in the male-dominated corporate world. The token, a numerical rarity of race, gender, or some other group characteristic, faces resistance from members of the majority group, who employ exclusionary practices to maintain their dominance in the workplace. Though Kanter intended the concept to be generic, research of the last two decades has embodied the token and revealed the asymmetrical experiences of men and women integrating occupations filled mostly by members of the opposite sex. Already gendered, in reality, masculinized, organizational and occupational structures ensure that male workers disproportionately rise to the top, regardless of whether their occupation is dominated by men or women. This study extends the findings of this line of research.

Women moving into jobs in men's prisons fare very differently from

men in women's institutions. While both men and women COs are restricted in cross-gendered situations, in both cases the restrictions advantage men and disadvantage women. In men's prisons, restrictions on
women's assignments due to a belief in the inherently greater ability of
men to deal with violent male inmates mean that women may be seen as
incapable of performing the job and as poor candidates for promotion.
In women's institutions, constraints on the assignments of men and the
link between masculinity and physical strength give rise to a situation in
which men are viewed by administrators and coworkers as essential to
the functioning of the institutions and receive preferred assignments.

My critique of the link in occupational discourse between masculinity and physical strength undoubtedly seems to some like willful denial.
Many of those in my study would see it this way; as one woman officer
puts it, "There's just no way to say that a woman is as strong as a
man," and men are necessary in any prison. Correctional officers' own
accounts deconstruct this notion in a myriad of ways, however. First,
they demonstrate that masculinity and strength are not merely linked
but conflated. To be a man is, by definition, to be bigger and stronger
than a woman, and this is true regardless of the size or physical abilities
of actual men and women. The identity relation between masculinity
and strength bars all women, a priori, from jobs that are held to require
this ability. Conflating the two also eclipses any discussion of the *kind*
of strength and the types of techniques that might really be necessary,
and whether these are the exclusive purview of men as a category. Skuratowicz (1996), for example, in her study of fire fighting, an occupation from which women were long categorically debarred due to their
presumably inherent weakness, finds that women broaden their interpretation of the physical requirements of their jobs from an exclusive
focus on masculine-identified brute strength to a more encompassing
conception combining strength, flexibility, endurance, and overall physical fitness.

Second, the experiences of officers in this study call into question the
assumption of an inherent relationship between physical strength and
the work. "Banging heads" is not a routine job requirement, and COs
repeatedly emphasize that the job requires more in the way of mental
than physical ability. Effective officers are often able to prevent violence
before it starts; women in men's prisons in particular often emphasize
their role as peacemakers. These findings mirror those of research on
women in policing, which finds that women officers stress the benefits

of defusing conflict rather than using physical force (Miller 1999; National Center for Women and Policing 2002).

Sexuality is a central concern in both men's and women's prisons, though in paradoxical and asymmetrical ways. Notions about women's essential heterosexuality and femininity combine to make jobs in men's prisons seem too degrading or too tempting due to the pull of "natural" heterosexual desire. This rhetoric distances resistance and discrimination, placing them in the hands of inmates, rather than in the hierarchy of authority in the institution. In women's prisons, structure, policy, and practice also reflect the assumption of heterosexuality, though the underlying image is of an aggressive and exploitative masculine sexuality. In this case, the prevailing discourse denies men's agency and positions women inmates as manipulative and beyond the bounds of desire.

Opportunities for advancement, though nominally governed by formal bureaucratic processes, still allow considerable space for the intervention of more subjective concerns. Informal ties to powerful supervisors and administrators are important, and these ties remain more accessible to white men than to other groups. The requirement that promoted officers must transfer undoubtedly places the greatest constraints on women. Sexual harassment and racism, while certainly less blatant than in earlier studies of prison officers, persist, though accounts of this kind achieve wide currency only among those groups most affected. This is perhaps one of the reasons that many white officers so vociferously espouse an anti–affirmative action discourse. Even so, many officers, among them a large number of women and African-American and Hispanic men, obviously derive great satisfaction from their work. Salary and benefits are obviously a draw, but factors intrinsic to the job matter as well. For many officers, satisfaction comes from the feeling that they can have a positive effect on people who are "at the lowest point in their lives." For others, the feeling of accomplishing seemingly impossible tasks is most important. Many "token" workers remain, however, ambivalent about their prospects in systems that sometimes offer opportunity with one hand and inequality with the other.

7

Conclusion

This book is, first and foremost, a study of the prison as a gendered organization. The theoretical foundation upon which I draw, and on which I hope to have built, remains an interloper in the field of organization studies, which has preferred to view gender, race, class, and sexuality as individual traits of workers instead of as essential components of organizations themselves (Martin and Collinson 2002). By arguing that the prison *qua organization* is gendered, I mean that rather than existing as a neutral bureaucratic entity, the prison was formed in and through a matrix of gender, race, class, and sexuality, and that it reproduces individuals, ideas, and inequalities along all these dimensions. As it is gendered, the prison is also raced and classed and sexualized. Though one may choose to emphasize a single dimension for analytical purposes, they never operate in exclusion from one another. Individuals possess these characteristics, of course, and they shape and confirm notions about their own "essential self," as well as the selves of others, through their work. Jobs are not generic slots in the organizational hierarchy but instead contain embedded assumptions about who the ideal worker is. The veracity of these assumptions is confirmed through policies and practices that privilege and reproduce this ideal.

The history of the prison is much more than a recounting of the linear progress of the "science" of penology. Indeed, such an account is incomplete without an understanding of the role of ideas about gender, race, class, and sexuality in the formation of the institution. The founders of America's adult prison system imagined the reform of the rational *man* and designed institutional structures and disciplinary practices with this image in mind. In early penitentiaries, most administrators viewed women at best as an afterthought, at worst as a nuisance. Housed in basements and attics, women inmates were denied even the benefits of exercise and fresh air out of the belief that their mere presence would drive men to disease at the hands of self-abuse. America's second prison system, the adult reformatory, arguably found its first institutional expression under Eliza Farnham, at the Mount Pleasant Female Prison, from 1844 to 1848. Criticized by the state legislature as a disciplinary regime with "nothing *masculine* in its composition" (quoted in Lewis 1965: 248, emphasis in original), reformatory practice gained wide legitimacy only after being transformed into a tool for the production of "Christian gentlemen" (Pisciotta 1994). Through the efforts of white middle-class reformers, a feminized version of the movement reemerged on a separate, and equally gendered, track, with the explicit intention of reconstituting "fallen" women in the mold of domestic femininity. The southern system of convict leasing and, eventually, prison farms was built on a foundation of ideas about freed black slaves that framed them as natural criminals. The plantation system was reproduced, and along with it the brutality of the overseer. As they had during slavery, by day black women worked the fields along with black men, and at night they were often subject to sexual abuse. White men served their time in southern penitentiaries; white women were often pardoned, adjudged too delicate to endure the rigors of incarceration. Elements of all three of these systems persist to the present day. History demonstrates that the raison d'être of the prison has never been the control or, at certain historical moments, the rehabilitation of the generic individual. From their inception, these institutions and their disciplinary regimes have been designed with particular "docile bodies" in mind (Foucault 1979).

So, too, were notions about gender and race embedded in prescriptions for the character and duties of the prison's ideal keepers. Even the occupation's gendered labels attest to this. In accord with a paramilitary model, men who served as prison *officers* in men's penitentiaries were to command masculine respect and mete out violence. Women, who served as *matrons* and later as cottage officers, were to act not as brute enforcers but as maternal mentors and guides, women who could gently set the fallen back on the path of true womanhood. Stereotypes about the allegedly inherent criminality of blacks shaped both occupations from the outset. This racist logic dictated that unless they were supervising inmates of their own race, black officers or matrons were a contradiction in terms. During the 1970s, administrators in men's prisons based their argument for the exclusion of women on what seemed to be self-evident—only real men could do the work of an officer. The last twenty years have seen the final defeat of legal barriers to women's employment in these institutions—though formal equality alone does not ensure the disappearance of informal obstacles to its achievement. Men's route to complete integration into the officer corps in women's prisons has been a very different, and equally gendered, one that is shaped even now by their original role as "brute force without benefit of a gun" (Giallombardo 1966: 32).

The sex- and race-segregated structure of the labor market fundamentally shapes the paths of those who become officers. Wage discrimination makes government-sector jobs as officers attractive to women and minority men and has fueled their influx into the occupation over the past three decades. Male officers in this study bring with them experience in the military or in other male-dominated, masculine gender–typed occupations. For them, the transition to the masculinized, paramilitary environment of the (men's) prison is a relatively smooth one. Women come largely from backgrounds in clerical work, and the connection between secretarial and correctional duties is much less than obvious. The gap between prison and free-world employment in these female-dominated, feminine gender–typed occupations is widened by the fact that like most of us, those who will be officers are steeped in media lore about the men's prison, a place where "everybody has a gun, and [there's] fighting every day." Training often builds on these images, emphasizing a worst-case scenario that many officers eventually realize is little more than a "fish story." The gendered construction of the typical prison and its characteristic inhabitant in culture and institutional practice means that women's prisons remain anomalies, and the needs of women inmates are exceptions to the rule.

Officers' perceptions of and interactions with inmates are profoundly influenced by gender, race, and sexuality. The persistent overrepresentation of inmates of color in the American prison system places Hispanic and African-American officers in a uniquely difficult position. Though they are more likely than their white colleagues to have experienced discrimination at the hands of the system, they are also responsible for enforcing its dictates. This standpoint contributes to the espousal of rehabilitation among these COs, as well as sympathy for the view, shared by many white officers, that inmates are human and have made mistakes. Like their coworkers, however, they also engage in the rhetoric of distancing—their charges "may be inmates but they are [still] human."

Without question, the most important theme in officers' comments about inmates is one that invokes gender distinctions, seeing male inmates as different from, and preferable to, their female counterparts. Correctional officers' descriptions draw on a host of gendered stereotypes, labeling women as emotional, manipulative, and petty. Men, on the other hand, are stoic (though potentially more dangerous) and obedient and have "real, legitimate complaints." Most officers—both men and women—express such disdain for women inmates that they eschew the prospect of work with them entirely. None of these gendered attributions are particularly surprising; indeed, all of these characteristics are associated with femininity and masculinity in culture, and those linked with the former constitute the negative half of a gendered dichotomy. They are given expression here in two very different, and deeply gendered, contexts. Men's institutions and the behaviors and needs of male inmates are transformed by ideology and practices such as training into those of the generic prison and its gender-neutral inmate; implied patterns of normative interaction in any prison follow from this. Women inmates are housed, generally, in lower-security facilities in which there is more ambiguity in policies and informal norms. The qualities officers attribute to the essential nature of women emerge from an environment in which there are simply more shades of gray.

In their work with male inmates, women officers find themselves welcomed, but this reception is often contingent on their acceptance of protection and willingness to assume roles as peacemakers and mother figures. These conditions invariably have the effect of discounting their authority, however, as culturally emphasized appropriate femininity generally does not involve the exercise of power over the lives of adult men. Sexual harassment, both verbal and visual, from inmates also presents obstacles for which women are usually unprepared by training, and with which their male counterparts simply do not have to deal. Conversely, the authority of men in women's prisons is augmented by a gendered "power multiplier" effect (Acker and Van Houten 1974: 154); men carry culturally legitimate masculine authority over women into the prison, which then amplifies this power through its use of men as intimidators and enforcers. The persistent discourse of fear around false allegations has the effect (though perhaps not the intention) of ensuring that this "natural" order will not be overturned.

Inmate violence and sexuality are also central concerns. Correctional officers' view of men's and women's violence is captured in the phrase "women have cat fights, men have gang fights." Women's assaults are irrationally motivated and involve trivial issues, such as girlfriends or "who's gonna sleep with who on *Melrose Place.*" Men deploy aggression for legitimate instrumental reasons, such as gang affiliation, money, or drugs. The normalization of their aggression through institutional policy and practice means that, paradoxically, officers say they prefer dealing with men's violence. The rare discussion of male inmates' sexuality takes the form of a discourse of gender inversion, with one partner in every pair transformed into a feminized "punk." In stark contrast to men's institutions, women's prisons are utterly sexualized. Gendered norms around the open expression of affection combine with institutional architecture and prison policy to heighten the visibility of women inmates' affectionate and sexual relationships. Though COs concede that these are largely consensual, heterosexism shapes some officers' perceptions that such interactions are "very sickening" and that dealing with them presents a serious management challenge.

In the case of the prison, as in most male- and female-dominated occupations, the underlying theme of men's and women's integration has been one of asymmetry. Cultural and institutional ideologies frame women as less able than men to deal with inmate violence and (for white women at least) too delicate to endure the sexual harassment they face in men's prisons. These presumptions then take form in practices that protect women or deploy them in "safe" assignments. Women themselves either resist or embrace this protection, but either strategy is dangerous. Those who choose the former risk creating animosity among their coworkers or being seen as less than "real" women; the latter gives rise to a view that women do not "pull their weight" or make viable candidates for promotion. The association of masculinity with physical strength makes men appear essential to the operation of both men's and women's prisons and is a fundamental cause of their overrepresentation as supervisors and administrators. Even the connection between masculinity and aggressive sexuality has advantages for men as it is played out through the medium of institutional policy and practice. Simply put, men's difference from women accrues benefits in the masculinized organizational context of the prison; women's difference from men does not.

At the system level, the persistent importance of a system of informal contacts means that those officers who have a mentor (a "daddy," as one CO puts it) are advantaged. Domestic responsibilities and the sexualization of women in institutional discourse mean that women are not as free to pursue these kinds of relationships as men are. Policies, such as transfer requirements, that are explicitly gender-neutral may also have a disproportionately negative impact on women. Sexual harassment and racism still affect the opportunities of women and minority men, though my study reveals that such practices are less widespread, or at least less blatant, than in the past. Many white officers, loath to acknowledge this, join in an anti–affirmative action discourse in which white men become the most disadvantaged of all groups. Even so, most officers in my study, regardless of race or gender, express satisfaction with their jobs, especially to the extent that they feel they can "make a difference" in the lives of their charges.

Implications for Theory

In chapter 1, I set out a theoretical framework which argues that organizations are gendered at the levels of culture, structure, and agency. In specifying these three facets, I do not mean to propose a rigid taxonomy or to oversimplify complex processes by wrapping them up in a neat typification (Martin and Collinson 2002). I offer these ways of viewing organizational gendering as heuristic categories, windows into organizations and occupations from which the combined views may tell us more than any one alone. Other researchers may prefer different levels of analysis or, indeed, reject such a project of delineation entirely. It seems worthwhile at this point, however, to bring together these three angles of vision on the case of the prison to assess the utility of the theoretical framework underlying this analysis.

Gendering through Culture

> I just feel that they're too easy here. I mean, I agree they're women, I don't think they can be treated the same, but I think there's just, what's the point, you know? I mean, this place is like summer camp. Some summer camps I've been to when I was a kid weren't as nice as this place. *Well, wait, what would you change?* I would put a fence up. I mean, if it's going to be a prison, it's going to be a prison. You know, just one fence. *And you'd put a fence because, I mean, are people escaping?* No. Because it's supposed to be a prison. (White male correctional officer)

Joan Acker defines gendering at the level of culture as the "construction of images, symbols, and ideologies that justify, explain, and give legitimacy" (1992: 568) to institutions, organizations, and occupations. These images are found in many sources, from language, to our commonsense notions about men's and women's work, and in popular culture. This study demonstrates quite clearly that our notions about prisons, inmates, and officers all contain embedded ideas about gender.

The "prison," generically speaking, is a men's prison. The overwhelming majority—nearly 90 percent—of cinematic depictions of the prison are set in men's institutions and almost invariably offer a cast of stock characters among whom are the brutal inmate and the sadistic prison officer. It is these images that recruits carry with them on their circuitous paths to prison. From the inception of the occupation, masculinity, with its presumed concomitant ability to use violence, has been an integral part of the package of desired attributes for prison officers. Today, training, assignment, and promotion practices in systems themselves, ostensibly gender-neutral, are undergirded by assumptions about typical prisons, their characteristic inmates, and their ideal officers. So, too, are the perceptions of all these among officers themselves shaped by these notions of what a "real prison" is. As the opening comment from an officer who works in a women's prison indicates, prisons have fences, whether they need them or not.

Images like these have important material effects. Historically, such notions fed the development of different kinds of institutions for men and women, as well as disciplinary regimes designed in accord with their "essential" natures. In the present, masculinized worst-case scenarios undoubtedly dissuade more women than men from the occupation, contributing to its continuing sex segregation. The ideological link between masculinity and violence is at the root of informal practices that restrict and protect women in men's prisons and deploy men as enforcers in women's prisons. Generic ideas about real prisons and real inmates come together to create a near-universal disdain for working in women's institutions, with their overly emotional inmates—from the perspective of officers, inmates, like big boys, simply don't cry.

Gendering through Structure

I had a sergeant, we have phone calls that we [monitor] for inmates, and I asked him, "You're always saying that women are going to do the same thing as the men. How come you won't assign a man to do a phone call?" He said, "No, I will never do that." I said, "That's not fair." *And men never get assigned to do that?* No. *Why not?* You know what, he could never explain that. All he could ever say was, that's a woman's job. And that offended me. (African-American woman officer)

"Structure" is among the most deceptively difficult of analytical concepts in social science. Though my sociological colleagues and I continually remind our students of the importance of social structure, or organizational structure, or community structure, we are not always clear about what we mean. Usually, we are not pointing at some physical edifice, though in the case of the prison, I have the opportunity to do so. Gender has shaped the architectural designs of men's and women's prisons from their earliest incarnations. Penitentiaries for men have been built in the mode of the panopticon, the design developed by Jeremy Bentham and famously appropriated by Michel Foucault (1979) as an analogy for the operation of social control in modern society. Women's institutions have replicated the domestic ideal embodied in the cottage design favored by reformatory advocates. These differences are now disappearing as "equity," in the actual form of a men's prison model, becomes the template for modern prison design.

What we usually mean by structure is something different, however. In the case of an organization, structure includes the distribution of power through hierarchical lines of authority, as well as institutional policies that have written form and unwritten rules that mandate normative practices. Gender may be constructed and reproduced through all these mechanisms. In both men's and women's prisons, men are usually at the top of the organizational hierarchy, predominating in top- and lower-level administration. As in most modern organizations, few policies whose intent is to differentiate staff by gender remain. Inequality is more likely to be perpetuated by seemingly neutral rules, such as requirements for shift work and transfer, that have a disproportionately negative impact on women. Structure may also have the effect of mitigating the effects of gender, as in the case of formal, bureaucratic rules in the federal system that govern the assignments of officers. Informal practices based on taken-for-granted notions about the abilities of men and women contribute to the sex segregation of tasks, even within the same job. As the woman's experience that opens this section indicates, as women have moved into jobs in men's prisons, duties previously performed by men have been redefined as "women's work."

Gendering through Agency

> I do like [my job]. The way I see it is, every man has had a woman in his life as a role model, mother, or an aunt, or a grandmother, tell him what to do at some point in his life. And they will do what you ask them to do as long you don't step on their ego too much. (White female officer)

> I like my job, and I get satisfaction out of, for instance, finding a knife. I get satisfaction out of that because that could not only hurt another inmate, but you know, staff. So, that's where I get my satisfaction from, finding guns, finding a knife. (Hispanic male officer)

As I use it here, agency is the micro level of gendering in organizations; it includes all the interactions in which workers are involved that, intentionally or not, invoke gender or reproduce gender inequality, as well as the process of identity construction through which individuals come to see themselves as appropriately gendered through their work. Officers describe their everyday contacts with inmates in language awash in gender stereotypes; male inmates resist through violence, women use manipulation. Officers' interactions with each other also reflect gendered notions about masculine strength and feminine vulnerability. Gendered identities are forged through work as well. The two officers just quoted represent the stereotypical extremes of this process. For the woman, being a correctional officer in a men's prison is an extension of her role as a mother. Her satisfaction with the work comes from providing maternal guidance to inmates, just as she would to her own children. Though this strategy of identity construction brings femininity into line with the duties of the officer, it is difficult to overemphasize how completely this notion conflicts with masculinized culturally and institutionally perpetuated ideas about men's prisons and their inmates. For the second officer, satisfaction comes from managing and preventing violence. He sees his role as that of a protector and undoubtedly does not find it particularly difficult to maintain this image in an occupation and an institution that explicitly privilege these qualities.

Though they are not representative, the standpoints of these officers do illuminate the boundaries of the interactional processes of gendered attribution in the masculinized occupational environment of the prison. West and Zimmerman argue that gender is "omnirelevant" in our daily interactions. They note, however, that "to 'do' gender is not necessarily to live up to normative conceptions of femininity or masculinity; it is to engage in behavior *at the risk of gender assessment*" (1987: 136, emphasis in original). For the present purposes, what this means is that regardless of the intention of a particular man or woman officer or how they interpret their own identities through work, virtually anything they do "can be assessed as to its womanly or manly nature" (136). Though a woman officer may not wish to fulfill the role of mother or counselor to her charges, she will undoubtedly be called upon to do so, as in the case of the African-American CO who describes the pressure she feels to "seem sensitive" in her interactions with inmates. Doing femininity is also about doing subordination. Though these are the duties allotted to women, they are rarely rewarded in this or any other masculinized work environment. Similarly, men will be called upon to serve as enforcers, whether or not they see themselves in this way. Doing masculinity reproduces dominance, however. The privileging of a masculinized image of the ideal officer means that men accrue substantial benefits for emphasizing their essential difference from women.

Implications for Change

If our goal is the creation of less oppressively gendered organizational environments (Britton 2000), then the most fruitful implications of this work are those that can help us to mitigate the effects of the connection between gender and inequality. Encouraging more realistic portrayals of prison life, depictions that do not revolve around hyperviolent images of animalistic inmates and sadistic wardens and officers, would be a first step toward changing the cultural construction of the prison and our preconceptions about the occupation. *Any* stories of women's real lives in prison would also be welcome. I suspect, however, that the popularity of the currently ubiquitous images of prison has much to do with the politics of race and the perpetuation of racism in American society. The animalistic inmate is also often black, and hence resonates with deeply racialized images of criminality. Changing these depictions will undoubtedly also involve breaking this link in the popular (white) imagination.

At the more immediate level of the institution itself, training that prepares officers for work in men's *and* women's institutions, and that provides men and women officers with information about the very different, and thoroughly gendered, environments they will face would serve all recruits more effectively. It might also go some distance toward removing the stigma attached to women inmates and women's prisons. Ostensibly neutral policies that have a disproportionately negative impact on women might be reconsidered, or at least reformulated in a way that is more accommodating of women's greater domestic responsibilities. Promotion practices that privilege the ability to deal with physical violence over other skills, like the ability to defuse it, should be made more equitable. Though I do not think bureaucratization is a panacea, formalized assignment policies contribute to less sex segregation of tasks in institutions; it also seems clear that efforts to lessen the influence of informal networks in hiring and promotion would greatly improve the advancement prospects of women and minority men. Racism and sexual harassment remain obstacles and should be more aggressively addressed.

Officers' interactions with inmates and other institutional actors would be affected by all these changes. Processes of identity formation in which men have an incentive to "prove themselves as different from and better than" (Williams 1995: 184) women are more difficult to alter. Changes in the institutional rewards that accrue to "essential" masculinity might matter to some extent but would probably have little lasting effect in a culture that privileges masculinity and devalues femininity. As Williams notes, "It is almost overwhelming to consider" (1995: 184) the extent of social change that would be necessary to disrupt the mechanisms of gendered identity construction of which inequality is inevitably the result.

I do not mean to end on an overly pessimistic note. I began this book by asking readers to "imagine a prison guard." My hope is that the image of the officer you now hold is more complex and multifaceted than the brutal turnkey of media-fed fantasies. The people who do this job are men and women and black and white and Hispanic (and people of all other races), and, to the extent that the prison's structure and policies allow, many are concerned about the inmates with whom they work. Day after day, they do society's "dirty work" in an institution that mandates enforcement of rigid rules of conduct but operates on the basis of order negotiated with the currency of discretion. Men no longer—if indeed they ever did—do their jobs by "banging heads." Women have proven that they can perform the previously unimaginable task of working in men's prisons. Many of those in my study, through their experiences and approaches to the work, are quietly and gradually transforming what it means to be an officer within the confines of the prison's iron cage.

Methodological Appendix

This study is based on in-depth interviews I conducted from 1993 to 1998 with seventy-two men and women correctional officers. To allow a wide basis for comparison, my objective in selecting sites and respondents for the research was to include men's and women's prisons, state and federal facilities, and men and women officers. I also sought to speak to a racially diverse group, with as many African-American and Hispanic officers as possible. Table A.1 depicts the distribution of the sample along all these dimensions. I have purposely constructed this table to obscure the numbers of officers in crosscutting categories of race, sex, system, and institution. I gave guarantees of confidentiality to those whom I interviewed and also promised not to reveal enough identifying characteristics about the prisons so that those facilities could be identified.

Gaining access to the sites was one of the most difficult aspects of the research. A long history of sensationalist media accounts of scandals and brutality has made prison administrators understandably wary of outsiders. In all, my proposal for research was rejected by administrators at six prisons (including one to which I later gained access). My initial proposal to a research committee at one institution was declined on the grounds that the study was not "scientific." The psychologist who headed the committee told me that the sample size was too small and that my findings would thus not be in any way generalizable. I drafted and redrafted my proposal more than a dozen times in the hope of making the research appear as innocuous (and "scientific") as possible. After a frustrating year of rejections, the prospect of getting into prison by a more conventional route even began to sound somewhat appealing. Gates were finally opened for me by contacts who had personal connections with administrators in both the state and federal systems. Once I gained the necessary introductions and my proposals for research were approved, I selected facilities with the assistance of staff in

TABLE A.1
*Distribution of Interviewed Officers by System,
Type of Institution, Sex, and Race*

	Total N = 72	Percent
System		
State	36	50
Federal	36	50
Type of institution		
Men's	40	56
Women's	32	44
Sample demographics		
Men	45	63
Women	27	37
White	51	71
African-American	14	19
Hispanic	7	10

central administrative offices in both systems. Even at that point, my proposal was rejected by administrators at two additional prisons. Wardens and (in the federal system) officer unions gave final approval to the project at individual institutions. Beyond the two dimensions of system and type, facilities were chosen on the basis of administrators' willingness to accommodate the research. In broad terms, they are: a federal medium-security men's prison, two low-security federal women's prisons, a maximum-security state men's prison, and a state women's prison that confines inmates at all security levels. Two of these institutions are located in the Midwest, three in the South.

All participants were volunteers. At the state prisons, I recruited officers by means of a short presentation at meetings prior to their shifts. I was given a few moments to describe the research and the interview process, and officers volunteered to be interviewed. At the federal prisons, administrators described my research to officers prior to my visit and collected names of those willing to participate. As table A.1 indicates, the resulting group is diverse in terms of race and gender and also represents a wide range of age and experience. The oldest officer to whom I spoke was sixty, the youngest, nineteen; the average age of officers in the sample was thirty-five. Officers ranged in experience from four months to twenty years, with an average of six years. The average officer in my study had attended some college but had not graduated; college degrees were more common among federal than state COs.

Interviews lasted from thirty minutes to three hours—the average was approximately forty-five minutes—and were tape-recorded and later transcribed for analysis. The original interview schedule was adapted from Williams (1989); a version that guided the interviews in one system is included at the end of the appendix. It is composed of five sections: background and career path information, general work environment issues, perceptions of personal safety and security, quality of life, and future plans. This schedule evolved over time as some questions were added to address issues I had not anticipated and others were dropped when it became clear that they were confusing or irrelevant. Interviews were semistructured; they followed the format of this schedule, but I pursued other topics as they arose. At four of the prisons, I conducted interviews inside the facility, during all three shifts, using offices and conference rooms provided for this purpose. At the fifth, I was not allowed to interview officers at work and instead obtained the telephone numbers of volunteers and called them to arrange interviews. The locations of these interviews varied widely; I talked to officers in restaurants, in private homes, and by phone and even conducted one interview in a car.

As I began this project, I initially considered interviewing inmates about their views of officers. Inmates are, after all, those most affected by the day-to-day work of COs. As my interviews progressed, however, I became convinced that it would be inadvisable to request permission to speak with inmates. The prison subcultures of officers and inmates are characterized in substantial part by a fundamental sense of distrust, an "us versus them" mentality in which any outsider or newcomer is assessed in terms of his or her loyalty to one group or another. While not every officer distrusts every inmate, or vice versa, a climate of suspicion is pervasive. Given that I had spoken to officers, I feared that inmates might be unwilling to be forthcoming with me. Similarly, I worried that if officers knew I would be speaking to inmates, I would have carried the taint, for some, of being "pro-inmate." Thus, for the purposes of the current study, I reluctantly chose not to pursue formal interviews with inmates.

Interviewing people about their work has obvious risks. Workers are understandably concerned that what they say will be relayed to administrators and that their livelihood may be endangered. A handful of officers in this study asked who would hear the tapes of their interviews; I assured them that the transcriber and I would be the only ones to listen to them and that the tapes would be destroyed after transcription. I gave respondents the option of turning off the tape recorder at any point during our conversation (only one did); four preferred that their interviews not be recorded. In these cases, I took extensive notes, which I later transcribed.

Though I provided guarantees of confidentiality to all respondents, some still worried about this issue. This white woman relates the views of her coworkers:

> I know a lot of male officers are thinking that they shouldn't do the interview. They think, she's probably working for [the governor], and this is going to come back on you. And I thought, that could possibly happen. [But] if you were working for [the governor], you probably would not have been allowed on the unit, because we cannot be interviewed by media. *I had to go through the research office, and then through the warden.* That's what I told these officers. And you know that's sad because there is so much that goes on that the public will never know because they cannot talk to us. All the media knows is what the inmates say.

Because my sample was composed of volunteers, I cannot know whether this kind of selection bias was operating. However, I was able to speak to a wide range of respondents, from the very dissatisfied to the extremely dedicated. This officer's comments also hint that officers may have been motivated to do interviews because they feel that no one really knows what goes on in prison. I got the sense that COs feel underappreciated and unfairly stereotyped, and many may have welcomed the opportunity to "set the record straight." It was also my perception (especially during the third shift, which can be monotonous, particularly after inmates have gone to bed) that officers enjoyed a diversion from routine and the opportunity to talk about their work. Most people feel like experts about our work environments, but few of us ever get the chance to tell others what we know.

Finally, interviews, like all interactions, are gendered. The fact that I am a woman undoubtedly made a difference in what respondents said to me. This does not mean that some interviews are more objectively honest than others; as Williams puts it "There is no archimedean point outside the gender system that allows for the collection of pure and unbiased data" (1995: 193–194). Instead, the gender (and race and class) of the respondent and that of the interviewer come together to structure the context and content of the interview (see also Williams and Heikes

1993). I felt this the most when a respondent began a statement with a disclaimer that referenced my gender (and presumably my sympathies), as in the case of this African-American man:

> Well, not to sound sexist or anything, but just to give you an honest observation, men tend to be more argumentative if they think that they have a good chance of winning or they believe in what they're saying to be correct. Women will use anything to have an argument based on their own belief, not even knowing, not even weighing the options if it's correct or not, and then trying to be manipulative based on the fact that you're a male, crying or winking, so there's a difference.

Even when talking to a woman, many officers espoused transparently sexist beliefs. One of the ways they did this was, as in this case, by drawing on the rhetorical separation between women in the free world (of whom I am a representative) and women inmates, though in some cases this line became blurry. Men in particular may have been more cautious in their statements about women coworkers, and women may have felt freer to discuss their concerns with me about male coworkers and supervisors, though I got the sense that they were also sometimes wary about this. This may well have been because they were unsure of whether I would be an ally, or because they were uncertain whether they had actually been discriminated against. Most officers, like most workers, go some distance to give colleagues and supervisors the benefit of the doubt.

Interview Schedule

A. Background Questions/Career Path Information

1. When did you first decide to become a correctional officer? Describe to me how you came to the occupation. What was going on in your life at this time? What were your options?
2. Did you have other jobs in corrections before you came to work at this facility? What were these? (If men's institution) Have you ever worked in a women's facility? (If women's institution) Have you ever worked in a men's facility?

B. General Work Environment Issues

TRAINING

1. Please describe your training experience. Do you think your training prepared you well for the job? Is there any part of your training that you think should be changed? What aspects ought to be maintained?

GENERAL ON-THE-JOB EXPERIENCE

2. What are your roles/duties at work? Where do you spend most of your time? Describe a typical day on the job. Are these the duties you would prefer? If not, what are these and why?

INTERACTIONS WITH COWORKERS

3. How many other men/women typically work with you as correctional officers? Would you say that men and women work together well as officers in this facility? What about other facilities in which you have worked? Do you think there are particular posts/duties that are more appropriate for men/women? Is there any racial tension between officers?

INTERACTIONS WITH INMATES

4. Think for a moment about your work with inmates. Overall, would you say that you enjoy this work? What would you say is your goal/purpose in working with inmates? Are there some types of inmates that are more difficult to manage than others? What kind of officer is most effective in working with inmates? Are there some strategies that are particularly dangerous/ineffective?
5. Do you think inmates react differently to officers on the basis of race/sex? Would you rather work with male/female inmates?

PERCEPTIONS OF SUPERVISION

6. Now we'll talk for a while about your relationships with supervisors. In general, would you say that they are supportive of you in your work? Have there been instances in which you think this has not been the case? If so, can you describe the situation?
7. In general, would you say that the standards for evaluating you/ your work are fair? In your opinion, what's the most important factor in receiving a good evaluation? Would you say that the

standards used for evaluating your coworkers are fair? Do you see any differences by race/sex in evaluations?

8. Are you interested in being promoted to a supervisory position? Why/why not? In your judgment, what are the most important criteria in getting a promotion? Is the process fair?

9. Would you be willing to transfer to another facility if you were promoted? How difficult would this be for you?

GENERAL SATISFACTION

10. For you, what is the most enjoyable aspect of your job? What aspect do you least enjoy? Would you say that coworkers, supervisors, or inmates are responsible for the majority of the problems with which you have to deal at work?

C. Personal Safety and Security

1. During the last six months, have there been instances of physical or sexual violence between inmates in this facility? Could you describe such an incident? On your shift, who usually deals with such incidents? Are you typically involved? Does dealing with violent incidents bother you?

2. Overall, how likely do you think it is that a staff member would be assaulted in this institution? Have there been incidents in which inmates have assaulted staff in this facility in the last six months? Can you give me an example? Were you involved? Does dealing with these kinds of incidents bother you?

3. Overall, would you say that this institution is safe? If not, do you think it's more unsafe for female officers? Male officers? Is there a difference?

D. Quality of Life

1. During the time you've worked here, has the type of inmate housed by this institution changed? If so, has that made your job easier? More difficult? How?

2. What kinds of work programs are provided for inmates at this institution? Are these programs adequate? What about educational programs? Recreation? Should these programs be improved or scaled back in any way?

E. Closing Questions

1. If you had to do it all over again, would you still become a correctional officer?
2. Where do you see yourself in ten years?
3. Any other issues you'd like to talk about/add?

Notes

NOTES TO CHAPTER 1

1. All data are author calculations from the Census of State and Federal Adult Correctional Facilities, 1995 (U.S. Department of Justice 1998). Throughout, calculations exclude community-based facilities (those from which 50 percent or more of inmates are allowed to depart) and co-correctional facilities (recoded as those in which more than 25 percent of inmates are of the opposite sex). Calculations are also restricted to those facilities operated by the Federal Bureau of Prisons or the various state systems. The base number of institutions is 1,147.

2. Data on labor force participation rates come from U.S. Department of Labor (2002a), table A.1. Data on the wage gap come from U.S. Department of Commerce (2001), table A.

3. Author calculation from U.S. Department of Labor (2002b), table 3. These seven job categories are secretaries (4 percent of women workers); elementary school teachers (4 percent); registered nurses (3 percent); nursing aides, orderlies, and attendants (3 percent); cashiers (2 percent); bookkeepers and accounting and auditing clerks (2 percent); and accountants and auditors (2 percent).

4. Data on the wage gap within occupations from U.S. Department of Labor (2002b), table 3.

5. The smaller wage gap for women correctional officers is partly due to the fact that they are in a labor market sector (government) in which recruitment and promotion practices are somewhat standardized. The wage gap by sex in almost all government occupations is smaller than in the private sector.

6. I draw on the "theory of gendered organizations" as set out by Joan Acker, but the levels of analysis I utilize differ slightly. In her 1990 statement of the theory, Acker argues that organizations are gendered at five levels (structure, policy and practice, ideology, interaction, and identity). In a 1992 restatement, the first two levels are combined. I have further simplified this scheme to three levels, structure, culture (ideology), and agency, including interactions as part of the third category.

7. I arrived at this number by subtracting the 91 unique titles of movies or series classified under the plot keywords "female-prison," "female-prisoner,"

"women's-correctional-facility," and "women-in-prison" from the 748 classified under the keyword "prison." I did not check the resulting list of "prison" films for duplications. Regardless, the point is clear—representations of men's prisons and male inmates on film drastically outnumber those of women.

8. I borrow the phrase "iron cage" from Max Weber's (1958 [1905]) classic analysis of the rationalization of modern society in *The Protestant Ethic and the Spirit of Capitalism*. Though he views ideal-typical bureaucracy as the most efficient of all forms of organization, he also sees its advance as a troubling sign of the loss of meaning in public life. In modern society, he argues, we are trapped in a cycle in which accumulation and efficiency serve not as means but as self-justifying ends. We thus find ourselves in an iron cage of ever-increasing technical rationality and bureaucratization. The modern prison, in which the goal of rehabilitation has been eclipsed by utilitarian discourses of safety and custody, is both a literal and a figurative iron cage.

NOTES TO CHAPTER 2

1. Author calculation from U.S. Department of Justice (2001). This is a sample survey; the total number of inmates interviewed in 1997 was 18,326.

2. An extensive academic literature traces the emergence of each of these prison systems, and I have drawn on it heavily here. On the rise of the penitentiary, see, for example, Hirsch (1992), McKelvey (1977 [1936]), Lewis (1965), Rothman (1980, 1990). On reformatories, see Pisciotta (1994). On convict leasing and the farm system, see Mancini (1996); Oshinsky (1996), Walker (1988). Of these, the standard literature on the penitentiary has perhaps paid the least attention to women. Pisciotta (1994), Mancini (1996); Oshinsky (1996), and Walker (1988) mention the presence of women in reformatories, in leasing camps, and on prison farms. In recent years, feminist historians have begun to fill in the gaps, documenting women's experiences in each system. Nicole Hahn Rafter (1990) has written perhaps the most exhaustive work on the treatment of women in men's penitentiaries, focusing on New York, Ohio, and Tennessee (see also Rafter 1982, 1983, 1985). Butler (1997) documents the experiences of women in western men's penitentiaries. On women in Illinois men's penitentiaries, see Dodge (1999). The classic history of the women's reformatory movement is Freedman (1981), though Rafter (1990) covers some of this terrain as well.

3. There is a long tradition of critical scholarship on the prison. Rusche and Kirchheimer (1939) were the first to offer a distinctly Marxist perspective, arguing that prisons operate at least in part to control a given society's supply of surplus labor. For other critical historiography, see Melossi and Pavarini (1981), Ignatieff (1978), and Foucault (1979). Howe (1994) provides a comprehensive review and feminist critique of this literature.

4. For a concise summary of Farnham's methods, see Colvin (1997).

5. For a complete history of the Lancaster facility, see Brenzel (1983).

6. Freedman (1981) gives the date of the opening of the Indiana facility as 1874. Rafter (1990) notes that the first women were transferred from the Jeffersonville, Indiana, men's prison in 1873. Unable to resolve this conflict, I use the earlier date.

7. The Bedford Hills institution was a rare exception. During her tenure as superintendent, Katharine Bement Davis refused to segregate inmates by race, though the facility (which received felons as well as misdemeanants) housed many black inmates (Rafter 1990).

8. The "Black Codes" specified offenses that could only be committed by free blacks. One of the most notorious of these codes, in Mississippi, specified that blacks were required annually to provide written evidence of employment for the year. This was usually a contract for plantation labor (Colvin 1997: 218).

9. This number excludes 304 community-based facilities, defined as those in which 50 percent or more of inmates are allowed to depart, as well as 110 private prisons and 16 joint local and state-operated facilities.

10. Author calculations from U.S. Department of Justice (1998). After restricting the sample, I found that seventy-seven prisons were classified as "co-correctional," meaning that both men and women can be housed there. On closer inspection, I discovered that the overwhelming majority of these held only a few inmates of the opposite sex. I reclassified men's facilities as those with an inmate population that was 75 percent or more male and recoded women's facilities in the same way. I then excluded the remaining eleven facilities from further analysis.

11. These differences are statistically significant.

12. I began the research with the criteria of including an equal number of men's and women's prisons and of interviewing officers at both federal and state-run institutions. One of the men's prisons in which I interviewed is nearby a women's prison, however, which allowed me to add another facility to the sample. Promises of confidentiality to those I interviewed and to those who gave me access to do the research prohibit me from identifying these institutions by name, or from providing enough detail such that they might be identified by other means. For this reason, I have chosen not to give the individual institutions pseudonyms, or to distinguish between them along enough unique dimensions as to make them easily identifiable.

NOTES TO CHAPTER 3

1. This number differs from that in table 3.1 because the reference categories are not the same. The designation "correctional institution officers," used by the Bureau of Labor Statistics and the Census Bureau, includes officers in jails, juvenile prisons and detention facilities, and community-based facilities. The Census

of State and Federal Correctional Facilities, as I have restricted the data, includes only correctional officers in adult prisons.

2. One of the most significant differences between men and women prison inmates is women's much higher level of previous physical and sexual abuse. According to the Bureau of Justice Statistics, 43 percent of female inmates (versus 12 percent of men) report physical or sexual abuse prior to incarceration. Women are six times more likely to have been sexually abused and three times as likely to have been physically abused. Of male and female inmates who had been abused, 50 percent of women experienced that abuse at the hands of an intimate, versus only 3 percent of men (Snell 1994).

NOTES TO CHAPTER 4

1. Author calculation from the National Longitudinal Survey of Youth, 1982 data, weighted.

2. All figures for "whites" are for non-Hispanic whites, as designated by the Census Bureau.

3. Numerous other studies find that correctional officers overwhelmingly report a pattern of occupational drift (Crouch and Marquart 1980; Jurik 1985; Kauffman 1988; Lombardo 1981; Martin and Jurik 1996; Zimmer 1986).

4. The advent of the "crime-fighting" model of policing in the United States in the 1930s solidified the historical trend toward a highly masculinized, paramilitary view of police officers and policing organizations. For a discussion of the development of this model, see Appier (1998). This approach has been challenged in recent years by community policing programs, which emphasize prevention and the building of positive relationships between officers and neighborhood residents. Miller (1999) notes that these programs often have particular appeal for women officers.

5. This pattern of previous military and law enforcement experience for men (but not women) is consistent with that reported in previous research (Jurik 1985; Martin and Jurik 1996; Zimmer 1986).

6. The situation is different for women in policing. This is a field in which the market is much more competitive, and women are adversely affected by hiring policies that give preferences to veterans (National Center for Women and Policing 2002). If the demand for prison officers abates, it is likely that women in corrections will be similarly affected.

7. In a "lockdown," inmates are confined to their cells for an extended period, typically, twenty-three hours per day. These are often imposed in the aftermath of escapes or riots; in this case, a riot at another prison in the system prompted the lockdown.

8. The physical abilities test has five separate components: Dummy drag—drag a seventy-five-pound dummy three minutes continuously for a minimum of

694 feet. Climb and grasp—maximum seven seconds. Obstacle course—maximum fifty-eight seconds. Run and cuff—quarter mile and apply handcuff within two minutes thirty-five seconds. Stair climb—participant with a twenty-pound weight belt will climb up and down 108 steps within forty-five seconds. All persons appointed to the Federal Bureau of Prisons, even those who are not correctional officers, are subject to these training requirements.

9. "Count time" is an integral part of prison routine. At the facilities I visited, inmates were counted and their locations noted as often as seven times a day. If at any time the actual count does not match the official total, all other activity ceases, and the institution may ultimately be "locked down" until the discrepancy can be reconciled.

10. Author calculation from U.S. Department of Justice (1998).

11. Though federal officers express some dissatisfaction with training, their accounts do not suggest that violence is the central focus of their preparation for the job. Federal training places more emphasis on communication and negotiation skills, which may be one of the factors that explains federal officers' higher level of satisfaction with the process.

12. As of this writing, these institutions are USP Florence (Colorado), USP Leavenworth (Kansas), USP Marion (Illinois), USP Terre Haute (Indiana), USP Allenwood (Pennsylvania), USP Lewisburg (Pennsylvania), USP Beaumont (Texas), USP Pollock (Louisiana), USP Atlanta (Georgia), and USP Lompoc (California).

13. Prison officers are not alone in this view. The idea that women are treated more leniently than men by the criminal justice system is taken as received wisdom by much of the general public, and any attempt to refute this notion is sure to elicit the apocryphal story of the woman who feigns crying to avoid receiving a traffic ticket. Systematic research on what has come to be known in the academic literature as the "chivalry" hypothesis reveals that it is largely false, however. On balance, similarly situated men and women (i.e., those who commit the same crimes, under the same circumstances, and who have the same prior records) are treated equally by the criminal justice system (for a review, see Belknap 2001). Similar findings do not hold for offenders of different classes and races, however.

NOTES TO CHAPTER 5

1. Lynn Zimmer (1986) reports similar storytelling about female officers' involvement with male inmates. Some of the accounts in her study had become folklore, with the same details adapted to different characters at a variety of institutions.

2. In the cultural iconography of the prison, the African-American inmate is the stock character—the African-American officer is almost a contradiction in

terms. This was certainly true in older films in the prison genre, but even in recent popular depictions officers are almost exclusively white.

3. This mirrors the findings of some quantitative research utilizing larger samples of officers. For studies finding that African-American and Hispanic officers are more oriented to rehabilitation, see Crouch and Alpert 1982; Van Voorhis et al. 1991; and Whitehead and Lindquist 1989. Other studies find no difference by race, e.g., Cullen, Lutze, and Link 1989; Jacobs and Kraft 1978; Toch and Klofas 1982.

4. A text search for the word "love" in the interview transcripts reveals no other such references to inmates. The only related use of the word is to refer derogatorily to cases in which officers had fallen in love with inmates, become sexually involved, and been fired.

5. Though women spoke of themselves as "mothers" to both men and women inmates, the only men who invoke their role as "father" speak in reference to women.

6. Usually, these are groups of male inmates detailed to perform construction or maintenance tasks at women's prisons.

7. Many quantitative studies find that COs exhibit a custody orientation. See for example, Crouch and Alpert (1982); Cullen, Lutze, and Link (1989); Jacobs (1977); Jurik and Musheno (1986); Poole and Regoli (1980); Van Voorhis et al. (1991).

8. This is not unique to the prison setting. Most people attribute behavior individually; when someone commits a crime or wins an award, our culture's individualist bias leads us to see this as the consequence of personal choices. A central focus of a sociological perspective, on the other hand, is the effect of social context and structure on individual outcomes.

9. This is a danger not unlike that posed by the "role traps" facing women managers described by Kanter (1977). For an application of this concept in the correctional context, see Jurik (1988).

10. There is an exception to women inmates' preference for male officers; inmates strongly favor assignment restrictions that bar men from posts, such as conducting strip searches or supervising showers, that involve viewing inmates naked or dressing and undressing (Owen 1998).

11. Men's fear of being accused of sexual impropriety extends beyond prison walls. Men in many female-dominated professions, such as nursing, elementary school teaching, and social work, take extraordinary steps, such as the use of female chaperones or a strict open-door policy when in the presence of female patients or clients, to avoid any suspicion (Williams 1995). Giuffre and Williams (2000) document male doctors' similar strategies with female patients.

12. The substantial differences between the median and mean values indicate the presence in the sample of a few facilities with extremely large inmate

populations and very high numbers of assaults. In 1995, 4 prisons (out of a total 1,147) reported more than 200 inmate assaults on staff; 17 reported more than 200 inmate assaults on other inmates.

13. There were 2.25 inmate assaults on other inmates for every 100 inmates incarcerated in women's prisons in 1995. For men's prisons, the comparable number is 2.42. The difference between these two values is not statistically significant.

14. In 1995, there were 0.94 staff assaults for every 100 women inmates versus 1.47 per 100 men. The difference between these two values is not statistically significant.

15. Staff can and do physically assault inmates, as the high-profile cases that appear periodically demonstrate. I collected no such accounts from officers, who may obviously have a vested interest in not reporting such behavior. However, I got the sense that this kind of violence is now less common—or at least less legitimate—than it had been in the past. Legal changes of the last two decades, in cases such as *Estelle v. Gamble*, 429 U.S. 97 (1976), *Hudson v. McMillan*, 503 U.S. 1 (1992), and *Ruiz vs. Estelle*, 503 F. Supp. 1295 (1980), have dramatically restricted officers statutory ability to use violence against inmates. Some COs in my study see these changes negatively, complaining that their "hands are tied"; others believe the restrictions create a more humane and safer environment for staff and inmates.

16. A recent soda commercial is just such an example. In the advertisement, a marketing executive is passing out cans of his product to male prison inmates. When he drops a can, he refuses to pick it up. At the end of the commercial, the marketer is sitting uncomfortably in a prison cell, the arm of a much larger inmate draped around his shoulder. This commercial was the subject of protest from groups working to call attention to the problem of prison rape and was eventually pulled from the air (Huber 2002).

17. For a description of the process through which certain male inmates become defined as "women" in prison discourse, see Coggeshall (1991).

18. There is some controversy in the literature on sexuality between men in prison. The tendency in past research was to see all sexual activity between male inmates as coercive or at least as a radical departure from past sexual behavior. More recent survey research suggests that many inmates experience their first same-sex sexual contact before they are incarcerated, and that a substantial amount of sexual activity between men in prison is consensual (Tewksbury 1989a, 1989b; see also Gebhard 1965).

19. Some critics argue that prison rape is systematically ignored by correctional officers and administrators, who believe that men should be able to fend for themselves (for a Web site maintained by the advocacy organization Stop Prisoner Rape, see www.spr.org). Other observers, including an officer in my study, contend that male victims, fearing retaliation from an offender with

whom they are literally locked in, are simply too afraid to report having been victimized. Both of these conditions could contribute to the lack of information I collected around this issue.

20. Some researchers (e.g., Owen 1998) make a distinction between "pseudo-families" and sexual relationships between women inmates in prison. Informal family structures may or may not involve sexual activity between members; one can belong to such a unit without being sexually involved with other inmates.

NOTES TO CHAPTER 6

1. Author calculation, U.S. Department of Justice (1998). "Administrators" is a broad category that includes wardens and superintendents as well as lower-level officials such as deputy and assistant wardens.

2. The first officer's observation suggests another gendered pattern. At the state men's prison, women officers are much more likely than men to be assigned clerical duties. Even within a single posting—that of roving officer—women's duties differ systematically from those of men in ways that reflect gendered notions. For women, the required tasks are much more likely to involve filing and paperwork; men are "runners" for supervisors, performing a variety of tasks throughout the prison.

3. In a "forced cell move," inmates are extracted by force from their cells by a team of officers.

4. I conducted interviews with three couples whose members both work in the same prison system, and with a handful of officers whose spouses also work in other prisons. The men in these couples are generally less concerned about their wives' work in prisons than those cited here.

5. James Fox argues that male officers' fears about women's seduction may be projection:

> Male guards' perceptions of prisoners' "uncontrollable sexual desire" is in part a reflection of their own sexual appetites (inhibited by organizational and social restraints). The prisoner, in this scheme, becomes a handy mirror for revealing male guards' sexual fantasies. (1982: 69)

6. A handful of officers admit that women may have a legitimate basis for their claim of being traumatized by pat searches by male COs. Almost all qualify this support, however, as in the case of the white male officer who asserts that while a "small percentage" of women have been "so abused by men that they have a real true fear of being touched by a man," "a much larger percentage" use the controversy to their advantage to manipulate the system.

7. The same reasoning is used by many women officers who object to the policy; they argue that if men are being paid the same salary, they should have the same duties.

8. The role of dealing with violence in creating opportunities for promotion is similar to that played by combat in the military, another deeply masculinized organization (Williams 1989).

9. Due to the small number of Hispanic women officers in the sample, I was unable to include their responses in my quantitative analysis. Neither Hispanic men nor white women differ significantly from white men in their reported levels of job satisfaction and job stress.

10. Only one African-American officer, a man, expresses any concern about affirmative action policies. He is ambivalent but thinks that in some cases minority officers may be advantaged in hiring and promotion.

11. Where affirmative action quotas have existed, they have been imposed by the courts as an after-the-fact remedy upon employers who have discriminated. The Supreme Court has ruled that such quotas must be temporary and "narrowly drawn" (Reskin 1998).

12. Public attitudes on affirmative action are enormously complex and are fundamentally influenced by the kind of program being described in a given survey question. As Reskin (1998) points out, we have very little data on the kinds of affirmative action that are actually being practiced. For a discussion of survey research on this issue, see Steeh and Krysan (1996).

13. There is little research on the issue of whether affirmative action programs have the effect of increasing "white backlash." One study (Taylor 1995) finds that workers in firms that have such programs are actually more supportive of race-targeted remedies than those who do not work for such companies.

14. This reflects the findings of a larger quantitative study of federal correctional officers (Camp, Steiger, and Batchelder 1995). This research finds that both women and minority COs (these two categories are compared separately) evaluate the opportunities of minorities less positively than do whites.

15. The fact that a rehabilitation orientation and job satisfaction are so intimately linked for many officers has important implications. To the extent that these COs feel that institutional structure and policy impede their efforts to work effectively with inmates, they are likely to be particularly dissatisfied with their work. This perhaps explains the persistent association between higher education and job dissatisfaction in a number of quantitative studies of correctional officers (Cullen et al. 1985; Jurik and Musheno 1986; Jurik and Halemba 1984).

References

Acker, Joan. 1989. *Doing Comparable Worth: Gender, Class and Pay Equity.* Philadelphia: Temple University Press.

———. 1990. "Hierarchies, Jobs, Bodies: A Theory of Gendered Organizations." *Gender and Society* 4:139–158.

——— 1992. "From Sex Roles to Gendered Institutions." *Contemporary Sociology* 21:565–568.

Acker, Joan, and Donald R. Van Houten. 1974. "Differential Recruitment and Control: The Sex Structuring of Organizations." *Administrative Science Quarterly* 19: 152–163.

Amnesty International. 1999a. "Not Part of My Sentence": Violations of the Human Rights of Women in Custody. London: Amnesty International. On-line: www.amnesty.org.

———. 1999b. A Visit to Valley State Prison for Women. London: Amnesty International. On-line: www.amnesty.org

Appier, Janis. 1998. *Policing Women: The Sexual Politics of Law Enforcement and the LAPD.* Philadelphia: Temple University Press.

Arneil, Barbara. 1999. *Politics and Feminism.* Oxford: Blackwell Publishers.

Ayers, Edward L. 1984. *Vengeance and Justice: Crime and Punishment in the Nineteenth-Century American South.* New York: Oxford University Press.

———. 1992. *The Promise of the New South: Life after Reconstruction.* New York: Oxford University Press.

Beck, Allen J., and Paige M. Harrison. 2001. Prisoners in 2000. Washington, DC: U.S. Department of Justice. On-line: www.usdoj.gov.

Belknap, Joanne. 2001. *The Invisible Woman: Gender, Crime, and Justice.* 2d ed. Belmont, CA: Wadsworth.

Belluck, Pam. 2001. "Desperate for Prison Guards, Some States Rob Cradles." *New York Times,* 21 April, national edition.

Bielby, William T., and Denise D. Bielby. 1992. "I Will Follow Him: Family Ties, Gender-Role Beliefs, and Reluctance to Relocate for a Better Job." *American Journal of Sociology* 97:1241–1267.

Blau, Judith R., Stephen C. Light, and Mitchell Chamlin. 1986. "Individual and Contextual Effects on Stress and Job Satisfaction: A Study of Prison Staff." *Work and Occupations* 13:131–156.

Blauner, Bob, ed. 1989. *Black Lives, White Lives: Three Decades of Race Relations in America.* Berkeley: University of California Press.

Blum, Linda M., and Peggy Kahn. 1996. "'We Didn't Hire You for Your Children': The Gendered Consequences of Nonstandard Working Hours in the Service Sector." Paper presented at the annual meetings of the American Sociological Association, New York.

Bose, Christine, and Peter Rossi. 1983. "Gender and Jobs: Prestige Standings of Occupations as Affected by Gender." *American Sociological Review* 48: 316–330.

Brenzel, Barbara M. 1983. *Daughters of the State: A Social Portrait of the First Reform School for Girls in North America, 1856–1905.* Cambridge: MIT Press.

Britton, Dana M. 1997a. "Gendered Organizational Logic: Policy and Practice in Men's and Women's Prisons." *Gender and Society* 11:796–818.

———. 1997b. "Perceptions of the Work Environment among Correctional Officers: Do Race and Sex Matter?" *Criminology* 35:85–105.

———. 1999. "Cat Fights and Gang Fights: Preference for Work in a Male-Dominated Organization." *Sociological Quarterly* 40:455–474.

———. 2000. "The Epistemology of the Gendered Organization." *Gender and Society* 14:418–435.

Britton, Dana M., and Christine L. Williams. 1996. "Don't Ask, Don't Tell, Don't Pursue: Military Policy and the Construction of Heterosexual Masculinity." *Journal of Homosexuality* 30:1–21.

Burkhart, Kathryn. 1973. *Women in Prison.* Garden City, NY: Doubleday.

Burrell, Gibson. 1984. "Sex and Organizational Analysis." *Organization Studies* 5:97–118.

Burrell, Gibson, and Jeff Hearn. 1989. "The Sexuality of Organization." Pp. 1–28 in *The Sexuality of Organization,* edited by Jeff Hearn, Deborah Sheppard, Peta Tancred-Sheriff, and Gibson Burrell. London: Sage Publications.

Butler, Anne M. 1997. *Gendered Justice in the American West: Women Prisoners in Men's Penitentiaries.* Urbana: University of Illinois Press.

Camp, Scott D., Thomas L. Steiger, and Jennifer A. Batchelder. 1995. "Perceptions of Job Advancement Opportunities: A Multilevel Investigation of Race and Gender Effects." Washington, DC: Office of Research and Evaluation, Federal Bureau of Prisons. On-line: www.bop.gov.

Carlen, Pat. 1983. *Women's Imprisonment.* London: Routledge and Kagan Paul.

Carlen, Pat, and Chris Tchaikovsky. 1985. "Women in Prison." Pp. 182–186 in *Criminal Women,* edited by Pat Carlen, J. Hicks, J. O'Dwyer, and D. Christina. Cambridge: Polity Press.

Cheek, F. E., and M. D. Miller. 1983. "The Experience of Stress for Correctional Officers: A Double-Bind Theory of Correctional Stress." *Journal of Criminal Justice* 11:105–120.

Chesney-Lind, Meda. 1996. "Sentencing Women to Prison: Equality without Justice." Pp. 127–140 in *Race, Class and Gender in Criminology: The Intersection*, edited by Martin D. Schwartz and Dragan Milovanovic. New York: Garland Press.

Chodorow, Nancy. 1978. *The Reproduction of Mothering*. Berkeley: University of California Press.

Cockburn, Cynthia. 1983. *Brothers: Male Dominance and Technological Change*. London: Pluto Press.

———. 1985. *Machinery of Dominance: Women, Men and Technical Know-How*. London: Pluto Press.

Coggeshall, John M. 1991. "Those Who Surrender are Female: Prisoner Gender Identities as Cultural Mirror." Pp. 81–95 in *Transcending Boundaries*, edited by Pamela Frese and John M. Coggeshall. New York: Bergin and Garvey.

Collins, Patricia Hill. 2000. *Black Feminist Thought: Knowledge, Consciousness, and the Politics of Empowerment*. 2d ed. New York: Routledge.

Collins, William C. 1991. "Legal Issues and the Employment of Women." Pp. 13–18 in *Change, Challenge, and Choices: Women's Role in Modern Corrections*, edited by Joann B. Morton. Laurel, MD: American Correctional Association.

Collinson, David L., and Margaret Collinson. 1989. "Sexuality in the Workplace: The Domination of Men's Sexuality." Pp. 91–109 in *The Sexuality of Organization*, edited by Jeff Hearn, Deborah Sheppard, Peta Tancred-Sheriff, and Gibson Burrell. London: Sage Publications.

Colvin, Mark. 1997. *Penitentiaries, Reformatories, and Chain Gangs: Social Theory and the History of Punishment in Nineteenth-Century America*. New York: St. Martin's Press.

Connell, Robert W. 1987. *Gender and Power*. Stanford: Stanford University Press.

Crouch, Ben M. 1980. "The Guard in a Changing Prison World." Pp. 5–45 in *The Keepers: Prison Guards and Contemporary Corrections*, edited by Ben M. Crouch. Springfield, IL: Charles C. Thomas.

Crouch, Ben M., and G. P. Alpert. 1982. "Sex and Occupational Socialization among Prison Guards." *Criminal Justice and Behavior* 9:159–176.

Crouch, Ben M., and James W. Marquart. 1980. "On Becoming a Prison Guard." Pp. 63–109 in *The Keepers: Prison Guards and Contemporary Corrections*, edited by Ben M. Crouch. Springfield, IL: Charles C. Thomas.

Cullen, Francis T., Bruce G. Link, Nancy T. Wolfe, and James Frank. 1985. "The Social Dimensions of Correctional Officer Stress." *Justice Quarterly* 2: 505–533.

Cullen, Francis T., Faith E. Lutze, and Bruce G. Link. 1989. "The Correctional Orientation of Prison Guards: Do Officers Support Rehabilitation?" *Federal Probation* 53:33–42.

Daniels, Jessie. 1997. *White Lies: Race, Class, Gender, and Sexuality in White Supremacist Discourse.* New York: Routledge.

Davies, Margery W. 1982. *Woman's Place Is at the Typewriter: Office Work and Office Workers 1870–1930.* Philadelphia: Temple University Press.

Dellinger, Kirsten, and Christine L. Williams. 2002. "The Locker Room and the Dorm Room: Workplace Norms and the Boundaries of Sexual Harassment in Magazine Editing." *Social Problems* 49:242–257.

Di Tomaso, Nancy. 1989. "Sexuality in the Workplace: Discrimination and Harassment." Pp. 71–90 in *The Sexuality of Organization*, edited by Jeff Hearn, Deborah Sheppard, Peta Tancred–Sheriff, and Gibson Burrell. London: Sage Publications.

Dodge, L. Mara. 1999. "'One Female Prisoner Is More Trouble Than Twenty Males': Women Convicts in Illinois Prisons, 1835–1896." *Journal of Social History* 32:907–930.

Du Bois, William Edward Burghardt. 1989 [1903]. *The Souls of Black Folk.* New York: Bantam Books.

Duffee, David. 1974. "The Correction Officer Subculture and Organizational Change." *Journal of Research in Crime and Delinquency* 11:155–172.

Dumm, Thomas L. 1987. *Democracy and Punishment.* Madison: University of Wisconsin Press.

Durkheim, Émile. 1950 [1985]. *The Rules of Sociological Method.* Translated by Sarah A. Solovay and John H. Mueller, edited by E. G. Catlin. Glencoe, IL: Free Press.

Elias, Norbert. 1978 [1939]. *The Civilizing Process I: The History of Manners.* New York: Urizen Books.

———. 1982 [1939]. *The Civilizing Process II: Power and Civility.* New York: Pantheon.

England, Paula. 1982. "The Failure of Human Capital Theory to Explain Occupational Sex Segregation." *Journal of Human Resources* 17: 358–370.

England, Paula, and Melissa Herbert. 1993. "The Pay of Men in 'Female' Occupations: Is Comparable Worth Only for Women?" Pp. 28–48 in *Doing "Women's Work": Men in Nontraditional Occupations*, edited by Christine L. Williams. Newbury Park, CA: Sage Publications.

England, Paula, Melissa Herbert, Barbara Kilbourne, Lori Reid, and Lori Megdal. 1994. "The Gendered Valuation of Occupations and Skills: Earnings in 1980 Census Occupations." *Social Forces* 73:65–99.

Epstein, Cynthia Fuchs. 1988. *Deceptive Distinctions: Sex, Gender, and the Social Order.* New Haven: Yale University Press.

Faith, Karlene. 1993. *Unruly Women: The Politics of Confinement and Resistance.* Vancouver: Press Gang Publishers.

Feagin, Joe R., and Melvin P. Sikes. 1994. *Living with Racism: The Black Middle-Class Experience.* Boston: Beacon Press.

Feagin, Joe R., Hernán Vera, and Nikitah Imani. 1996. *The Agony of Education: Black Students at White Colleges and Universities.* New York: Routledge.

Feinman, Clarice. 1994. *Women in the Criminal Justice System.* 3d ed. Westport, CT: Praeger Publishers.

Ferguson, Anne Arnett. 2000. *Bad Boys: Public Schools in the Making of Black Masculinity.* Ann Arbor: University of Michigan Press.

Fitzpatrick, Ellen. 1990. *Endless Crusade: Women Social Scientists and Progressive Reform.* New York: Oxford University Press.

Fletcher, Joyce K. 1998. "Relational Practice: A Feminist Reconstruction of Work." *Journal of Management Inquiry* 7:163–186.

Foucault, Michel. 1979. *Discipline and Punish: The Birth of the Prison.* Translated by Alan Sheridan. New York: Pantheon Books.

Fox, James G. 1975. "Women in Crisis." Pp. 181–205 in *Man in Crisis*, edited by Hans Toch. Chicago: Aldine-Atherton.

———. 1982. *Organizational and Racial Conflict in Maximum-Security Prisons.* Lexington, MA: Lexington Books.

Freedman, Estelle B. 1981. *Their Sisters' Keepers: Women's Prison Reform in America, 1830–1930.* Ann Arbor: University of Michigan Press.

———. 1996. *Maternal Justice: Miriam Van Waters and the Female Reform Tradition.* Chicago: University of Chicago Press.

Garfinkel, Harold. 1967. "Passing and the Managed Achievement of Sex Status in an 'Intersexed' Person, Part One." Pp. 116–185 in *Studies in Ethnomethodology.* Oxford: Polity Press.

Garland, David. 1990. *Punishment and Modern Society: A Study in Social Theory.* New York: Oxford University Press.

Gebhard, Paul H. 1965. *Sex Offenders: An Analysis of Types.* A publication of the Kinsey Institute for Sex Research. New York: Harper and Row.

General Accounting Office. 1999. Women in Prison: Sexual Misconduct by Correctional Staff. Washington, DC: General Accounting Office. On-line: www.gao.gov.

Giallombardo, Rose. 1966. *Society of Women: A Study of a Women's Prison.* New York: John Wiley.

Giuffre, Patti, and Christine L. Williams. 2000. "Not Just Bodies: Strategies for Desexualizing the Physical Examination of Patients." *Gender and Society* 14: 457–482.

Goffman, Erving. 1961. *Asylums: Essays on the Social Situation of Mental Patients and Other Inmates.* New York: Anchor Books.

———. 1977. "The Arrangement between the Sexes." *Theory and Society* 4: 301–331.

Gould, Stephen Jay. 1981. *The Mismeasure of Man.* New York: W. W. Norton.

Granovetter, Mark. 1995. *Getting a Job: A Study of Contacts and Careers* 2d ed. Chicago: University of Chicago Press.

Gwaltney, John Langston. 1980. *Drylongso: A Self-Portrait of Black America.* New York: Vintage Books.

Hartmann, Heidi I. 1976. "Capitalism, Patriarchy, and Job Segregation by Sex." *Signs: Journal of Women in Culture and Society* 1:137–169.

Hawkes, Mary G. 1991. "Women's Changing Roles in Corrections." Pp. 100–110 in *Change, Challenge and Choices: Women's Role in Modern Corrections,* edited by Joann B. Morton. Waldorf, MD: American Correctional Association.

Hawkins, Gordon. 1980. "Correctional Officer Selection and Training." Pp. 49–62 in *The Keepers: Prison Guards and Contemporary Corrections,* edited by Ben M. Crouch. Springfield, IL: Charles C. Thomas.

Hearn, Jeff, and Wendy Parkin. 1987. *"Sex" at "Work": The Power and Paradox of Organization Sexuality.* New York: St. Martin's Press.

Heffernan, Esther. 1972. *Making It in Prison: The Square, the Cool, and the Life.* New York: John Wiley.

Held, Virginia. 1993. *Feminist Morality: Transforming Culture, Society, and Politics.* Chicago: University of Chicago Press.

Hirsch, Adam J. 1992. *The Rise of the Penitentiary.* New Haven: Yale University Press.

Hochschild, Arlie Russell. 1983. *The Managed Heart: Commercialization of Human Feeling.* Berkeley: University of California Press.

Howe, Adrian. 1994. *Punish and Critique: Towards a Feminist Analysis of Penality.* London: Routledge.

Huber, Emily. 2002. 7-Up Bubbles over Prison Rape. Mother Jones News Updates, May 13. On-line: www.motherjones.com.

Human Rights Watch. 1996. All Too Familiar: Sexual Abuse of Women in U.S. State Prisons. New York: Human Rights Watch. On-line: www.hrw.org.

———. 1998. Nowhere to Hide: Retaliation against Women in Michigan State Prisons. On-line: www.hrw.org

Ignatieff, Michael. 1978. *A Just Measure of Pain.* New York: Pantheon.

Jacobs, James B. 1977. *Stateville: The Penitentiary in Mass Society.* Chicago: University of Chicago Press.

Jacobs, James B., and Harold G. Retsky. 1975. "Prison Guard." *Urban Life* 4:5–29.

Jacobs, James B., and Lawrence J. Kraft. 1978. "Integrating the Keepers: A Comparison of Black and White Prison Guards in Illinois." *Social Problems* 25:304–318.

Jencks, Christopher, L. Perman, and Lee Rainwater. 1988. "What Is a Good Job? A New Measure of Labor Market Success." *American Journal of Sociology* 93:1322–1357.

Jenne, D. L. and R. C. Kersting. 1998. "Gender, Power, and Reciprocity in the Correctional Setting." *Prison Journal* 78:166–185.

Jurik, Nancy C. 1985. "An Officer and a Lady: Organizational Barriers to Women Working as Correctional Officers in Men's Prisons." *Social Problems* 32:375–388.

―――. 1988. "Striking a Balance: Female Correctional Officers, Gender Role Stereotypes, and Male Prisons." *Sociological Inquiry* 58:291–305.

Jurik, Nancy C., and Gregory J. Halemba. 1984. "Gender, Working Conditions, and Job Satisfaction of Women in a Non-traditional Occupation: Female Correctional Officers in Men's Prisons." *Sociological Quarterly* 25:551–566.

Jurik, Nancy C., and Michael C. Musheno. 1986. "The Internal Crisis of Corrections: Professionalization and the Work Environment." *Justice Quarterly* 3:457–480.

Kanter, Rosabeth Moss. 1977. *Men and Women of the Corporation.* New York: Basic Books.

Kauffman, Kelsey. 1988. *Prison Officers and Their World.* Cambridge: Harvard University Press.

Kaufman, D., and M. Fetters. 1980. "Work Motivation and Job Values among Professional Men and Women: A New Accounting." *Journal of Vocational Behavior* 16:251–262.

Kessler, Suzanne, and Wendy McKenna. 1978. *Gender: An Ethnomethodological Approach.* New York: John Wiley.

Kissel, Peter J., and Paul L. Katsampes. 1980. "The Impact of Women Corrections Officers on the Functioning of Institutions Housing Male Inmates." *Journal of Offender Counseling, Services and Rehabilitation* 4:213–231.

Lamming, George. 1983. *In the Castle of My Skin.* New York: Schocken Books.

Leidner, Robin. 1991. "Selling Hamburgers and Selling Insurance: Gender, Work, and Identity in Interactive Service Jobs." *Gender and Society* 5:154–177.

―――. 1993. *Fast Food, Fast Talk: Service Work and the Routinization of Everyday Life.* Berkeley: University of California Press.

Leonard, Eileen B. 1983. "Judicial Decisions and Prison Reform: The Impact of Litigation on Women Prisoners." *Social Problems* 31:45–58.

Lewis, W. David. 1965. *From Newgate to Dannemora: The Rise of the Penitentiary in New York, 1796–1848.* Ithaca: Cornell University Press.

Lombardo, Lucien. 1981. *Guards Imprisoned: Correctional Officers at Work.* New York: Elsevier.

Lunden, Walter A. 1965. *The Prison Warden and the Custodial Staff.* Springfield, IL: Charles C. Thomas.

Lynch, Frederick R. 1991. *Invisible Victims: White Males and the Crisis of Affirmative Action.* New York: Praeger.

MacKinnon, Catharine. 1987. *Feminism Unmodified: Discourses on Life and Law.* Cambridge: Harvard University Press.

Mancini, Matthew J. 1996. *One Dies, Get Another: Convict Leasing in the American South, 1866–1928.* Columbia: University of South Carolina Press.

Marini, Margaret Mooney, and Mary C. Brinton. 1984. "Sex Typing and Occupational Socialization." Pp. 192–232 in *Sex Segregation in the Workplace*, edited by Barbara Reskin. Washington, DC: National Academy Press.

Martin, Patricia Yancey. 2001. "'Mobilizing Masculinities': Women's Experiences of Men at Work." *Organization* 8:587–618.

Martin, Patricia Yancey, and David Collinson. 2002. "'Over the Pond and across the Water': Developing the Field of Gendered Organizations." *Gender, Work and Organization* 9:244–265.

Martin, Steve J., and Sheldon Ekland-Olson. 1987. *Texas Prisons: The Walls Came Tumbling Down*. Austin: Texas Monthly Press.

Martin, Susan E. 1980. *"Breaking and Entering": Policewomen on Patrol*. Berkeley: University of California Press.

———. 1995. "The Interactive Effects of Race and Sex on Women Police Officers." Pp. 383–397 in *The Criminal Justice System and Women: Offenders, Victims, and Workers*, edited by Barbara Raffel Price and Natalie J. Sokoloff. New York: McGraw-Hill.

Martin, Susan E., and Nancy C. Jurik. 1996. *Doing Justice, Doing Gender: Women in Law and Criminal Justice Occupations*. Thousand Oaks, CA: Sage Publications.

Masur, Louis P. 1989. *Rites of Execution: Capital Punishment and the Transformation of American Culture, 1776–1865*. New York: Oxford University Press.

McClellan, Dorothy. 1994. "Disparity in the Discipline of Male and Female Inmates in Texas Prisons." *Women and Criminal Justice* 5:71–97.

McKelvey, Blake. 1977 [1936]. *American Prisons: A History of Good Intentions*. Montclair, NJ: Patterson Smith.

McMahon, Maeve. 1999. *Women on Guard: Discrimination and Harassment in Corrections*. Toronto: University of Toronto Press.

Melossi, Dario, and Massimo Pavarini. 1981. *The Prison and the Factory*. Totawa, NJ: Barnes and Noble Books.

Miller, Jerome. 1996. *Search and Destroy: African-American Males in the Criminal Justice System*. New York: Cambridge University Press.

Miller, Susan L. 1999. *Gender and Community Policing: Walking the Talk*. Boston: Northeastern University Press.

Miller, Teresa A. 2000. "Sex and Surveillance: Gender, Privacy and the Sexualization of Power in Prison." *George Mason University Civil Rights Law Journal* 10:291–356.

Mitford, Jessica. 1973. *Kind and Usual Punishment: The Prison Business*. New York: Vintage Books.

Morris, Allison, and Ania Wilczynski. 1995. "Rocking the Cradle: Mothers Who Kill Their Children." Pp. 198–217 in *Moving Targets: Women, Murder and Representation*, edited by Helen Birch. Berkeley: University of California Press.

Moyer, Imogene L. 1978. "Differential Social Structures and Homosexuality among Women in Prison." *Prison Journal* 64:45–56.

National Center for Women and Policing. 2002. *Equality Denied: The Status of Women in Policing, 2002.* On-line: www.feminist.org/police/ncwp.asp.

O'Brien, Patricia. 2001: *Making It in the "Free World": Women in Transition from Prison.* Albany: SUNY Press.

O'Farrell, Bridget, and S. Harlan. 1982. "Craftworkers and Clerks: The Effect of Male Coworker Hostility on Women's Satisfaction with Nontraditional Jobs." *Social Problems* 29:252–265.

Omi, Michael, and Howard Winant. 1986. *Racial Formation in the United States: From the 1960s to the 1980s.* New York: Routledge and Kagan Paul.

Omolade, Barbara. 1994. *The Rising Song of African-American Women.* New York: Routledge.

Oshinsky, David M. 1996. *"Worse Than Slavery": Parchman Farm and the Ordeal of Jim Crow Justice.* New York: Free Press.

Owen, Barbara. 1988. *The Reproduction of Social Control: A Study of Prison Workers at San Quentin.* New York: Praeger.

———. 1998. *"In the Mix": Struggle and Survival in a Women's Prison.* Albany: SUNY Press.

Pateman, Carole. 1988. *The Sexual Contract.* Oxford: Polity Press.

Peña, Manuel. 1981. "Class, Gender, and Machismo: The 'Treacherous-Woman' Folklore of Mexican Male Workers." *Gender and Society* 5:30–46.

Pierce, Jennifer L. 1995. *Gender Trials: Emotional Lives in Contemporary Law Firms.* Berkeley: University of California Press.

Pisciotta, Alexander W. 1994. *Benevolent Repression: Social Control and the American Reformatory-Prison Movement.* New York: NYU Press.

Pollock-Byrne, Jocelyn M. 1986. *Sex and Supervision: Guarding Male and Female Inmates.* New York: Greenwood Press.

Poole, Eric D., and Robert M. Regoli. 1980. "Role Stress, Custody Orientation, and Disciplinary Actions: A Study of Prison Guards." *Criminology* 18:215–226.

Preyer, Kathryn. 1982. "Penal Measures in the American Colonies: An Overview." *American Journal of Legal History* 26:326–353.

Pringle, Rosemary. 1989. *Secretaries Talk: Sexuality, Power, and Work.* London: Verso.

———. 1993. "Male Secretaries." Pp. 128–151 in *Doing "Women's Work": Men in Nontraditional Occupations,* edited by Christine L. Williams. Newbury Park, CA: Sage Publications.

Prokos, Anastasia, and Irene Padavic. 2002. "'There Oughtta Be a Law against Bitches': Masculinity Lessons in Police Academy Training." *Gender, Work and Organization* 9:438–458.

Putnam, Robert D. 2000. *Bowling Alone: The Collapse and Revival of American Community.* New York: Simon and Schuster.

Rafter, Nicole Hahn. 1982. "Hard Times: Custodial Prisons and the Example of the New York State Prison for Women at Auburn, 1893–1933." Pp. 237–260 in *Judge, Lawyer, Victim, Thief: Women, Gender Roles, and Criminal Justice*, edited by Nicole Hahn Rafter and Elizabeth Stanko. Boston: Northeastern University Press.

———. 1983. "Chastizing the Unchaste: Social Control Functions of a Women's Reformatory, 1894–1931." Pp. 288–311 in *Social Control and the State: Historical and Comparative Essays*, edited by Stanley Cohen and Andrew Scull. Oxford: Martin Robertson.

———. 1985. "Gender, Prisons, and Prison History." *Social Science History* 9: 233–247.

———. 1990. *Partial Justice: Women, Prisons, and Social Control.* 2d ed. New Brunswick, NJ: Transaction Publishers.

———. 2000. *Shots in the Mirror: Crime Films and Society.* New York: Oxford University Press.

Reskin, Barbara F. 1998. *The Realities of Affirmative Action in Employment.* Washington, DC: American Sociological Association.

Reskin, Barbara F., and Irene Padavic. 1988. "Supervisors as Gatekeepers: Male Supervisors' Response to Women's Integration in Plant Jobs." *Social Problems* 35:536–550.

Reskin, Barbara F., and Patricia A. Roos. 1990. *Job Queues, Gender Queues: Explaining Women's Inroads into Male Occupations.* Philadelphia: Temple University Press.

Ridgeway, Cecilia L. 1997. "Interaction and the Conservation of Gender Inequality." *American Sociological Review.* 62:218–235.

Roos, Patricia A. 1990. "Hot-Metal to Electronic Composition: Gender, Technology, and Social Change." Pp. 275–298 in *Job Queues, Gender Queues: Explaining Women's Inroads into Male Occupations*, edited by Barbara F. Reskin and Patricia A. Roos. Philadelphia: Temple University Press.

Rothman, David J. 1980. *Conscience and Convenience: The Asylum and Its Alternatives in Progressive America.* Boston: Little, Brown.

———. 1990. *The Discovery of the Asylum: Social Order and Disorder in the New Republic.* 2d ed. Boston: Back Bay Books.

Rowe, R., and W. E. Snizek. 1995. "Gender Differences in Work Values: Perpetuating the Myth." *Work and Occupations* 22:215–229.

Rusche, Georg, and Otto Kirchheimer. 1939. *Punishment and Social Structure.* New York: Columbia University Press.

Schulz, Rockwell, James R. Greeley, and Roger Brown. 1995. "Organization, Management and Client Effects on Staff Burnout." *Journal of Health and Social Behavior* 36:333–345.

Schur, Edwin M. 1984. *Labeling Women Deviant: Gender, Stigma, and Social Control.* New York: Random House.

Semple, Janet. 1993. *Bentham's Prison: A Study of the Panopticon Penitentiary*. New York: Oxford University Press.

Sheppard, Deborah L. 1989. "Organizations, Power and Sexuality: The Image and Self-Image of Women Managers." Pp. 139–157 in *The Sexuality of Organization*, edited by Jeff Hearn, Deborah Sheppard, Peta Tancred-Sheriff, and Gibson Burrell. London: Sage Publications.

Shihadeh, Edward S. 1991. "The Prevalence of Husband-Centered Migration: Employment Consequences for Married Mothers." *Journal of Marriage and the Family* 53:432–444.

Skuratowicz, Eva. 1996. "Damping down the Fires: Male Dominance and the Second Stage of Women's Integration into the Fire Service." Paper presented at the annual meetings of the American Sociological Association, August, New York.

Smith, Dorothy E. 1979. "A Sociology for Women." Pp. 135–187 in *The Prism of Sex: Essays in the Sociology of Knowledge*, edited by Julia A. Sherman and Evelyn Torton Beck. Madison: University of Wisconsin Press.

Snell, Tracy L. 1994. Women in Prison. Washington, DC: Bureau of Justice Statistics. On-line: www.ojp.usdoj.gov.

Steeh, Charlotte, and Maria Krysan. 1996. "Trends: Affirmative Action and the Public, 1970–1995." *Public Opinion Quarterly* 60:128–158.

Steinberg, Ronnie J. 1990. "Social Construction of Skill: Gender, Power and Comparable Worth." *Work and Occupations* 17:482–499.

Stephan, James J. 1997. Census of State and Federal Correctional Facilities, 1995. Washington, DC: U.S. Department of Justice. On-line: www.ojp.usdoj.gov.

Sykes, Gresham M. 1958. *The Society of Captives: A Study of a Maximum Security Prison*. Princeton: Princeton University Press.

Szockyj, E. 1989. "Working in a Man's World: Women Correctional Officers in an Institution for Men." *Canadian Journal of Criminology* 31:319–328.

Taylor, Marylee C. 1995. "White Backlash to Workplace Affirmative Action: Peril or Myth?" *Social Forces* 73:1385–1414.

Teeters, Negley K. 1955. *The Cradle of the Penitentiary: Walnut Street Jail at Philadelphia, 1773–1835*. Philadelphia: Temple University Press.

Teeters, Negley K., and John Shearer. 1957. *The Prison at Philadelphia: Cherry Hill*. New York: Columbia University Press.

Tewksbury, Richard. 1989a. "Fear of Sexual Assault in Prison Inmates." *Prison Journal* 69:62–71.

———. 1989b. "Measures of Sexual Behavior in an Ohio Prison." *Social Science Research* 74:34–39.

Toch, Hans, and J. Klofas. 1982. "Alienation and Desire for Job Enrichment among Correction Officers." *Federal Probation* 46:35–44.

Tucker, William H. 1994. *The Science and Politics of Racial Research*. Urbana: University of Illinois Press.

U.S. Department of Commerce. Bureau of the Census. 2000. Money Income in the United States, 1998. Washington, DC. On-line: www.census.gov.

———. 2001. Money Income in the United States, 2000. Washington, DC. On-line: www.census.gov.

———. 2002. *Statistical Abstract of the United States, 2001.* Washington, DC. On-line: www.census.gov.

U.S. Department of Justice. Bureau of Justice Statistics. 1998. Census of State and Federal Adult Correctional Facilities, 1995 [Computer file]. Conducted by U.S. Department of Commerce, Bureau of the Census. ICPSR ed. Ann Arbor: Inter-university Consortium for Political and Social Research [producer and distributor]. On-line: www.icpsr.umich.edu. ICPSR study no. 6593.

———. Federal Bureau of Prisons. 2001. Survey of Inmates in State and Federal Correctional Facilities, 1997 [Computer file]. Compiled by U.S. Dept. of Commerce, Bureau of the Census. ICPSR ed. Ann Arbor: Inter-university Consortium for Political and Social Research [producer and distributor]. On-line: www.icpsr.umich.edu. ICPSR study no.2598.

U.S. Department of Labor. Bureau of Labor Statistics. 2000. Occupational Outlook Handbook. Washington, DC. On-line: www.bls.gov.

———. 2001a. Census of Fatal Occupational Injuries, 2000. Washington, DC: U.S. Department of Labor. Washington, DC. On-line: www.bls.gov.

———. 2001b. Highlights of Women's Earnings in 2000. Washington, DC. On-line: www.bls.gov.

———. 2001c. Survey of Occupational Injuries and Illnesses, 2000. Washington, DC. On-line: www.bls.gov.

———. 2002a. Employment Situation: June 2002. Washington, DC. On-line: www.bls.gov.

———. 2002b. Highlights of Women's Earnings in 2001. Washington, DC. On-line: www.bls.gov.

Van Voorhis, Patricia, Francis T. Cullen, Bruce G. Link, and Nancy Travis Wolfe. 1991. "The Impact of Race and Gender on Correctional Officers' Orientation to the Integrated Environment." *Journal of Research in Crime and Delinquency* 28:472–500.

Walker, Donald R. 1988. *Penology for Profit: A History of the Texas Prison System, 1867–1912.* College Station: Texas A&M University Press.

Walker, J., C. Tausky, and D. Oliver. 1982. "Men and Women at Work: Similarities and Differences in Work Values within Occupational Groupings." *Journal of Vocational Behavior* 21:17–36.

Ward, David, and Gene Kassebaum. 1965. *Women's Prison: Sex and Social Structure.* Chicago: Aldine-Atherton.

———. 1971. "Homosexual Behavior among Women Prisoners." pp. 42–53 in *Total Institutions*, edited by Samuel E. Wallace. New York: Transaction Books.

Webb, G. L., and David G. Morris. 1985. "Prison Guards." Pp. 204–214 in

Correctional Institutions, edited by Robert M. Carter, Daniel Glaser, and Leslie T. Wilkins. New York: Harper and Row.

Weber, Max. 1958 [1905]. *The Protestant Ethic and the Spirit of Capitalism.* Translated by Talcott Parsons. New York: Charles Scribners.

West, Candace, and Sarah Fenstermaker. 1995. "Doing Difference." *Gender and Society* 9:8–37.

West, Candace, and Don Zimmerman. 1987. "Doing Gender." *Gender and Society* 1:125–151.

Whitehead, J., and C. Lindquist. 1989. "Determinants of Correctional Officer Professional Orientation." *Justice Quarterly* 6:69–87.

Williams, Christine L. 1989. *Gender Differences at Work: Women and Men in Nontraditional Occupations.* Berkeley: University of California Press.

———. 1992. "The Glass Escalator: Hidden Advantages for Men in the 'Female' Professions." *Social Problems* 39:253–268.

———. 1995. *Still a Man's World: Men Who Do "Women's" Work.* Berkeley: University of California Press.

———. ed. 1993. *Doing "Women's Work:" Men in Nontraditional Occupations.* Newbury Park, CA: Sage Publications.

Williams, Christine L., and E. Joel Heikes. 1993. "The Importance of Researcher's Gender in the In-Depth Interview: Evidence from Two Case Studies of Male Nurses." *Gender and Society* 7:280–291.

Witz, Anne. 1990. "Patriarchy and Professions: The Gendered Politics of Occupational Closure." *Sociology* 24:675–690.

Wooden, Wayne S., and Jay Parker. 1982. *Men behind Bars: Sexual Exploitation in Prison.* New York: Da Capo Press.

Zedner, Laura. 1995. "Wayward Sisters: The Prison for Women." Pp. 329–361 in *The Oxford History of the Prison: The Practice of Punishment in Western Society*, edited by Norval Morris and David J. Rothman. New York: Oxford University Press.

Zimmer, Lynn E. 1986. *Women Guarding Men.* Chicago: University of Chicago Press.

———. 1987. "How Women Reshape the Prison Guard Role." *Gender and Society* 1:415–431.

Zupan, Linda L. 1992a. "Men Guarding Women: An Analysis of the Employment of Male Correction Officers in Prisons for Women." *Journal of Criminal Justice* 20:297–309.

———. 1992b. "The Progress of Women Correctional Officers in All-Male Prisons." Pp. 323–343 in *The Changing Roles of Women in the Criminal Justice System: Offenders, Victims, and Professionals*, edited by Imogene L. Moyer. Prospect Heights, IL: Waveland Press.

Index

Acker, Joan, 3, 6, 7–8, 11–12, 219, 221, 235n. 6
administrators, 5, 11, 52, 63, 66–67, 68, 77, 79, 110, 116, 159, 167, 172, 210–212, 225, 242n. 1; informal ties to, 192–194, 215, 220; men's penitentiaries, 10, 28–32, 53–54, 70–71, 135, 178, 216, 217, 220, 227–228, 241n. 19; men's reformatories, 33–37, 55, 61; officer views of, 64, 65–66, 178, 187, 202, 229, 230; prison farms, 45–47, 55–57, 61; racism among, 29, 46–48, 61, 202, 217; representation of women as, 5, 167, 211, 223; representation of Blacks and Hispanics as, 110, 167, 211; social class and, 58–59; views on women inmates, 28–32, 65, 216; women's prisons/reformatories, 31, 34–35, 37–41, 57–60, 65, 72, 74, 101, 186–187, 214, 217, 237n. 7
advancement. *See* promotion
affirmative action, 62, 192, 204–208, 215, 243n. 10, 243n. 11, 243n. 12, 243n. 13. *See also* discrimination/prejudice
agency: gendering through, 2, 6–7, 14–19, 21, 129, 167, 174–177, 189–190, 208–209, 216, 221, 224–226, 235n. 6; inmates and, 125; sexuality and, 161, 190, 215. *See also* female inmates; female officers; femininity; male inmates; male officers; masculinity
Amnesty International, 76, 186
Anthony, Susan B., 38
Appier, Janis, 167, 238n. 4
architecture, 20, 128, 149, 216, 223; men's prisons, 25–26, 28, 35, 159; women's prisons, 34, 39–40, 41, 50, 59, 61, 101, 220
assaults. *See* violence/brutality

assignments/postings of officers: administrative segregation, 172, 151, 152, 154, 159, 198; cellblocks/dormitories/housing units, 47, 72, 74–75, 86, 106–107, 141, 146, 172–174, 176–177, 186–190; chow hall, 172; control room, 150, 155, 171, 172–174; roving, 172, 174, 186, 188, 189, 242n. 2; "safe" postings, 174–175; showers, 3, 72, 73, 146, 158, 172, 173, 187, 240n. 10; tower, 9, 172; yard/compound, 172
Asylums (Goffman), 106–107, 164
Auburn (congregate) system, 25–33, 42, 53–55, 58
authoritarian personality, 51, 64, 80

Barton, Clara, 58
Bentham, Jeremy, 223
Black Codes, 42, 43, 237n. 8
Bona fide occupational qualification (BFOQ), 10, 71
Brenzel, Barbara, 34, 237n. 5
Brockway, Zebulon, 34–37, 48, 55, 61
bureaucracy, 98, 166, 173, 205, 215, 216, 223, 226, 236n. 8
Butler, Anne, 27, 29, 58, 236n. 2

"camp mentality," 102–103
Carpenter, Mary, 34
chain gangs, 43
chivalry, 141, 179; theory, 239n. 13
co-corrections, 48, 235n. 1, 237n. 10
Coggeshall, John, 159, 241n. 17
Colvin, Mark, 22, 25–26, 28, 30, 32, 34–35, 42–44, 53–55, 236n. 4, 237n. 8
Connell, Robert, 145, 171
contraband, 32, 37, 53, 75, 107, 133, 180, 190; drugs, 55, 126, 127, 152, 157, 219–220; weapons, 156, 224

About the Author

Dana M. Britton is Associate Professor of Sociology at Kansas State University. She received her B.A. in 1987 and M.A. in 1989 from the University of Oklahoma, and her Ph.D. from the University of Texas at Austin in 1995. She has published numerous essays on gender, work, and gendered organizations, including "The Epistemology of the Gendered Organization"; "Feminism in Criminology: Engendering the Outlaw"; and "Don't Ask, Don't Tell, Don't Pursue: Military Policy and the Construction of Heterosexual Masculinity" (with Christine Williams).